THE BIG SIX
HISTORICAL THINKING CONCEPTS

Authors
Dr. Peter Seixas
Tom Morton

Senior Program Advisor
Jill Colyer, The Historical Thinking Project

Reviewers
Stefano Fornazzari, York Region District School Board, ON
Jan Haskings-Winner, Toronto District School Board, ON
Martin May, Saskatoon Public Board of Education, SK
Ian S. Pettigrew, Peel District School Board, ON
Dr. Alan Sears, University of New Brunswick, NB
John Stewart, Department of Education,
Culture and Employment, NWT

Contributing Authors, DVD-ROM
Jill Colyer
Stefano Fornazzari

NELSON EDUCATION

NELSON EDUCATION

The Big Six Historical Thinking Concepts

Authors
Dr. Peter Seixas
Tom Morton

Editorial Director
Linda Allison

Publisher, Social Studies
Paula Smith

Managing Editor, Development
Alexandra Romic

Product Manager
Jessie MacKinnon

Program Manager
Kim Toffan

Developmental Editors
Margaret Hoogeveen
Susan Hughes

Editorial Intern
Leona Burlew

**Director, Content and Media
Production**
Linh Vu

Content Production Editor
Janice Okada

Copyeditor
Linda Jenkins

Proofreader
Linda Szostak

Production Manager
Helen Jager Locsin

Senior Production Coordinator
Kathrine Pummell

Production Coordinator
Huddy Wang

Design Director
Ken Phipps

Interior Design
Trinh Truong

Cover Design
Trinh Truong

Illustrators
MPS Limited
Trinh Truong

Compositor
MPS Limited

Photo/Permissions Researcher
Strand Acquisitions Inc.:
David Strand, Jennie Peddlesden

Cover Research
Debbie Yea

Printer
Transcontinental Printer Inc.

Contents

ACKNOWLEDGMENTS

The Big Six Historical Thinking Concepts would not have been written without a suggestion from David Steele, nor come to fruition without the positive, exploratory spirit of Jill Colyer, the good-hearted perseverance of Margaret Hoogeveen, and the big-picture perspective of Paula Smith.

Peter acknowledges his indebtedness: to my colleagues at UBC and in the Canadian and international history education community; to my students over the years, who push me always toward clarity; to teachers, museum educators, and others in the Historical Thinking Project, who keep my feet on the ground; and, with love, to Susan Inman, fierce advocate, inspirational teacher, reliable critic, emotional anchor, life partner, and mother of our two amazing children.

Tom acknowledges that he is a magpie: My contribution to this book is such a bricolage of borrowings that it is hard to single out only a few sources of inspiration. But I gratefully credit John Myers and our collaboration over the years and, more recently, the dedicated educators and students in the Heritage Fairs program. I am certainly indebted to the love and support of *ma compagne de vie*, Rose-Hélène, and daughter Chloé, who smiles blithely when I talk to her of history.

What you have in front of you, dear reader, is the product of two very well-nurtured guys who have worked together over the course of their professional lives in a variety of shared projects, none more intense or more rewarding than writing this book.

Peter Seixas   *Tom Morton*

FOREWORD

Most people agree that schools should teach history, though they often disagree over just what that history should be and how it might best be taught. Obviously, the study and teaching of history must be rooted in some selection of facts about the past. The task is to decide which facts should be selected for study and what students should do with them. Are they something to be memorized and tested—and, more often than not, quickly forgotten—or should they serve a more ambitious educational purpose?

Since at least the 1890s, historians and history educators have largely agreed that students must learn to approach the facts of history critically, not least by understanding the relationship between "the past" and "history." To do this, students must investigate how we come to know anything about the past at all and what makes any particular fact "historical" in the first place. In addition, they should come to understand how historians research and write history; the nature of historical evidence and arguments; what makes some historical arguments more satisfactory than others, and by what criteria; and how historians use their data to create historical accounts and interpretations.

However, researchers have repeatedly shown that classroom practice often lags far behind the principles formulated by historians and history educators. There have always been exceptional teachers who bring history to life for their students, but school inspectors' reports and national inquiries have shown that the teaching of history has too often been confined to textbook coverage and the recitation of facts that are devoid of any meaning for students and equally devoid of any defensible educational purpose. The result is that, all too often, history is not a stimulus to thought and imagination, but merely a charge on the memory, and usually a short-lived charge at that.

Not the least of the attractions of this book is its demonstration of how this long-standing gap between the theory and practice of history education can be eliminated. Peter Seixas and Tom Morton not only offer their readers a persuasive rationale for the study and teaching of history that is rooted in their "big six" concepts of historical thinking, but they also show how these concepts can be applied in the history classroom.

To do this, the authors draw on Tom Morton's many years of successful history teaching and on Peter Seixas's widely acclaimed model of historical thinking. To design the teaching strategies described in this book, Tom Morton brings to bear his experience developing and testing activities in his own history classroom, as well as extensive research on the pedagogy of the discipline of history. Peter Seixas's approach to historical thinking is rooted in the findings of a growing body of classroom-based research and the scholarly practice of historians, thereby combining disciplinary substance with pedagogical practicality.

The result is a welcome blend of theory and practice that will be of great service to history teachers while also making history more accessible and thus more educationally rewarding for students.

The "big six" concepts that comprise historical thinking as described by Seixas and Morton are not mere add-ons to be mechanically applied to some selection of facts once they have been taught. Rather, they are designed to be integrated into all aspects of teaching, from the formation of objectives, through the selection of resources and teaching strategies, to the assessment of students' performance. They are best thought of not as "skills" and certainly not as "outcomes," but rather as "habits of mind" or, as Morton and Seixas describe them, "competencies."

Best of all, what Seixas and Morton significantly call "guideposts" are just that—indicators of a path to follow, not demarcated itineraries from which no deviation is allowed. The "big six" concepts are intended to help students explore the forest of historical data, not confine them to a single prescribed path. Indeed, students who are guided appropriately might well arrive at their own grounded definitions of such concepts as significance, change, or cause and consequence. If so, they will be well on the way to thinking historically.

All of the "big six" concepts are important, but my personal favourite is what Morton and Seixas call "historical perspectives"—the ability to set hindsight aside and see the past, so far as we ever can, through the eyes of the people who lived it, to understand why they thought the way they thought and did the things they did, and in so doing gain a richer understanding of what it means to be human. Here, it seems to me, is history's greatest educational value: to enlarge students' possibly limited experience of life by visiting the "foreign country" of the past and returning home with fresh insights and new ways of looking at what we might otherwise have taken for granted or never even noticed.

In 1895, the pioneer Canadian historian G.M. Wrong told a University of Toronto audience that students of history had to be "something more than passive receivers" of information and had to "earn the right to do their own thinking on historical questions."* For the last hundred years we have been trying, often against long odds, to convert Wrong's words into classroom reality. In this book, Peter Seixas and Tom Morton show us how it can be done.

Ken Osborne
Professor Emeritus
Faculty of Education, University of Manitoba

---

* Wrong, G.M. (1895). Historical Study in the University: An inaugural lecture. Cited in Wright, D. (2005). *The professionalization of history in English Canada* (p. 31). Toronto: University of Toronto Press.

INTRODUCTION

Histories are the stories we tell about the past. They can be simple stories about going shopping yesterday; they can be complex stories about how nations formed or global trade developed. But the past itself is gone. By definition it is no longer present, so we can't observe it directly. We have a need for meaningful, coherent stories about what came before us. Yet a gap exists between the present we live in and the infinite, unorganized, and unknowable "everything that ever happened." How we overcome that gap gives rise to history.

> ... a gap exists between the present we live in and the infinite, unorganized, and unknowable "everything that ever happened."

But is the past really gone? As William Faulkner famously wrote, "The past is never dead. It's not even past." Whether or not we are conscious of it, whether it enters our minds at all, every aspect of the world we inhabit today is the product of yesterday. The chair you sit in as you read this page was designed, manufactured, sold, bought, shipped, and placed in its current spot at some point in the past—its existence today is thus an extension of the past. Not only the objects, buildings, streets, and cities through which you move, but also the social, political, and cultural worlds in which you navigate daily are the embodiment of everything that came before. And what is true of the world *around* you is equally true of *yourself*: your body—from the scars left by old injuries to the DNA in your cells left by your parents—and your mind—from the ideas you read about in this passage to the words you will use to write your next email. All is inherited. How can we become more conscious of the past that lies within every aspect of the present? Can understanding our ties to the past help us live in the present? How we answer these questions gives rise to history education.

What Is Historical Thinking?

As the discipline of history has developed over time, certain principles of historical thinking have evolved as historians attempt to deal with these questions, as well as other questions fundamental to history: How do we know what we know about the past? How can we represent the knowledge of something that is no longer here (i.e., the past)? What are the relationships between us, today, and those who lived in the past? What do we believe when two accounts of the same events conflict with each other?

Recall the definition of history given in our opening: "Histories are the stories we tell about the past." This definition sets up the most fundamental problem in the discipline of history: the relationship between the historian and the past that he or she is thinking, reading, or writing about. This problem can be seen in the *distance* between the present (in which the historian exists) and the past (which no longer exists); in the *choices* the historian must make in order to draw coherence and meaning from an infinite and disorderly past; and in the *interpretive lenses* that the historian brings as a result of being who he or she is. History is created through the solutions to these problems. It takes shape neither as the result of the historian's free-floating imagination, nor as the past presenting itself fully formed in an already coherent and meaningful story, ready to be "discovered" by the historian. Rather, history emerges from the tension between the historian's creativity and the fragmentary traces of the past that anchor it.

Historical thinking is the creative process that historians go through to interpret the evidence of the past and generate the stories of history. It would be naive to expect to find one universal structure of historical thinking that would apply to all cultures for all time. Different cultures have various ways of understanding the relationships between past, present, and future. The differences between oral and written histories are only the most obvious of examples. Consider the enormous challenge of constructing histories for our own moment—the most complex era in which human beings have ever lived. How do we, how *can* we, construct histories in a time of unprecedented mixing, mobility, and communication among different cultures while living with an accelerating pace of change, and while being driven by global economies and technologies that are revolutionized within years rather than generations or centuries?

The historian's expertise lies in being able to handle this challenge creatively. Historians become experts in dealing with the problems of history through their academic training. As part of a community of inquiry, they know when their colleagues violate the norms of evidence, when claims of significance are inadequately argued, and when causal explanations omit relevant conditions or events.[1] Sometimes historians explain the rules of the game and show us the process they follow to construct history, but more commonly we read

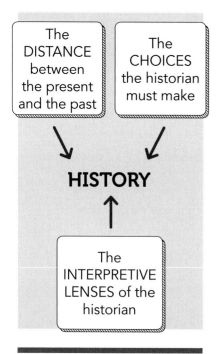

How do we know what we know about the past?

The DISTANCE between the present and the past

The CHOICES the historian must make

HISTORY

The INTERPRETIVE LENSES of the historian

Figure 1 History is made when historians find solutions to three problems.

---

1 Seixas, P. (1993). The community of inquiry as a basis for knowledge and learning: The case of history. *American Educational Research Journal 30*(2), 305–24.

---

in their histories only the end product—their historical narratives. In some sense, they are like the directors of a play. Too often, our students see only the play. We want them to peer backstage, to understand how the ropes and pulleys work that make the play possible.

Rethinking the Teaching of History

Some students have been lucky enough to learn history from a truly great teacher. Generally, however, what has passed for history curriculum in schools has rarely paid close attention to historians' methods and ways of thinking. As educators, we have been content to tell stories about the past and to have students tell them back in essays or, in the creative history classroom, in projects and skits. This approach does not aim high enough.

Science curriculum does not work this way. Students learn about the scientific method and do increasingly complex experiments so they can understand the basis of scientific claims. The mathematics curriculum does not work this way. Students learn to solve math problems at a young age and, over the course of their schooling, are expected to become increasingly sophisticated at doing so. Why shouldn't the history classroom have comparably high goals?

In answer to this challenge, we present the historical thinking concepts in this book as a starting point for rethinking how we teach history. These concepts constitute a six-part framework for helping students to think about how historians transform the past into history and to begin constructing history themselves. The concepts give us a vocabulary to use while talking with students about how histories are put together and what counts as a valid historical argument. These concepts are relevant for the most elementary histories—those that a child might tell—but also for the most advanced texts that an academic historian with specialized training might write. Thus, this framework allows for *progression*: students can use the concepts to move from depending on easily available, commonsense notions of the past to using the culture's most powerful intellectual tools for understanding history.

> These concepts are relevant for the most elementary histories—those that a child might tell—but also for the most advanced texts.

Six Concepts of Historical Thinking

The ideas that we refer to as "the big six" historical thinking *concepts* reveal *problems* inherent to constructing history. When carefully considered and thoroughly analyzed, each historical thinking concept reveals a tension, or difficulty, that may be irresolvable in any ultimate way. Taking an historical perspective, for example, asks us to take the viewpoint of an historical actor whose worldview was likely very different from our own. But our reconstructions of the world of the past are inevitably products of our own frames of reference—we can't escape them. Historians are therefore forced to reach workable accommodations. To address the problem revealed by the historical perspectives concept, for example, historians make limited but justifiable inferences based on available primary source evidence. Naive historical thinkers generally fail even to recognize the problems related to constructing

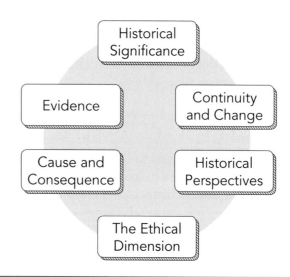

Figure 2 The six historical thinking concepts constitute a framework for helping students to think about how historians transform the past into history and to begin constructing history themselves. The concepts do not function independently; instead, they work together as various aspects of the thinking process.

history. Many school history curricula and most textbooks fail to define them. It should come as no surprise, then, that most students don't learn to grapple with the problems, and never learn the workable accommodations that historians use. Instead, they take intellectual shortcuts and, in so doing, miss out on both the challenge and much of the excitement of doing history.

If the concepts reveal inherent problems, confronting those problems can lead to competencies, to use a word common in current educational discourse. How successfully students grapple with the tensions, complexities, and problems embedded in historical thinking concepts is a basis for measuring their progress toward competency in historical thinking. The purpose of this book is to explore the concepts, articulate the problems, and suggest pathways for helping students achieve greater competency in historical thinking.

The six historical thinking concepts make no sense at all without the material, the topics, the substance, or what is often referred to as the "content" of history. For example, one key idea of the historical significance concept is that significance varies from group to group. This key idea makes sense only when tied to a real example: The year 1867 is significant for Canadians, but far less so for Americans (except, perhaps, for Alaskans, whose state was purchased from Russia in that year). Just as the concepts make no sense without historical content, historical content cannot be truly understood as anything other than a series of disconnected bits of data to be memorized without a grasp of the historical thinking concepts. The concepts and content are thus mutually dependent for historical understanding.

The six concepts can be presented as the strategies that historians use in response to six key problems. These problems are expressed in the questions that head the next six paragraphs.

> Just as the concepts make no sense without historical content, historical content cannot be truly understood ... without a grasp of the historical thinking concepts.

How Do We Decide What Is Important to Learn about the Past?

Historians **establish historical significance**. We can't know all of the past—there is simply too much there. Why do we care, today, about certain events, people, and trends in the past, and not others? Particular facts become significant when we see them as part of a larger narrative that is relevant to important issues that concern us today. Thus, for example, the Battle of the Plains of Abraham is significant for Canadians because it occupies a key place in the story of French–English relations in Canada, a narrative that continues to be a live issue for us today.

How Do We Know What We Know about the Past?

Historians **use primary source evidence**. Ultimately, the foundations for all claims in history are the traces left over from the times in which past events occurred. If we rely on the work of earlier historians, we do so knowing that these historians (or the historians *they* relied on) went back to primary sources. Making an historical claim that others can justifiably believe, then, requires finding, selecting, contextualizing, interpreting, and corroborating sources for an historical argument. For example, if we wanted to build an historical argument about wartime attitudes toward German Canadians, we might choose to refer to a reliable history of German immigration to Canada, a 1916 newspaper article from Berlin, Ontario (which would soon become Kitchener, Ontario), and a diary kept by a German immigrant during the period.

How Can We Make Sense of the Complex Flows of History?

Historians **examine continuity and change**. History is often defined as the story of change over time. But history is more complex: some things don't change at all; some things change quickly and then slowly; and, at any given moment, some things change while others remain the same. Sensitivity to all of these aspects of continuity and change is crucial to narrating history. For example, we might look for what *didn't* change over the tumultuous years of the French Revolution, or what *did* change through the placid 1950s in North America. Moreover, some changes have resulted in better living conditions for some groups of people, while leading to economic hardship, cultural impoverishment, or enslavement for others. The ideas of progress and decline are thus part of the discussion of continuity and change. Finally, periodization—the selection of a set of events that make up a period of history—helps make sense of the flows of continuity and change.

Why Do Events Happen, and What Are Their Impacts?

Historians **analyze cause and consequence**. Causation is fundamental to history, as it is to any storytelling: We want to know how certain conditions and actions led to others. Without a sense of causation, sets of events—even if organized chronologically—become mere disconnected lists. The role of human choice is a central problem here: How were particular decisions shaped, made possible, or constrained by the historical circumstances of the moment? How, in other words, does the interaction between human agency and existing conditions shape the course of events? For any event—as large as the colonization of India or as small as the birth of an individual child—we can trace both the conditions and the decisions that allowed, or precipitated, its taking place. Similarly, we can identify the short-term and long-term consequences that result from virtually any event.

How Can We Better Understand the People of the Past?

Historians **take historical perspectives**. "The past is a foreign country"[2] with its different social, cultural, intellectual, and even emotional contexts that shaped people's lives and actions. Our ancestors were not simply early versions of us, differing only in their styles of clothing and their lack of cellphones. We can attempt to see through the eyes of the people of the past by making evidence-based inferences about what they thought and believed. Yet we examine the past through our own present-day lenses, with concerns and questions that arise from the present. Can we avoid "presentism," the imposition of the present on the past? For example, what did it mean for Prime Minister John A. Macdonald to compare Chinese immigrant workers to "threshing machines" in 1886? The challenge is to figure out what Macdonald was thinking and why he used that metaphor, without calling him a racist and leaving it at that.

How Can History Help Us to Live in the Present?

Historians **attempt to understand the ethical dimension** of history. As we look back on the devastation of conquests or the injustices of enslavement, an ethical stance is unavoidable. By the same measure, an ethical judgment is involved when we try to decide what were the victories and achievements of the past. Yet those who were involved lived in circumstances so different from those of today that we must use caution in applying our own moral sensitivities. This raises a series of interrelated questions: How should we judge historical actors? What are the implications for us, today, of the horrors and heroisms of the past? How can we use the study of the past to inform judgments and actions on controversial issues in the present? All of these questions are relevant, for example, to an historical study of Canada's residential school system for First Nations, Métis, and Inuit children.

---

2 The complete opening line of L.P. Hartley's 1953 novel *The Go-Between* is "The past is a foreign country: they do things differently there."

Our Approach to Historical Thinking in the Classroom

Our model of historical thinking—the six concepts—comes from the work of historians. It is rooted in how they tackle the difficult problems of understanding the past, how they make sense of it for today's society and culture, and thus how they get their bearings in a continuum of past, present, and future. As history educators, our goal is to enable students to begin to do the same, in a step-by-step process that is challenging but not overwhelming. Otherwise, in their reading of history, they remain simply the passive, and often unwilling, recipients of someone else's work.

> Our model of historical thinking ... is rooted in how [historians] tackle the difficult problems of understanding the past ...

Seeing through the Eyes of an Historian: Thinking about the Concepts

The structure of *The Big Six Historical Thinking Concepts* flows directly from these ideas. We begin each chapter with an essay that explores one of the six concepts through the work of a particular Canadian historian. We made our selections in part on the basis of the historians' academic reputations but also on their popular appeal. None of them is closeted in an ivory tower (or a dusty archive), oblivious to the issues that energize people today.

In addition to telling fascinating stories, each of our chosen authors opens a window for us to see the way they put their histories together, and how they got from the big questions of history, through the evidence that has been left from the past, to the interpretive achievement that we can recognize in the pages of their books.

> ... each of our chosen authors opens a window for us to see the way they put their histories together.

- In *Vermeer's Hat: The Seventeenth Century and the Dawn of the Global World*, historian Timothy Brook takes a detail from one of Johannes Vermeer's paintings and shows its significance for the beginnings of globalization. We examine his work in order to understand historical significance in Chapter 1: Historical Significance.
- In *The Power of Place, the Problem of Time: Aboriginal Identity and Historical Consciousness in the Cauldron of Colonialism*, historian Keith Thor Carlson searches for, finds, and analyzes a mountain of evidence to answer a huge question about First Nations identities in the Fraser Valley of British Columbia. Examination of Carlson's use of evidence begins our consideration of the concept in Chapter 2: Evidence.
- Historian Margaret Macmillan showcases a turning point in world history in the title of her book, *Paris 1919: Six Months That Changed the World*, and thereby opens her discussion of continuity and change surrounding the events that followed World War I. We use this discussion as our starting point in Chapter 3: Continuity and Change.
- Popular historian Charlotte Gray's *Gold Diggers: Striking It Rich in the Klondike* features six "self-made" adventurers, thereby setting up a host of questions: How and when do individuals' decisions cause historical change? What are the consequences down the road? How do conditions

shape those decisions in the first place? These questions frame our discussion of the concept in Chapter 4: Cause and Consequence.

- Historian and journalist Julie Wheelwright documents her efforts to peer into the world of her ancestor in *Esther: The Remarkable True Story of Esther Wheelwright: Puritan Child, Native Daughter, Mother Superior*. Attention to her meticulous historical methods sparks our consideration of the concept in Chapter 5: Historical Perspectives.
- And finally, in *The Book of Negroes*, historical novelist Lawrence Hill leads his readers on a painful journey through the historical crime that fuelled the early American economy—the enslavement of Africans. His confrontation with the ethical dimension of the slave trade opens the door to our own consideration of the concept in Chapter 6: The Ethical Dimension.

Marking a Path: The Guideposts

Each chapter essay is followed by discussion of the four or five "guideposts" to the concept that were revealed through discussion of the historian's approach. Guideposts are the big ideas related to each concept—the "way in" to the historian's way of thinking. They mark a path from the historian to the classroom. Of course, we don't expect students to replicate the work of these mature academics and journalists who have spent years in training and a lifetime honing their craft. But, as in any apprenticeship, the masters provide the models.

> Guideposts are the big ideas related to each concept—the "way in" to the historian's way of thinking.

What *can* we expect from students? The guideposts pull from the historians' methods what students need to know about the concept. We then translate these guideposts into students' understandings. These appear in a table entitled "Generating Powerful Understandings," which leads to the practical section of each chapter. Many students will arrive in the history classroom with very limited understandings of the way the discipline of history works. For each guidepost, we describe this possible "starting point" of limited understanding, as well as a demonstration of a powerful understanding of the guidepost.

Moving toward Powerful Understanding: Working with the Concepts

The final section of each chapter moves to the task of helping students develop competencies in each of the powerful understandings. This practical section includes (1) an activity for introducing the chapter concept to students, (2) guidance and three to five activities to help students develop powerful understandings of the guideposts, and (3) an activity to consolidate student understanding of the historical thinking concept. Some activities include blackline masters, which appear at the end of each chapter and in modifiable form on the DVD-ROM. The activities are either generic or model activities that you can revise to apply to the content of the courses you are teaching. As you work through the activities, students will generate measureable demonstrations of powerful understanding.

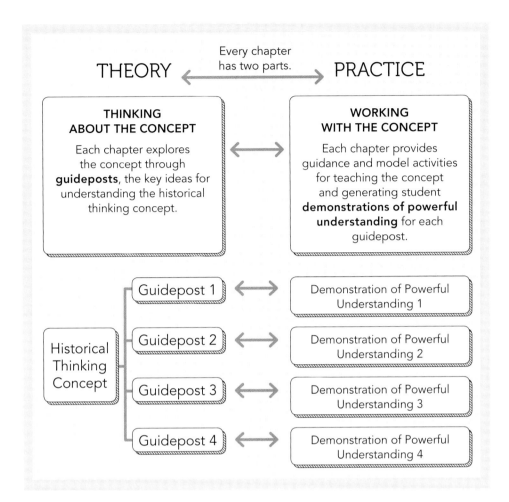

THEORY ⟵ Every chapter has two parts. ⟶ PRACTICE

THINKING ABOUT THE CONCEPT

Each chapter explores the concept through **guideposts**, the key ideas for understanding the historical thinking concept.

⟷

WORKING WITH THE CONCEPT

Each chapter provides guidance and model activities for teaching the concept and generating student **demonstrations of powerful understanding** for each guidepost.

Historical Thinking Concept

Guidepost 1 ⟷	Demonstration of Powerful Understanding 1
Guidepost 2 ⟷	Demonstration of Powerful Understanding 2
Guidepost 3 ⟷	Demonstration of Powerful Understanding 3
Guidepost 4 ⟷	Demonstration of Powerful Understanding 4

Figure 3 Every chapter helps you teach one historical thinking concept by providing the theory in the first half, followed by practical guidance. The two-way arrows indicate that you may wish to consult both sections as you expand the use of historical thinking in your history classroom.

Inquiry: Integral to Historical Thinking

Engaging students through thought-provoking questions is integral to our approach to teaching history. The right questions should prompt them to take an active stance toward engaging with the past. Inquiry questions demand more than memorizing pieces of information or looking up solutions. They involve grappling with evidence, weighing choices, and making interpretations.

So, we pose big questions to be answered and significant problems to be solved. These questions, which are woven into our lesson scaffolding, variously form the foundations for discussions, analyses, and whole lessons. Along the way, we provide students with guidance without eliminating the demand for creativity and deliberation. Like the historical thinking concepts, an inquiry-based approach takes as a model the questions that Brook asks about the origins of globalization, or that Carlson asks about First Nations identities, in a scaled-back and pedagogically appropriate way.

Doing history should be fun and serious, difficult and rewarding, meaningful and creative. If some of those elements are missing, students are not getting the whole package. We hope that you will find what follows useful in helping students develop active and fulfilling engagements with the past.

> Doing history should be fun and serious, difficult and rewarding, meaningful and creative.

Guideposts to Historical Thinking

Historical Significance *How do we decide what is important to learn about the past?*

Guidepost 1   Events, people, or developments have historical significance if they **resulted in change**. That is, they had deep consequences, for many people, over a long period of time.

Guidepost 2   Events, people, or developments have historical significance if they are **revealing**. That is, they shed light on enduring or emerging issues in history or contemporary life.

Guidepost 3   Historical significance is **constructed**. That is, events, people, and developments meet the criteria for historical significance only when they are shown to occupy a **meaningful place in a narrative**.

Guidepost 4   Historical significance **varies** over time and from group to group.

Evidence *How do we know what we know about the past?*

Guidepost 1   History is **interpretation** based on **inferences** made from primary sources. Primary sources can be accounts, but they can also be traces, relics, or records.

Guidepost 2   **Asking good questions** about a source can turn it into evidence.

Guidepost 3   Sourcing often begins before a source is read, with questions about **who** created it and **when** it was created. It involves inferring from the source the author's or creator's **purposes, values,** and **worldview**, either conscious or unconscious.

Guidepost 4   A source should be analyzed in relation to the **context of its historical setting**: the conditions and worldviews prevalent at the time in question.

Guidepost 5   Inferences made from a source can never stand alone. They should always be **corroborated**—checked against other sources (primary or secondary).

Continuity and Change *How can we make sense of the complex flows of history?*

Guidepost 1   Continuity and change are **interwoven**: both can exist together. **Chronologies**—the sequencing of events—can be a good starting point.

Guidepost 2   Change is a **process**, with varying paces and patterns. **Turning points** are moments when the process of change shifts in direction or pace.

Guidepost 3   **Progress and decline** are broad evaluations of change over time. Depending on the impacts of change, progress for one people may be decline for another.

Guidepost 4   **Periodization** helps us organize our thinking about continuity and change. It is a process of interpretation, by which we decide which events or developments constitute a period of history.

Cause and Consequence *Why do events happen, and what are their impacts?*

Guidepost 1 Change is driven by **multiple causes**, and results in **multiple consequences**. These create a complex web of interrelated short-term and long-term causes and consequences.

Guidepost 2 The **causes** that lead to a particular historical event **vary in their influence**, with some being more important than others.

Guidepost 3 Events result from the interplay of two types of factors: (1) **historical actors**, who are people (individuals or groups) who take actions that cause historical events, and (2) the social, political, economic, and cultural **conditions** within which the actors operate.

Guidepost 4 Historical actors cannot always predict the effect of conditions, opposing actions, and unforeseen reactions. These have the effect of generating **unintended consequences**.

Guidepost 5 The events of history were **not inevitable**, any more than those of the future are. Alter a single action or condition, and an event might have turned out differently.

Historical Perspectives *How can we better understand the people of the past?*

Guidepost 1 An ocean of **difference** can lie between current **worldviews** (beliefs, values, and motivations) and those of earlier periods of history.

Guidepost 2 It is important to avoid **presentism**—the imposition of present ideas on actors in the past. Nonetheless, cautious reference to universal human experience can help us relate to the experiences of historical actors.

Guidepost 3 The perspectives of historical actors are best understood by considering their **historical context**.

Guidepost 4 **Taking the perspective of historical actors** means inferring how people felt and thought in the past. It **does not mean identifying with** those actors. Valid **inferences** are those **based on evidence**.

Guidepost 5 Different historical actors have **diverse perspectives** on the events in which they are involved. Exploring these is key to understanding historical events.

The Ethical Dimension *How can history help us to live in the present?*

Guidepost 1 Authors make **implicit or explicit** ethical judgments in writing historical narratives.

Guidepost 2 Reasoned ethical judgments of past actions are made by taking into account the **historical context** of the actors in question.

Guidepost 3 When making ethical judgments, it is important to **be cautious about imposing contemporary standards** of right and wrong on the past.

Guidepost 4 A fair assessment of the ethical implications of history can inform us of our **responsibilities to remember and respond** to contributions, sacrifices, and injustices of the past.

Guidepost 5 Our understanding of history can help us make **informed judgments** about contemporary issues, but only when we **recognize the limitations** of any direct "lessons" from the past.

Chapter 1

HISTORICAL SIGNIFICANCE

How do we decide what is important to learn about the past?

Guideposts to Historical Significance

> **Guidepost 1**

Events, people, or developments have historical significance if they **resulted in change**. That is, they had deep consequences, for many people, over a long period of time.

> **Guidepost 2**

Events, people, or developments have historical significance if they are **revealing**. That is, they shed light on enduring or emerging issues in history or contemporary life.

> **Guidepost 3**

Historical significance is **constructed**. That is, events, people, and developments meet the criteria for historical significance only when they are shown to occupy a **meaningful place in a narrative**.

> **Guidepost 4**

Historical significance **varies** over time and from group to group.

Figure 1.1 Johannes Vermeer's seventeenth-century painting *Officer and Laughing Girl* becomes a doorway to the past in the hands of historian and author Timothy Brook. In his book *Vermeer's Hat: The Seventeenth Century and the Dawn of the Global World*, Brook shows how the man's hat in this painting opens a "passageway that leads out into the wider world" (Brook, 2008, p. 29). It is made from beaver pelts, a product of the fur trade in Canada. The hat gains historical significance for us because the author ties it to the narrative of globalization, an issue of interest to us today.

Thinking about
HISTORICAL
SIGNIFICANCE

Of the myriad events that have ever happened, and the many people who have ever lived, how do we decide which ones our students should learn about? For that matter, how do historians decide what to research and write about? Both questions lead to a related question: What makes an event that took place two centuries ago or a person who lived five centuries ago historically significant? This question does not have a simple answer. Nonetheless, historians have attempted to answer it by embracing the responsibility to decide what is significant enough to research; educators have similarly made choices about what is significant enough to teach. We believe that students should take responsibility for understanding how and why particular historical events, people, and developments are significant enough for them to learn about.

Before the introduction of historical thinking in a classroom, students may go no further than the textbook in thinking about significance: "If it is in the textbook, it must be significant. Why else would they put it in there?" While this logic has some justification, it renders students entirely passive in the face of the authority of the text. When students are taught to think critically about what is historically significant, they learn not only the results of the work of historians (dates, names, and places deemed to be significant) but more importantly how to make reasoned decisions about historical significance, as an historian would do.

How One Historian Approaches Historical Significance

As we begin to think about how to teach students about historical significance, let us consider what we can learn from the experience of historian Timothy Brook, a specialist in the history of the sixteenth and seventeenth centuries. A native of Toronto, Brook now teaches at the University of British Columbia. In his book *Vermeer's Hat: The Seventeenth Century and the Dawn of the Global World*,[1] Brook explores the early development of globalization. (The image shown on the cover of his book is featured on page 13.) Of interest to our discussion, Brook offers some clues as to how he managed the problems inherent to constructing history, though we have to read between the lines to really understand his reasoning.

On Starting Points

Brook begins his argument by saying that the small Dutch town of Delft, where he begins his narrative, is *not* particularly significant: he had many choices about where to locate his history. Delft, in other words, did not have the kind of profound impact that would give it a traditional form of historical significance. So what reasons does Brook offer to explain his choice?

> I could offer any number of reasons to explain why a global history of the intercultural transformations of seventeenth-century life must start from Delft.... I start from Delft simply because I happen to have fallen off my bike there, because Vermeer happened to have lived there, and because I happen to enjoy looking at his paintings. (pp. 4, 5)

Brook makes it sound as if it were mere personal experience and preference that led him to situate the book where he did. While it is true that Brook's falling off his bike in Delft and his attraction to Vermeer's paintings may serve as starting points for a research project, they do not create historical significance on their own. Indeed, Brook's choice of Delft turns out to be not as serendipitous as he implies in the lines above. In the seventeenth century, the Dutch republic had just escaped the grip of Spain's Habsburg Empire and was building new trade relations with the rest of the world. As Brook states, it was a time when "people were weaving a web of connections and exchanges as never before" (p. 6). Delft was therefore a central node for the phenomenon that is the subject of the book. That phenomenon, as the book's subtitle states, is "the seventeenth century and the dawn of the global world."

1 Brook, T. (2008). *Vermeer's hat: The seventeenth century and the dawn of the global world*. London: Bloomsbury Press, Profile Books.

TEACHING TIP

The potential of historical thinking to engage and animate students can be seen when any group of students tries to rank a small set of events, people, or developments for their historical significance. See the activity **Ranking Topics in a Unit** on page 28.

One of the major trends—perhaps *the* major trend—that we are grappling with in the twenty-first century is the process of globalization. Brook's history reveals that globalization is not a phenomenon of the last 50 years but of the last 500. He uncovers the origins of some of our most fundamental present-day concerns in Delft, not because seventeenth-century Delft was just like twenty-first-century Canada, but because it was the "dawn" of a phenomenon that interests us passionately today.

On Finding Connections

Brook chose Delft for a second reason: Vermeer lived and worked there, painting representations of scenes with "hints of broader historical forces that lurk in their details" (p. 7). The hat in the painting *Officer and Laughing Girl* that supplies the title of his book provides a good example. This image of the hat, at the centre of a scene between a man and a woman in the 1650s, provides a "passageway that leads out into the wider world" (p. 29). From here, Brook tells the story of the hat's North American raw material; the development of the market in beaver pelts, and its impact on relations among French, English, Algonquin, Wendat (Huron), and Mohawk peoples; and, crucially for the big idea of globalization, Champlain's motivation for fur trade and exploration: a passage to China. Delft, Vermeer, and the hat achieve their significance as Brook demonstrates the part they play in a larger story that ends up in the twenty-first century, with us.

Thus, two elements come together in Brook's project that help us understand the process of constructing historical significance.

- The first element consists of big, compelling concerns that exist in our lives today, such as environmental sustainability, justice, power, welfare, or, in Brook's case, globalization.
- The second element involves the much more particular events, objects, and people whose historical significance is in question—in Brook's case, the hat in the painting.

Historical significance emerges when the historian links the two elements.

The historical significance of "Vermeer's hat" arises not from Vermeer as an important painter, much less from the painting or the hat itself, but rather from the story through which the historian *links* the hat to the larger processes that result in twenty-first-century globalization. The hat is not significant without the story.

How can Brook's experience help us teach about historical significance? Primarily, it demonstrates that historical significance is not intrinsically located in a particular event, object, or person, but rather that it is relative to

---

CONNECTIONS BETWEEN CONCEPTS

The evidence concept tells us that asking insightful questions about sources, including paintings, can turn them into evidence. This is what Brook did with Vermeer's paintings, asking such questions as "How is the hat in this painting connected to global trade?" This process helped him construct the historical significance of the details in the paintings.

the narrative in which the particular is situated. In Brook's narrative, the beaver hat and other details of Vermeer's paintings shed light on issues and problems that concern us today. This helps to explain why historical significance is not fixed and unchanging. It shifts in relation to the changing problems of society and culture. Historical significance expresses a flexible *relationship* between ourselves (historians, teachers, and students) and the past.

Now that we have an overview of the process an historian takes to construct historical significance, let us investigate the process further by examining four guideposts—or big ideas—about historical significance, and how we can bring those big ideas into the classroom.

> Historical significance expresses a flexible **relationship** between ourselves ... and the past.

Criterion: Did It Result in Change?

We can teach students to determine historical significance by testing an event or individual against two specific criteria.[2] The first and most straightforward of these criteria concerns the degree of impact of an event, person, or development. Canadian students learn about the exploits of Samuel de Champlain, for example, because of the impact of his actions: he explored what is now Canadian territory on behalf of a European power, and he founded and administered the first colonies of New France. These activities had deep consequences for many people over a long period of time. Canadian history textbooks are filled with similar characters whose actions resulted in profound change that affected the development of this country. (There are, of course, the people and actions that are significant for just the opposite reason: they *prevented* profound change.)

Because the impact criterion is fairly straightforward, it makes a good starting point for a classroom consideration of historical significance. You can begin by analyzing with students a particular event, person, or development that is historically significant by virtue of having "resulted in change." Choose an example that is quite obvious and familiar to students, such as Prime Minister Sir John A. Macdonald or Wayne Gretzky, and create a concept web with the class to explore the various impacts. Your initial goal is to help students develop the competency of explaining the significance of events, people, or developments that had deep impact for many people over a long period of time. This task demands considerable knowledge of historical events, context, and chronologies, but is not cognitively difficult.

Historical Significance

 Guidepost 1

Events, people, or developments have historical significance if they **resulted in change**. That is, they had deep consequences, for many people, over a long period of time.

---

2 The choice of two criteria for historical significance was a pragmatic one. In the considerable empirical research on students' understanding of historical significance, the definition of numerous and various types of (or criteria for) significance remains unresolved. Our typology reflects a pragmatic compromise: what it loses from having only two criteria for historical significance it gains in utility and relative simplicity of explanation. Among the contributors to the debate are Geoffrey Partington (1980), Lis Cercadillo (2001), and Christine Counsell (2004), each of whom presents five overlapping but incongruous types.

Partington, G. (1980b). What history should we teach? *Oxford Review of Education, 6*(2), 157–176. Cercadillo, L. (2001). Significance in history: Students' ideas in England and Spain. In A. Dickinson, P. Gordon, & P. Lee (Eds.), *Raising standards in history education: International review of history education* (Vol. 3, pp. 116–145). London: Woburn Press. Counsell, C. (2004). Looking through a Josephine-Butler-shaped window: Focusing pupils' thinking on historical significance. *Teaching History, 114*(March), 30–36. Carla Peck reviews the literature in her dissertation *Multi-ethnic high school students' understandings of historical significance: Implications for Canadian history education* (Vancouver, UBC, 2009). See also Conway, R. (2006). What they think they know: The impact of pupils' preconceptions on their understanding of historical significance. *Thinking History, 125*, 10–15.

Figure 1.2 In 2009, actors performed the musical *Strike!* in front of Winnipeg City Hall. The event this theatrical production represents—the 1919 Winnipeg General Strike—can be measured against the criterion of impact. The strike was a very dramatic event in Canadian history, but does it have historical significance? Did it result in a profound impact on the lives of many people over a long period of time? Questions like these can generate heated discussion among historians and students alike.

Criterion: Is It Revealing?

The criterion of "resulting in change" is key to understanding significance, but it does not provide the whole story. It does not explain why historians now devote so much attention to the histories of women, workers, immigrants, ethnic and sexual minorities, and many others who *did not* have the economic clout of a Rockefeller or the political power of a Churchill, and to events that were not necessarily the great turning points in world history. How can we explain the current significance of "ordinary" people and events, previously dismissed as insignificant? Why are the history journals and the history textbooks devoting so much attention to *them*?

The answers to these questions lie in the second criterion for historical significance. Otherwise insignificant flotsam of history *becomes* historically significant when it reveals to us something about the time period in question, and more importantly, about an issue that interests us today. For example, the particulars of the life of an Inuk hunter in the eighteenth century could inform a current debate about the responsibility to protect the environment. As you teach about the "revealing" criterion, your goal should be to develop in students the competency of explaining how an event, person, or development that *did not* meet the first criterion of "resulting in change" can nonetheless be significant for what he or she "reveals" to us about issues and concerns that are compelling to us today.

Discovering what an event, person, or development reveals about a larger issue—as Brook did with the beaver hat in *Officer and Laughing Girl*—is inherently more challenging than identifying impacts, so you may have to spend more time helping students understand this criterion. Work with students to develop inquiry questions that can bring historical significance to a personal interest. For example, at the outset of a research project, students may begin by citing simple personal interest or preference: "I like hockey. Therefore, it is historically significant." Insufficient as this statement is by itself, it could be a starting point, in the same way that Brook's love of Vermeer's paintings offered an entryway to exploring broader issues. You might encourage the young hockey fan to conduct research to answer the question "How has hockey fostered a common northern identity to the geographically dispersed, linguistically divided country of Canada?" Or "How has machismo in competitive mass spectacle changed, or not, over time?" The narratives that the hockey fan would create in response to these questions would help to establish the historical significance of a development: the invention and diffusion of hockey.

Consider the case of a student who undertakes a research project about her grandmother for a history fair. The personal interest is obvious; the historical significance is not. The historically sophisticated student will link her grandmother to a larger story by showing what her experience revealed about immigration, war and peace, or perhaps social mobility. The grandmother's life becomes significant for its part in enlightening us about driving concerns of today. The student thereby establishes the significance of her grandmother, just as Timothy Brook establishes the significance of Vermeer's hat.

Historical Significance

 Guidepost 2

Events, people, or developments have historical significance if they are **revealing**. That is, they shed light on enduring or emerging issues in history or contemporary life.

Figure 1.3 In 1999, teacher Fumiko Ishioka (shown here) asked officials at the Auschwitz Museum for an artifact to make the Holocaust more real for her students in Japan. They gave her the suitcase of Hana Brady, who was killed in the gas chambers at the age of 13. The story of Hana and her suitcase led to the opening of eyes, a book, a play, and a movie.[3] This photograph shows Ishioka on a visit to Toronto in 2003 opening the suitcase for students at Seneca Hill Public School. The Nazis thought that Hana was of no significance. But the story of her suitcase touched many people and made Hana historically significant.

Narrative and the Construction of Historical Significance

History is not everything that happened in the past. Instead, history consists of the meaningful stories, or narratives, that we tell about what happened in the past. Our first two guideposts were *criteria* for judging whether an event, person, or development is historically significant. The third guidepost is not another criterion; rather, it explains how the historian *establishes* the significance by means of a story. Narrative is crucial for both the "resulting in change" and the "revealing" criteria. The significance arises as the historian writes or tells the story, whether it is about Champlain's exploration leading to new European knowledge of America, or Vermeer's hat revealing the origins

---

3 Canadian journalist Karen Levine wrote the 2002 non-fiction book *Hana's Suitcase*. The suitcase referred to in the title sits on the table in the photograph (Figure 1.3). The book has been published in 30 countries and translated into 17 languages. Emil Sher adapted the book into a stage play of the same name. Larry Weinstein created the CBC documentary *Inside Hana's Suitcase* in 2009.

of globalization. Consequently, to establish historical significance themselves, students need to know enough about the period in question to be able to see the possible connections to concerns we have today. Only then will they be able to build a narrative through which historical significance emerges.

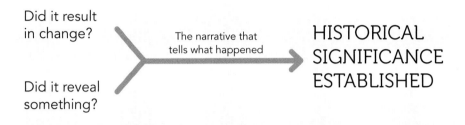

Figure 1.4 The historical significance of an event, person, or development emerges through the construction of a narrative.

To develop historical thinking in students, teach them to recognize specific examples of authors of historical accounts *constructing* historical significance through narrative (in books, film, exhibits, and historical fiction). By *construction*, we do not mean "to make up," but rather "to build" using the building blocks of the story. Guide students through three steps of the process.

1. **Identify the large question:** First, help students learn to identify the large questions or issues that authors address through their histories. It will be helpful, initially, to provide students with a list of the kinds of issues that historians often address, such as the building of nations, conflicts over power, and struggles for rights and recognition.

2. **Describe the plot:** A second step in analyzing narrative concerns plot. Guide students in asking questions about the plot: Is the story one of success and triumph, or of failure and destruction? Or is it a more complex mixture of the two?

3. **Identify the role of the particular:** Finally, help students recognize the role of the particular event, person, or development *within* the story. Again, providing some suggestions at the outset will help students. Was the event (the execution of Charles I, D-Day) the beginning, the climax, or the end of the story? Was the person (John A. Macdonald, Poundmaker) a hero who achieved good things against great odds, a villain who obstructed justice, or a human being whose life took twists and turns that reveal something important for us today? Was the development (the invention of gunpowder, the growing awareness of human rights) a benefit to humanity, or did it lead to great harm the world over? In other words, how is the particular event, person, or development connected to the issues and the plot? In the example of Hana's suitcase, what did Hana—brought to life through the suitcase—reveal to us about the Holocaust?

How Historical Significance Varies

Awareness that historical significance is constructed can help us understand how and why historical significance varies, which it does in two ways.

Variance over Time

First, knowing that historical significance is constructed *in relation to today's concerns* explains why and how significance can vary over time. Concerns about gender relations and sexuality today demand a different account of the Victorian era in Canada than would have been written 60 years ago. Historians were not writing histories about midwives or homosexuality in the 1950s, any more than they were writing about globalization, as Brook did in 2008. These were not pressing topics—at least not in the public sphere—for people in the mid-twentieth century. The issues of contemporary life and culture shift over time, and therefore historical significance cannot be fixed and unchanging; it must shift over time as well. As explained above, historical significance changes over time because it expresses a flexible *relationship* between ourselves (historians, teachers, and students) and the past.

You might wish to introduce students to the concept of variance over time by presenting data such as that in Figure 1.5. It shows the number of mentions of the word *Passchendaele*, a key battle from World War I, in the print version of the *Globe and Mail*. The number of mentions is modest in the decade in which the event takes place and then drops for at least five decades. It climbs a bit in the 1970s when a book and a play about the event appear, but then skyrockets in the 2000s when a film about the battle hits the theatres, and the battle again looms large in the Canadian imagination. Practically overnight, Passchendaele became an historically significant event.

Historical Significance

> **Guidepost 4**
> Historical significance **varies** over time and from group to group.

Mentions of "Passchendaele" in the *Globe and Mail*

Decade	Number of Mentions
1910–1919	16
1920–1929	7
1930–1939	6
1940–1949	4
1950–1959	2
1960–1969	5
1970–1979	11
1980–1989	33
1990–1999	11
2000–2009	1016

Figure 1.5 Can we measure historical significance? Not directly. But we do have indicators that can tell us if people were reading and writing about an event. Consider the data at right, which tell us the number of mentions in the print version of the *Globe and Mail*[4] for the name of a key 1917 battle for Canadians in World War I.

4 Mentions are for the *Toronto Globe*, 1910–1936, and *The Globe and Mail*, 1937–present. "Canada's Heritage from 1844—The Globe and Mail." Retrieved January 11, 2012, from http://www.proquest.com/en-US/catalogs/databases/detail/canada_heritage.shtml

Figure 1.6 The Great Peace of Montréal was a major treaty between New France and 40 First Nations that was signed in 1701. It heralded a new peace in a region wracked by hostilities. Fifty years ago, this historical event was not considered significant enough for public celebration. Today, this spectacular mural stands as a testament to the coming together of nations. Note, in particular, that the French and First Nations are depicted as equals. What changed in 50 years to make this into an historically significant event worthy of commemoration?

Variance from Group to Group

Knowing that historical significance is constructed allows us to better understand a second source of variability: the author. Every author of history, whether a student, teacher, or historian, will bring his or her own perspective, knowledge, and concerns to the table. The authors of history will bring their worldviews to the table as well: an historian of a nation that lost a war may have a radically different perspective on the historical significance of certain events than would an historian from the nation that won that war. Authors from different groups, peoples, or nations will write different histories. Students only need to be shown early European paintings depicting early contact with First Nations to see how worldview can affect the recording of history. Why are Europeans shown as tall, active, and noble, while First Nations people are not? How would the paintings be different if the artists had been Mi'kmaq or Beothuk?

Showing how significance can change over time and can vary depending on the perspective of different groups may be the most challenging competency for students to meet regarding historical significance.

Generating Powerful Understandings of Historical Significance

Use the lessons and activities in the second half of this chapter to enable your students to move from limited to powerful understandings of the ideas embodied in the guideposts.

> Guidepost 1 Events, people, or developments have historical significance if they **resulted in change**. That is, they had deep consequences, for many people, over a long period of time.

DEMONSTRATION OF LIMITED UNDERSTANDING	DEMONSTRATION OF POWERFUL UNDERSTANDING
Student shows an unexamined faith in the textbook or other authority as a basis for significance, or relies on simple personal preference as the basis for historical significance.	Student explains the historical significance of events, people, or developments by showing that they **resulted in change**.

> Guidepost 2 Events, people, or developments have historical significance if they are **revealing**. That is, they shed light on enduring or emerging issues in history or contemporary life.

DEMONSTRATION OF LIMITED UNDERSTANDING	DEMONSTRATION OF POWERFUL UNDERSTANDING
Student limits his or her criteria for historical significance to the level of impact of an event, person, or development.	Student explains the historical significance of events, people, or developments by showing what they **reveal** about issues in history or contemporary life.

> Guidepost 3 Historical significance is **constructed**. That is, events, people, and developments meet the criteria for historical significance only when they are shown to occupy a **meaningful place in a narrative**.

DEMONSTRATION OF LIMITED UNDERSTANDING	DEMONSTRATION OF POWERFUL UNDERSTANDING
Student is unable to identify how significance is constructed in textbooks or other historical accounts.	Student identifies how historical significance is **constructed through narrative** in textbooks or other historical accounts.

> Guidepost 4 Historical significance **varies** over time and from group to group.

DEMONSTRATION OF LIMITED UNDERSTANDING	DEMONSTRATION OF POWERFUL UNDERSTANDING
Student assumes that significance is fixed and unchanging (i.e., is inherent in an event, person, or development).	Student shows how historical significance **varies** over time and from group to group.

Working with
HISTORICAL
SIGNIFICANCE

To design lessons and units that help students achieve the powerful understandings of historical significance, frame your lessons around a discipline-based inquiry, beginning with a carefully crafted question. An inquiry question can provide the "conceptual Velcro" that gives a purpose and direction to activities that might otherwise seem disconnected.

An inquiry question
- captures and sustains student interest
- guides students toward a better understanding of the concept
- results in a tangible, lively, substantial, enjoyable "performance task" that wraps up the lesson sequence. Through this task, students should be able to generate an answer to the inquiry question.[5]

It can be difficult to find a question that meets all three criteria for a good inquiry question. "Why is Champlain historically significant?" may require historical thinking, but it is hardly engaging. It could, however, be reworded to increase interest: "Does Champlain deserve to be called the father of New France?" Likewise, "What was the importance of the Charter of Rights and Freedoms?" could be more provocatively worded as "Was the Charter really that important?"

Inquiry questions can and should be asked often. You can introduce them at the start of a lesson or unit, and then make them a point of reference: post them on a wall, print them on blackline masters, and discuss them at various times—particularly before a culminating task that requires students to answer them.

Introducing Historical Significance

Like the introductory activities for the other concepts in this book, the following activity is generic—independent of course content—and is intended to help you explore students' preconceptions about the concept and raise their curiosity. So, before engaging in an inquiry to investigate a specific example of historical significance, use the following activity to introduce the idea that the topics that appear in history textbooks and other accounts

---

5 Riley, M. (2000, May). Into the key stage 3 history garden: Choosing and planting your enquiry questions. *Teaching History, 99,* 8.

are chosen based on criteria. Many students never consider this. The past is a given. The stories in the history text just are. If we are to see progress in students' facility in historical thinking, we need to help them examine these usually unspoken ideas, as they do with the "sketch and reflect" activity that follows.

ACTIVITY: Sketching Significance

In this activity, students make personal decisions about what is historically significant, and then consider the criteria that they used to make those decisions. The sketch that students produce can be saved for reflection and revision as the school year goes forward. It is adaptable to most grade levels and can be used to assess content knowledge as well.

- Ask students to draw a diagram on a blank sheet of paper to show the most significant events, people, or developments in the history of the world (or of Canada or a defined region or time period, depending on the unit you are teaching). Tell them that
  - they may use pictures, icons, or words to create their elements
  - they should arrange their elements in a way that makes sense to them personally
- State the task limitation: they have only *15 minutes* to complete their sketches. Explain that the task is really too big to complete in 15 minutes, but that the time limit is meant to force them to think on their feet—to choose carefully but quickly.[6]
- Before students begin, warn them that afterwards they will be explaining their choices, as well as their arrangement of figures. This knowledge will encourage them to take the task seriously.
- After providing 15 minutes for students to work independently, ask them to add themselves to their sketches, if they have not already done so.
- Once they are finished, distribute **BLM 1.1: Analyzing Your Significance Sketch**, and ask students to write the answers to the questions.
- Invite students to share their sketches and answers with a partner. Then, hold a class discussion to compare and contrast the criteria that students used to decide what to include in their sketches. Take note of student answers, perhaps by listing the most common answers on the board, so that you can refer to these as you move on to discuss explicitly the criteria for historical significance.
- Explain to students that they have just completed the task—using criteria to rank according to importance—that all historians use to decide what is worthwhile studying or researching, or in other words, to decide what is historically significant.

---

6 See Seixas, P. Mapping the terrain of historical significance. *Social Education*, (61.1), 22–27, and Létourneau, J. & Moisan, S. (2004). Young people's assimilation of a collective historical memory: A case study of Quebeckers of French-Canadian heritage. In P. Seixas (Ed.), *Theorizing historical consciousness* (pp. 109–128). Toronto: University of Toronto Press.

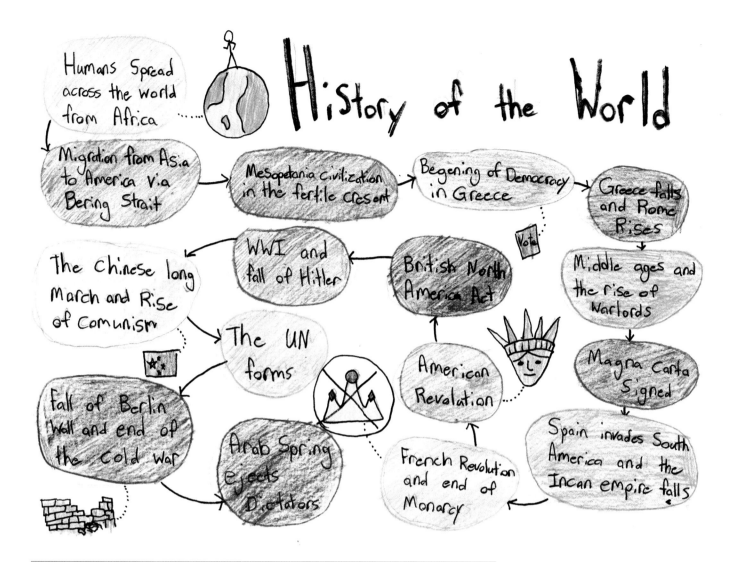

Figure 1.7 This history of the world sketch was made by a Grade 8 student who says she chose a political theme because "that's what interests me," and the specific events because they "changed things for a lot of people." Note that she was permitted a little more time than the 15 minutes recommended for this activity.

Alternative

Another introductory activity, especially appropriate for elementary students, is to ask them to write, draw, or make a timeline of their life story that includes the five most significant events or developments in their life. Ask them to explain why they made the choices they did.

Teaching Guidepost 1

Broad inquiries to begin a unit or lesson that focus on historical significance could be developed using question stems such as these:

- Why should we bother to learn about X?
- Why does everyone remember Y?

As you develop your own inquiry questions, it is best to be pithy. A short preamble giving context, however, can make the inquiry more student friendly. For example, "What were the most significant social welfare laws passed after World War II?" could be made more engaging by adding the preamble below in the first sentence of the assignment. You can also add specific instructions to indicate a specific performance task, as in the final sentence:

> The opening sentence of the Canadian Museum of Civilization's "Social Progress Gallery" says that "Social progress is the weight of laws designed to alleviate human suffering." What laws have done the most to alleviate suffering? Which ones deserve to be in the gallery? Your task will be to prepare a "Hall of Fame of Progressive Laws" with an explanation of your criteria for your choices.

Similarly, giving students an imaginary but authentic role can give the activity more meaning. For example, the task in the final sentence could ask students to be the museum's historian; in the activity **Ranking Topics as the Textbook Author** on page 30, students take on the role of a textbook author making selections for inclusion in a textbook chapter.

The first criterion for historical significance, "resulting in change," as described in Guidepost 1, is usually the easiest for students to recognize. Students readily grasp that a person or event can become historically significant by affecting many people (quantity) in a deep way (profundity) over a long period of time (durability).

To introduce students to the first criterion, draw on the criteria that they used to justify their choices in the activity **Sketching Significance** on page 26. Identify instances in which students used quantity, profundity, or durability of impact to signify historical significance. You may wish to develop a list of events, people, or developments that the whole class agrees resulted in profound impact for many people over a long period of time. Leave the wording of the guidepost in plain view, and use one or more of the following three activities to give students practice in using this criterion.

If your students are familiar with the "revealing" criterion, you may also use the activities below for practice in using this criterion.

ACTIVITY: Ranking Topics in a Unit

PURPOSE

To provide students with an overview of a unit and with practice using a specific criterion, such as "resulting in change," to determine historical significance

Give students a list of topics that will be covered in an upcoming unit. Ask students to draw on their prior knowledge of the time period or theme to rank the topics from most to least historically significant based on the "resulting in change" criterion, and then to defend their choices. Display the guidepost for reference. Students can rank the list individually or in small groups.

In addition to giving students practice in using the "resulting in change" criterion to weigh significance at the beginning of a unit, this activity can provide students with an overview and chronology of the time period to be studied. As well, as with the introductory activity, a ranking can help to uncover students' preconceptions about significance. Finally, this activity can give you an opportunity to "sell" the unit, that is, to answer in advance the omnipresent question, "Why are we learning this?" The activity can be repeated after the unit of study is complete, and the results compared.

Alternative

A diamond ranking adds variety to this exercise. Divide students into pairs and give each pair an envelope containing brief descriptions of nine events, people, or developments that will be part of the upcoming unit. Ask pairs to rank their historical significance in a diamond formation like the one below.

The most significant event, person, or development should be placed at the top of the diamond. The next two are both placed in second position. The three across the centre row share fourth position. The next two, in the fourth row, share seventh position. The least historically significant is placed at the bottom of the diamond.

When pairs have completed their ranking, join pairs to form groups of six. Each pair then explains and seeks to justify its ranking to the other two pairs. The six try to negotiate a consensus ranking for the group as a whole. The groups of six then explain their consensus to the whole class.

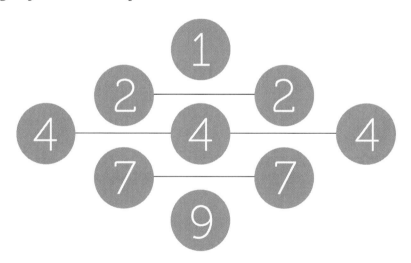

Figure 1.8 This diamond-shaped ranking model acknowledges that events, people, and developments can have equal historical significance, though possibly for different reasons. After students use this model at least once, ask them to compare the pros and cons of this ranking model with a linear ranking model (i.e., ranking 1–10).

ACTIVITY: Survivor in a Hot-Air Balloon

The Hot-Air Balloon Debate is a well-known learning game, and one of the few to have its own Wikipedia entry.

- Before class, choose a selection of events, people, or developments that are featured in a unit that students have already studied. These will be "passengers" in a hot-air balloon that students must rate for historical significance.
- Divide the class into small groups. The number of groups should be the same as the number of "passengers."

PURPOSE

To improve student familiarity with the criteria for historical significance

- The debate begins when you make an announcement, as follows:

  You are in a hot-air balloon that is losing height rapidly and will soon crash because it is overweight! Your task is to choose three (or more) passengers to get rid of so the others can survive. Who will you choose to save? The passengers are ...

... and then list off your selection of "passengers." Explain that the class will take the following steps to decide on the relative historical significance of each passenger. The most historically significant passengers get to stay in the balloon.

- Assign each group a passenger and direct group members to work together to find reasons why their assigned passenger is historically significant enough to deserve to stay in the sinking balloon.
- One representative from each group presents the group's arguments to the class. The class then votes to decide which of the passengers are more significant than the others.
- Debrief, focusing on the reasons *why* students chose to save some passengers but not others.[7]

Alternatives

You may wish to use other imaginary life-or-death scenarios in place of a sinking hot-air balloon, such as a lifeboat lost at sea, a stranded spaceship, or a mine that has caved in on trapped miners. The imagined situations are useful merely to add interest. You may wish to think of a scenario relevant to the unit topic, such as sailors trapped on a sinking submarine during the Battle of the Atlantic.

ACTIVITY: Ranking Topics as the Textbook Author

The decision-making format can also be used toward the end of a unit of study to consolidate learning. For example, provide students with the following scenario:

You are a famous author. Your publishing company hired you—on a lucrative contract—to write a textbook chapter on the Cold War [or the topic of the unit], but it has suddenly fallen on hard times and now has a small budget. The editor-in-chief can only afford a short chapter. So, she asks you to write about only the five most historically significant events, people, or developments. Make a proposal to the editor-in-chief listing the five topics you plan to write about (in order of importance), giving the reasons why you choose them.

If you have already introduced the criterion of "revealing," it could be included as well as "resulting in change" as the basis for students' decisions.

PURPOSE

To give students an opportunity to demonstrate their understanding of criteria for determining historical significance

CONNECTIONS BETWEEN CONCEPTS

If you choose one of the alternative tasks, such as designing a mural, this exercise overlaps with the ethical dimension, which concerns, in part, who from the past should be celebrated and why.

---

7 Matthew Bradshaw warns against unwarranted simplification of a complex concept—a risk of this exercise. Bradshaw, M. (2006, December). Creating controversy in the classroom: Making progress with historical significance. *Teaching History, 125,* 21–22.

Alternatives

Other scenarios might include telling students they are on a committee that is assigned to design a poster, monument, or mural illustrating the most significant events in the life of a historical figure or in the history of your community. Invite students to rank the topics in a similar way.

Teaching Guideposts 2 and 3

The second criterion for historical significance involves an event, person, or development that did *not* have impact according to the first criterion. According to many historians, events, people, and developments with little or no impact can nonetheless have historical significance if they *reveal* something about the past that is of concern to us today. This was the reasoning that Brook used to bring significance to Delft.

It can be hard for students to recognize the significance of topics that had few major consequences, such as Vermeer's hat or the Dionne quintuplets. Yet these can reveal much to us. For example, the quintuplets' experience can cast light on the position of children and poor families in 1930s Canada, as well as on issues of power and rights.

The key to helping students master the "revealing" criterion is to assist them in recognizing how historical significance is contingent on giving the event, person, or development a place within a historical narrative. Vermeer's hat has a place in the narrative of globalization. The Dionne quintuplets have a place in the story of the social history of the 1930s and the broad movement toward human rights continuing today.

As you introduce the "revealing" criterion to students, it is important to note that the historian *constructs*, or creates, the figure's significance. Historical significance, in fact, cannot exist without being created or constructed. Historians, filmmakers, and textbook authors make choices about what to feature in their works. They make these choices to serve a purpose, answer a question, or throw light on an issue in the past or present. The storytellers of history then link their choices to a larger narrative to meet their goals, as Adam Hochschild links a meeting in a print shop to the larger story of abolition of slavery (as you will see in the activity **Analyzing Bury the Chains** on page 32).

Significance then is relative and contingent, not inherent in the event, person, or development itself. Although students may need considerable guidance to develop this understanding, small, personal, revealing stories readily engage their interest. Students are fascinated, for example, by the secret of Hudson's Bay Company employee John Fubbister when they discover that "he" was Isabel Gunn, who was only revealed as a woman when she gave birth

> **DEMONSTRATION OF POWERFUL UNDERSTANDING 2**
>
> Student explains the historical significance of events, people, or developments by showing what they **reveal** about issues in history or contemporary life.

> **DEMONSTRATION OF POWERFUL UNDERSTANDING 3**
>
> Student identifies how historical significance is **constructed through narrative** in textbooks or other historical accounts.

after a holiday celebration at Fort Pembina in December 1807. Although interesting in its own right, the story sparks further student inquiry into the position of women in the larger narrative of the fur trade.

Students become adept at recognizing the construction of historical significance by practising with a variety of historical accounts, as they do in the activity **Analyzing Bury the Chains** below. Text that has not been questioned is like courtroom testimony that has not been examined. This form of critical thinking aligns with "Questioning the Author"—a well-researched reading strategy that is intended "to help students become more actively engaged as readers with a voice."[8] Students skilled in historical inquiry, moreover, may be better able to challenge those who would misuse history.

Inquiry questions to explore the criteria of revealing and the role of narrative can be quite direct, such as "Who or what does the creator of this narrative think is historically significant?" However, this hardly qualifies as a good inquiry for capturing student interest. An inquiry needs to begin with what John Dewey called "some perplexity, confusion, or doubt." Toward this end, such a question could be reworded as

- Why does the writer, director, or artist include X but not Y?
- What did the writer, director, or artist leave out or downplay?
- Whose voices don't we hear, and why?

Key concepts such as historical significance must be questioned, played with, and explored if they are to be understood. Content that has not been questioned is like courtroom testimony that has not been examined. All of the above inquiry questions challenge students to think for themselves and make reasoned judgments about historical significance.

ACTIVITY: **Analyzing Bury the Chains**

PURPOSE

To gain practice in identifying how an historian constructs historical significance by connecting to a narrative

MATERIALS

- BLM 1.2: Bury the Chains (1 per student)

In this activity, students identify the construction of historical significance in an excerpt from a recent history about the antislavery movement: *Bury the Chains: Prophets and Rebels in the Fight to Free an Empire's Slaves* by Adam Hochschild.[9] This exercise can be done as a whole class activity, in groups, or individually.

- Distribute **BLM 1.2: Bury the Chains**. Ask students to read the passages excerpted from *Bury the Chains* by Adam Hochschild on **BLM 1.2a: Bury the Chains**. After they are finished reading, ask students to answer the questions on **BLM 1.2b: Bury the Chains**.
- Discuss student responses together as a class. Pay particular attention to question 6, and ensure that students grasp how Adam Hochschild constructed historical significance by connecting an event with a larger narrative.

---

8 Ogle, D., Klemp, R., & McBride, B. (2007). *Building literacy in social studies: Strategies for improving comprehension and critical thinking* (p. 19). Arlington, VA: ASCD.

9 Hochschild, A. (2005). *Bury the chains: Prophets and rebels in the fight to free an empire's slaves.* New York: Houghton Mifflin.

Teaching Guidepost 4

Because historical significance is constructed, the choices of what is considered historically significant vary according to a person's background, knowledge, and worldview, among other factors. Similarly, people's choices change over time primarily because the issues that interest us also change over time.

You can encourage students to consider these two forms of variance by presenting questions such as the following, adapting them to the periods of history you are studying:

- Why do people tell different stories about X?
- Why do today's textbooks include more material on group X than did textbooks of 50 years ago?

An example you can use to illustrate changing historical significance over time is the story of Tekahionwake, commonly known as Pauline Johnson. This poet of mixed Mohawk and British ancestry wrote and performed poetry in Canada in the late nineteenth and early twentieth centuries. She was one of very few female writers in Canada at that time to make a living in her field. Thousands of Canadian schoolchildren read her signature poem, "The Song My Paddle Sings."

Although her funeral in 1913 was at that point the largest in Vancouver history, Johnson soon faded into historical "insignificance." Recently, however, historians have re-evaluated her importance as their interest in the artistic work of First Nations and women has increased. Historians now appreciate her resistance to dominant ideas about race, gender, and Canada. Actor Donald Sutherland quoted a Johnson poem at the opening ceremony to the 2010 Olympics in Vancouver, something that would have been unheard of 50 years ago during her temporary period of insignificance.

Reflection on the changing historical significance of people such as Pauline Johnson can contribute to anti-racist or human rights education when we ask the inquiry question, "Why was Pauline Johnson 'insignificant' for so many years? Why is she historically significant now?"

ACTIVITY: Moving beyond the Textbook Timeline

Most history textbooks include timelines that highlight the events that the textbook authors believe are the most historically significant. Rarely does a text provide alternative chronologies displaying choices made from different perspectives. Rarely are the choices ever examined as choices. To adapt Socrates' dictum to historical thinking, the unexamined timeline is not worth reading.

Walk students through a comparison of a variety of timelines, aiding students in identifying the differences.

- Begin by helping students examine a timeline in your class textbook. If one is not available, show a straightforward example from the

---

DEMONSTRATION OF POWERFUL UNDERSTANDING 4

Student shows how historical significance **varies** over time and from group to group.

CONNECTIONS BETWEEN CONCEPTS

Inquiries that provide opportunities to raise issues such as sexism and civil rights lend themselves to consideration of the ethical dimension of historical thinking, because when we decide who is historically significant, we are also deciding who is "worthy" of our attention.

PURPOSE

To practise identifying how historians' choices regarding historical significance reflect their different perspectives

sources on **BLM 1.3: Sources for Timelines**. Using a "think aloud" strategy, model for students how to use criteria to interpret the significance and perspective of the entries on the timeline. Most entries will have been included because they "resulted in change." When taken together, some sets of entries will suggest a coherent narrative.

- Ask students to conduct a similar analysis with the Environmental History Timeline[10] or another in the selection offered on **BLM 1.3: Sources for Timelines**. Students should identify the criteria and perspectives behind the selection of events, people, and developments included. Alternatively, different groups of students could be given different timelines from the blackline master. Ask each group to report to the class on the kinds of events, people, and developments listed in their timeline. They should share what they infer are the points of view and criteria for the timeline creators' selection of these items.

- After students have examined two or more timelines, conduct a class discussion by working through the questions below. Responses to the final question in particular provides feedback about students' understanding of the variability of historical significance.
  - What do you notice is the same about these timelines? What is different?
  - What might explain these differences?
  - Are some of these timelines better than others? On what basis do you think this?
  - How do you think the contents of our textbook and its timelines might look if this were a textbook in another province? In another country?
  - What topics do you think were important in a history textbook written 50 years ago? How about in one written 50 years from now?
  - If two authors of history textbooks or websites look at the same facts, will they tell the same stories? Why or why not?
  - What can you conclude from this exercise about the nature of history?

Consolidating Understanding

Something or someone can become historically significant by resulting in large-scale change or by revealing something about the past that is important to us today. In either case, historical significance is always demonstrated through the particular's place in a larger story.

ACTIVITY: Write Me a Story

This class activity invites students to review topics they have already covered, reconsider their historical significance, and write an historical story that demonstrates their conclusions. This activity is appropriate for the end of a unit, term, or year.

---

10 Kovarik, W. *Environmental history timeline.* Retrieved May 18, 2012, from http://www.radford.edu/wkovarik/envhist/index.html

---

- Begin by identifying the themes you have studied. You may define these themes yourself, or arrive at them through discussion with the class. They can be themes related to politics, economics, demographics, or society; or they can be defined in terms of issues such as immigration, French-English relations, gender relations, and international relations. Your goal is to have enough themes that every group of four will write a story on a different theme, although there could be repeated themes. (Divide the number of students by four to determine the number of themes needed.)
- Write the names of your chosen themes on eight large pieces of paper and post them around the classroom.
- Create a list of specific events, people, or developments (i.e., topics) that go with the chosen themes. These, too, may be arrived at through discussion with the class, or through your own definition. Ensure that several topics fit comfortably into each determined theme. Generate enough topics so every student has a different one, although here, too, topics could be repeated, if necessary.
- Assign one topic to each student. All students review their assigned topics and decide why the event, person, or development was historically significant.
- Ask students to think about which theme or themes would make the best home for their topic.
- Direct students to gather next to the theme poster that best fits their topic. To help students make their choice, ask them to consider by what criteria their topic is historically significant. For example, did it result in economic change or reveal something important about minority rights? If students have trouble deciding which group they should join, open the question to the class to help in the decision.
- Before moving to the next stage, you may need to adjust the size of groups if they are out of balance. Students should be in groups small enough to work effectively, that is, a maximum of five.
  - For large groups, ask students if there is anyone who is uncertain that they are with the correct theme.
  - For small groups, ask the whole group if there are any other significant events, people, or developments that should be included in their group. Explain that many of the topics could be grouped with more than one theme.
- Finally—and this is the key to the exercise—each group of students composes an historical story that links all of their topics and presents it to the class. The story can be imaginative, but it must be faithful to a plausible interpretation of evidence. Remind students that a good story has a plot and a clear beginning and ending, and it explores its theme in a meaningful way. The significance of the individual events, people, or developments should be demonstrated by their place in the story.
- In a follow-up class discussion, make explicit the criteria and larger narrative in each of the students' stories.

BLM 1.1 Analyzing Your Significance Sketch

Name: _____ Date: _____

Answer the following questions to help you identify the criteria you used to decide which events, people, or developments were most historically significant.

1. Does your sketch show well-known events and powerful people? Or does it show the ordinary lives that most people live?

2. Are there any references to nations or countries in your sketch?

3. Does your sketch show connections to local, national, or international issues?

4. Do your choices feature big historical changes?

5. Did your choices change people's lives?

6. If you added yourself to the sketch, how did you position yourself in relation to the other elements, and why?

7. Does your sketch tell a story? If so, what is the message in your story?

8. Considering your answers to questions 1 to 7, what reasons or criteria helped you decide what to include in your sketch?

BLM 1.2a **Bury the Chains**

Name: _____ Date: _____

Read the following passages from Adam Hochschild's book *Bury the Chains*.[11] As you read, think about what each passage is contributing to your understanding of the story of the abolition movement.

1   *Strangely, in a city [London, England] where it seems that on almost every block a famous event or resident is commemorated by a blue and white glazed plaque, none marks this spot. All you can see … are a few low, nondescript office buildings, an ancient pub, and, on this site itself, 2 George Yard, a glass and steel high-rise. Nothing remains of the bookstore and print shop that once stood here.*

2   *At the end of the eighteenth century, well over three quarters of all people alive were in bondage of one kind or another … of slavery or serfdom. The age was a high point in the trade in which close to eighty thousand chained and shackled Africans were loaded onto slave ships and transported to the New World each year …*

3   *This is the story of the first, pioneering wave of that campaign [to abolish slavery].… England is where the story really begins, and for decades it was where American abolitionists looked for inspiration and finally for proof that the colossally difficult task of uprooting slavery could be accomplished. If we were to fix one point when the crusade began, it would be the late afternoon of May 22, 1787, when twelve determined men sat down in the printing shop at 2 George Yard.*

4   *The British abolitionists were shocked by what they came to learn about slavery and the slave trade. They were deeply convinced that they lived in a remarkable time that would see both evils swept from the face of the earth. Like anyone who wages such a fight, they discovered that injustice does not vanish so easily. But their passion and optimism are still contagious and still relevant to our times, when, in so many parts of the world, equal rights for men and women seem far distant.*

5   *The movement they forged is a landmark for another reason.… Slaves and subjugated people have rebelled throughout history, but the campaign in England was something never seen before: it was the first time a large number of people became outraged, and stayed outraged for many years, over someone else's rights. And most startling of all, the rights of another colour, on another continent.*

---

11 Hochschild, A. (2005). *Bury the chains: Prophets and rebels in the fight to free an empire's slaves* (pp. 1–5). New York: Houghton Mifflin.

The Big Six Historical Thinking Concepts   Copyright © 2013 by Nelson Education Ltd.

BLM 1.2b **Bury the Chains**

Name: _____ Date: _____

After reading the passages from *Bury the Chains*, answer these questions.

1. Passage 1 sets the scene today. What does it convey, if anything, about the significance of what is to come?

2. Passage 2, which is from the beginning of the historical narrative, lays out the conditions at the end of the eighteenth century. What is the most notable point?

3. Passage 3 tells the beginning of the real, detailed, specific action of the story, with an event and some people. Who, what, when, and where was the event?

4. Passage 4 tells us why this story is important. In your own words, tell why it is important.

5. Passage 5 follows up and expands on why the story is important. Again, in your own words, what does this paragraph add?

6. Explain, in your own words, why twelve men sitting down at a table in 1787 could be an historically significant event.

7. Create a list of steps the author took to construct or create the historical significance of the event by giving it a place in the narrative of the abolition movement.

BLM 1.3 **Sources for Timelines**

- The **HistoryWorld** website gives a wide range of summaries of history and timelines from chemistry to the crusades to Canada. Get to the site by searching "historyworld timesearch" and then select "historyworld timelines."

- Oriented toward the British classroom, the award-winning **Timelines.tv** website combines video narratives with timelines. Get to the site by searching "timelines tv."

- The **BBC News** (British Broadcasting Corporation News) website includes country profiles. These include timelines of the countries' national histories. Get to the site by searching "bbc news country profiles." On the profiles page, select a country or region to get to a specific profile. Then click on the timeline link for that profile.

- The **Encyclopedia of Canada** website has a page with a 100 Greatest Events in Canadian History timeline that begins in 985 CE when Bjarni Herjolfsson is said to have sighted Canada and ends in 1996 when Donovan Bailey wins the Olympic gold medal for the 100 metres. Get to the site by searching "encyclopedia of canada 100 greatest events in canadian history timeline."

- The **Canadian Geographic** website includes a First Peoples timeline slideshow that begins in 40 000 BCE and ends in 1999 with the establishment of Nunavut. Get to the website by searching "canadian atlas first peoples timeline."

- The **Simon Fraser University** website hosts a timeline on Chinese Canadian history: From C to C: Chinese Canadian Stories of Migration. It covers events from 1788 to 2010 in a "moving" timeline linked to primary source images and clips of commentaries from historians. Get to the website by searching "from c to c."

- The **Black History Canada** website is home to a timeline of Canadian Black history that begins in 1605 with the arrival of Mathieu Da Costa and includes personal profiles and descriptions of key events. Get to the website by searching "black history canada," and then click on "Timeline."

- The **Smithsonian** website includes a timeline of the Lakota winter counts. These are traditional calendars of the Lakota First Nation from the nineteenth century. Winters are represented in symbolic drawings of battles with other nations, deaths of horses, capturing a medicine arrow, and smallpox epidemics, among others. Get to the website by searching "lakota winter counts."

Chapter 2

EVIDENCE

How do we know what we know about the past?

Guideposts to Evidence

> **Guidepost 1**

History is **interpretation** based on **inferences** made from primary sources. Primary sources can be accounts, but they can also be traces, relics, or records.

> **Guidepost 2**

Asking good questions about a source can turn it into evidence.

> **Guidepost 3**

Sourcing often begins before a source is read, with questions about **who** created it and **when** it was created. It involves inferring from the source the author's or creator's **purposes**, **values**, and **worldview**, either conscious or unconscious.

> **Guidepost 4**

A source should be analyzed in relation to the **context of its historical setting**: the conditions and worldviews prevalent at the time in question.

> **Guidepost 5**

Inferences made from a source can never stand alone. They should always be **corroborated**—checked against other sources (primary or secondary).

Figure 2.1 Members of the Coast Salish Nation celebrate a land use agreement announced by British Columbia Premier Gordon Campbell in 2006. In his book *The Power of Place, The Problem of Time: Aboriginal Identity and Historical Consciousness in the Cauldron of Colonialism* (2011), historian Keith Thor Carlson tells the history of the Stó:lō [STOH-lo] First Nation, one of the Coast Salish First Nations. He examined literally thousands of primary sources for this project, asking the questions that turned some of these sources into evidence. How might the work of historians like Carlson be a help in settling the land claims of First Nations?

Thinking about EVIDENCE

The process of writing history using primary sources involves a three-way interplay among the inquiry questions that propel the study, the close analysis of available sources, and knowledge of the context of the sources. Each informs and refines the other two. The mutual interplay is what makes doing history possible but, at the same time, what makes doing history so difficult.

Figure 2.2 Constructing history using primary sources involves three interrelated tasks. Each informs and refines the other two.

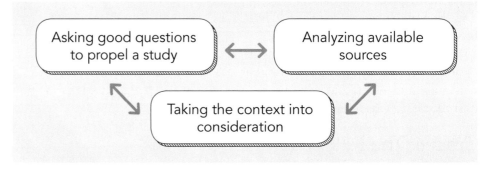

Before the introduction of historical thinking in a classroom, students may go no further in their analysis of sources than to ask "What does it say?" or "What facts does it give me?" Even when they consider primary sources instead of secondary sources, they may be unable to make history from these puzzle pieces from the past. If we can help them grasp that history is *interpretation of evidence*, then they will see the purpose of developing their own ability to interpret. By teaching students how to think like historians, we enable them to engage with history by seeking appropriate sources, analyzing those sources, and considering their context. Students learn not only how to make inferences about their sources but also how to corroborate those inferences.

How One Historian Approaches Evidence

As we begin to think about strategies for teaching students how to use evidence to make history, let us consider what we can learn from the experience of historian Keith Thor Carlson, author of *The Power of Place, The Problem of*

Time.[1] This is the fourth book Carlson has written about the Stó:lō peoples, whose traditional territories lie in southern British Columbia. He worked for some years as an historian and research coordinator for the Stó:lō Nation.

Carlson's most recent book explores the Stó:lō history of social relations, cultural change, and the historical meanings of Stó:lō identity. Of interest in our discussion about the use of evidence in research are his insights into the methods he used to make history from thousands of primary sources. First, though, let us give thought to the question that he was trying to find an answer for: Who are the Stó:lō?

The Question: Who Are the Stó:lō?

The Stó:lō people have occupied lands surrounding the lower reaches of the Fraser River for centuries. Carlson tells the story of a complex Stó:lō identity that has shifted over time. Do the Stó:lō constitute a single Stó:lō Nation throughout the region, or are their identities more tied to local places? Throughout their history, the answer to this question has had implications for political power, cultural status, and economic well-being.

The issue has immediate, contemporary relevance as well: Who can legitimately represent the First Nations of the Fraser River in negotiations with the federal government about Aboriginal rights and land title in the region? Can the Stó:lō negotiate with the federal government as a single political unit, or must individual Stó:lō bands negotiate separately? The answers Carlson sought could not be found in a single source. They would require a deep historical investigation involving literally thousands of sources. Carlson met the challenge by seeking out relevant sources, analyzing them as evidence, and corroborating what that evidence suggested.

Traces: The Raw Material of History

Although we would never expect high school students to conduct research involving thousands of sources, we do want them to understand the process and to learn to analyze sources. In order to examine closely Carlson's use of primary source evidence, it may be helpful to focus on a small piece of his story. In July 1879, Joint Indian Reserve Commissioner Gilbert Malcolm Sproat reported the following:

> All the tribes living between Yale and the mouth of the Fraser [want to organize into a single government].... They must not be in too much a hurry. (pp. 247, 253)

This was the meagre trace of history where Carlson began his construction of an historical account.

1 Carlson, K.T. (2011). *The power of place, the problem of time: Aboriginal identity and historical consciousness in the cauldron of colonialism.* Toronto: University of Toronto Press.

2 Sam Wineburg coined the use of *source* as a verb in 1991 in his definition of the *sourcing heuristic,* as "the practice of reading the source of the document before reading the actual text." (See Wineburg, S. [1991]. On the reading of historical texts: Notes on the breach between school and academy. *American Educational Research Journal, 28*(3), 495–519).

KEY TERMS

account: a narrative or story

context: the circumstances at the time of the creation of a source; the society and belief system in which the source was created as well as the historical events taking place at the time

corroboration: crosschecking; comparing and contrasting one or more sources with an interpretation, with the intention of confirming or refuting the interpretation

evidence: what a source becomes when it is analyzed, thereby becoming pertinent in an historical inquiry

inference: conclusion based on "reading between the lines" of a source

interpretation: an account of the past reached by making inferences from sources; a single event can have multiple interpretations

source: a trace, relic, record, written account, oral testimony, archaeological artifact, or even DNA, that is being analyzed in the course of an historical inquiry

sourcing: asking questions related to the creator of the source and the intended audience[2]

trace: a scrap left over from the past, anything from a menu to a telegram or an email

Figure 2.3 This 1906 photograph shows a First Nation fisher on the Fraser River. Much of what we know of history comes from the examination of traces—the leftovers of the past. This photograph is a good example of a trace: raw material just waiting for analysis.

> Most primary sources ... are ... the detritus of everyday life that just happens to be preserved.

Note that Sproat's words do not *tell the story* of his encounter with the Stó:lō, much less explain *why* he responded as he did. Rather, he was simply doing his job: recording a request and his response. This example clarifies a distinction between traces and accounts. Many primary sources are accounts written in the time period in question, such as eye-witness descriptions of historical events. Most primary sources, however, are like the Sproat quotation: a trace of the past that is left behind by accident—the detritus of everyday life that just happens to be preserved. Traces are not organized as stories, that is, as accounts of a situation; their authors did not intend to provide one. But they do form the material for historians to write theirs. Sproat was not acting like an historian. As we shall see, it is Carlson who thought like an historian by asking questions that would turn Sproat's words into the evidence for the history Carlson would write.

Building a History

Carlson's next step was to ask questions stemming from his source. Why did the Stó:lō wish to be represented by a single government? Why would Sproat not support a politically unified Stó:lō Nation?

Sources that could answer these questions directly were not to be found. Carlson looked elsewhere (he *had* to) to find a parallel encounter with more evidence to support an explanation. Carlson uncovered such an encounter between Sproat and the Nlakapamux Nation (farther up the Fraser River), from which more documentation survived. In this case, there was a different outcome: Sproat supported the Nlakapamux request to be treated as a singular entity. Carlson was puzzled. Why would Sproat support the Nlakapamux in their formation of a central governing institution and remain hesitant about the Stó:lō efforts to do the same?

Geography and demography supplied Carlson with some context to help him work toward an interpretation. The Stó:lō lived in the general area where several communities of newcomers were developing. The total Stó:lō population of 1900 (in 1879) outnumbered even the largest of the newcomers' settlements (New Westminster, at 1500 in 1881). The context of worldviews prevalent at the time gave Carlson further insight: colonial societies generally viewed First Nations as a threat. By putting the context of relatively large First Nations populations alongside the context of the colonial mindset of fear, Carlson could propose an interpretation:

> Colonial society [in the Stó:lō area] was simply not ready to allow that much concentrated power to manifest itself in the hands of Indians. (p. 253)

Thus, Carlson takes the step toward "making history" by using context to help him interpret the evidence and write an historical account.

Corroborating the Interpretation

Carlson knew that he would need to corroborate such an interpretation. He did find documentary evidence that provided this support. Six months before Sproat's communication, the *Victoria Daily Standard*— the largest local newspaper at the time—editorialized as follows:

> Singly the Indian tribes are easily dealt with, but once bind them together by ties, whether political or social, and they will be much more difficult to coerce or persuade. (p. 253)

Carlson found further documentation showing that Sproat's colleagues in the Department of Indian Affairs Pacific office held similar views. Superintendent I.W. Powell endorsed a statement from "Concerned Citizens" fearing that

> ...the future peace of the province is being seriously jeopardised [sic] in this proposed combination of semi-civilized natives.... We desire especially to bring to your notice, that the past safety and security which we have enjoyed in the Province is owing to the fact that the large Indian population of the Country has been divided into small bands without a head Chief possessing the general authority or influence, and without the ability to unite and constitute themselves a powerful and formidable force. (pp. 253, 254)

As it happened, shortly after Sproat's report, the Stó:lō organized to present a coherent voice to Indian Affairs. Sproat retired, but his successors continued to resist Stó:lō efforts to gain recognition. Nevertheless, as Carlson demonstrates, this resistance was not the end of the story. The Stó:lō continued to actively confront new circumstances and face new challenges, with awareness of their place and their past, and an eye to the future.

This small episode in Carlson's larger story of the Stó:lō has been worth considering here because it highlights aspects of the nature of primary sources, their uses by historians, and, in turn, what students need to learn about them. Carlson demonstrated all three components of the process for using evidence in historical research:

1. He asked big, important questions that propelled his research.
2. He conducted close analysis of available sources.
3. He considered those sources in the context of the time period.

Now that we have an overview of the process that an historian takes to conduct historical research using primary sources, let us investigate the process further by examining five guideposts—or big ideas—about evidence, and how we can bring those big ideas into the classroom.

Understanding History as Interpretation

Evidence

> **Guidepost 1**
History is **interpretation** based on **inferences** made from primary sources. Primary sources can be accounts, but they can also be traces, relics, or records.

It can be a revelation to students when they start to understand the difference between *history* and *the past*. The past is everything that has ever happened. Histories are the meaningful stories that we tell about what happened, that is, interpretations. Primary sources, the leftovers from the past, provide the link between the past that is gone and the histories that we write and tell today. As noted above, a phrase like Sproat's "They must not be in too much a hurry" is, like most relics and records, a *trace* of the past. Documents, emails, photographs, videos, databases, restaurant menus, toothpaste ads—these are all the raw material of history. To create a history, one must select relevant sources, ask questions and make inferences about them, and, most important, interpret them. This is the process Carlson went through, first finding a relevant quotation (as above), then making inferences about it (Sproat seemed to disapprove of unification), and finally developing an interpretation (Sproat was reflecting a colonial mindset, prevalent at the time, that Aboriginal peoples were better "handled" if kept disunited).

You will want to help your students recognize the difference between secondary accounts, or histories, and the primary sources on which they are based. This can be achieved by examining the pairing of an historical account with a few pieces of the evidence that the historian used in his or her research. This examination will allow students to see not only the difference between secondary and primary sources but also the process by which historians build an interpretation using inferences drawn from primary sources.

Evidence

> **Guidepost 2**
Asking good questions about a source can turn it into evidence.

Turning a Source into Evidence

Carlson asked two types of questions. The first type were inquiry questions—the questions about Stó:lō identity that propelled his research and guided him to a relevant quotation. Guidepost 2 highlights the second type of questions: the questions that Carlson asked *about* the quotation, and that turned this trace into evidence useful to him in his inquiry. These are questions about not just what the source says or shows, but about what is not said, whose purposes and perspectives are expressed, what generated the source, and what impact it might have had.

Help students develop the competency of framing questions about sources that will help them use these traces of the past as evidence for an argument or an account. Editorial cartoons are useful for teaching this competency because they usually contain fairly obvious messages. Further, students will be able to develop and sometimes answer questions about purpose and perspective, such as "What is the artist's message?"

Sourcing: Starting an Analysis

Sourcing is the first step in analyzing virtually any source. Sourcing questions begin with straightforward queries, such as "When was this written?" "Who wrote this?" and "What was his or her position?" More accomplished students will then move on to questions that are much more difficult to answer, such as "What was the author's attitude toward...?" or "Why would the journalist focus on...?" The latter sort of questions require inference making— suggesting reasonable explanations by reading between the lines and linking to other period sources.

When analyzing stories (or accounts or narratives, all of which are synonyms for our purposes), historians can ask questions about bias, objectivity, and proximity to the events. In dealing with the quotations from Sproat, however, Carlson did not ask these questions because Sproat is not telling a story—he is an historical character *in* the story. So Carlson was interested in Sproat's position, motivation, and purposes, as well as the impact of his words.

Note that Sproat's words did not *tell* Carlson about motivation or purpose; Sproat did not articulate these in the document. Even if he had set them down in writing, however, the historian must necessarily ask whether what he wrote was actually what motivated him. Students need to be able to read meanings that are not actually on the page.

Taking the Context into Account

Contextualizing documents encourages us to analyze sources considering the perspective of the time and in the society in which the source was created. It is unlikely that historical figures would set down the assumptions and worldviews within which they were operating. These constitute the atmosphere they inhaled, and were no more visible to them than the air they breathed. However, this is context that can help us understand and interpret their words accurately. It is the historian's job to map the currents and changes—"the climates of opinion," in Carl Becker's words—of the past. Students need to develop the ability to contextualize documents in the time and place they were created, as Carlson did when he drew on his awareness about colonial attitudes to contextualize Sproat's comments.

Evidence

 Guidepost 3

Sourcing often begins before a source is read, with questions about **who** created it and **when** it was created. It involves inferring from the source the author's or creator's **purposes**, **values**, and **worldview**, either conscious or unconscious.

Evidence

 Guidepost 4

A source should be analyzed in relation to the **context of its historical setting**: the conditions and worldviews prevalent at the time in question.

Figure 2.4 This 1943 poster was created by the Wartime Information Board to send a message to Canadians. The purpose and world-view of the artist, Hubert Rogers, can be inferred by asking good questions about the poster: "What does each character represent?" (soldiers, industrial workers, and women who tend Victory Gardens or keep up the farm while the men are at war) "How does the artist portray these characters?" (good looking, determined, and acting in unison) "What makes this government propaganda?" (purpose is to convince Canadians that contributions on the home front were just as important as soldiering) "Why didn't the artist portray the soldier as a woman?" (women were employed in the armed forces but not as combat soldiers)

The Final Step: Corroboration

Historians comb through a multitude of documents to find relevant sources. Carlson's unearthing of Sproat's July 29, 1879, letter to the Superintendent General of Indian Affairs involved delving through a lot of *other* detritus before he finally got to File 10692, Volume 3669, Reel C-10117, Record Group 10 of the Department of Indian Affairs in Library and Archives Canada, page 338.

The letter proved relevant. Carlson's job of sifting through documentation was not over, however. His next task was to corroborate the inferences he drew from the letter. He corroborated his interpretation of Sproat's thinking about the Stó:lō by comparing it with Sproat's previous statements about the Nlakapamux, as well as comparing it with the views of the "Concerned Citizens" and other officials in Indian Affairs, and with the findings in other secondary sources. Carlson followed the same process with hundreds of other documents, transcripts, and recordings, many of which he then used to write an account of this episode. To be able to construct accounts of events—to "make" history—students need to learn how to handle multiple primary documents—to assess where they reinforce each other and, perhaps even more important, where and why they contradict each other.

Evidence

Guidepost 5

Inferences made from a source can never stand alone. They should always be **corroborated**— checked against other sources (primary or secondary).

Generating Powerful Understandings of Evidence

Use the lessons and activities in the second half of this chapter to enable your students to move from limited to powerful understandings of the ideas embodied in the guideposts.

> **Guidepost 1** History is **interpretation** based on **inferences** made from primary sources. Primary sources can be accounts, but they can also be traces, relics, or records.

DEMONSTRATION OF LIMITED UNDERSTANDING
Student shows an unexamined faith in the trustworthiness of all sources.

DEMONSTRATION OF POWERFUL UNDERSTANDING
Student **makes insightful inferences** from primary sources.

> **Guidepost 2** **Asking good questions** about a source can turn it into evidence.

DEMONSTRATION OF LIMITED UNDERSTANDING
Student is confused about how to ask questions about a source.

DEMONSTRATION OF POWERFUL UNDERSTANDING
Student **asks good questions** that turn primary sources into evidence for an inquiry, argument, or account.

> **Guidepost 3** Sourcing often begins before a source is read, with questions about **who** created it and **when** it was created. It involves inferring from the source the author's or creator's **purposes, values,** and **worldview,** either conscious or unconscious.

DEMONSTRATION OF LIMITED UNDERSTANDING
Student fails to consider questions about the creation of the source.

DEMONSTRATION OF POWERFUL UNDERSTANDING
To begin analyzing a document or visual, student engages in **sourcing,** that is, asking questions about **when** and **why** the source was created, and by **whom.**

> **Guidepost 4** A source should be analyzed in relation to the **context of its historical setting:** the conditions and worldviews prevalent at the time in question.

DEMONSTRATION OF LIMITED UNDERSTANDING
Student makes judgments about the language and messages of sources without taking into account the time period when they were written.

DEMONSTRATION OF POWERFUL UNDERSTANDING
Student **contextualizes** sources—he or she keeps in mind the conditions and worldviews prevalent at the time the source was created.

> **Guidepost 5** Inferences made from a source can never stand alone. They should always be **corroborated**—checked against other sources (primary or secondary).

DEMONSTRATION OF LIMITED UNDERSTANDING
Student makes unwarranted claims on the basis of a single source.

DEMONSTRATION OF POWERFUL UNDERSTANDING
Student **corroborates** inferences from a single source with information from other sources (primary or secondary), and expresses degrees of certainty about those inferences.

Working with EVIDENCE

Introducing Evidence

To introduce students to the idea that history is constructed from traces of the past, we suggest two introductory activities unconnected to the course content. The first engages students by having them analyze their personal experience; the second involves direct instruction.

ACTIVITY: I Left a Trace

Ask students to jot down everything that they have done in the last 24 hours (and that would be appropriate for classroom discussion). After describing what a trace is, ask students to

1. make a list of traces that might have been left of their life in the past 24 hours (including digital traces)
2. identify which traces were purposeful and which were accidental
3. offer an opinion about whether the traces are likely to be preserved[3]

Student answers will provide concrete reference points to introduce words such as *historical record*, *relic*, and *testimony*, as well as add to their understanding of *trace*.

Use the following questions to build from this concrete example to consider broader questions of historical knowledge and the role played by traces:

- Were there any things you did that left no trace or that left only traces that would not be preserved? What does this suggest about the historical record?
- What would future historians think about you if they were able to study your traces? What if they were able to see only those traces that you left *purposefully*?
- What if all the traces of everyone on Earth disappeared and your traces were the only ones to survive? How much would future historians be able to learn about our society by studying only your traces?
- What other kinds of traces, relics, testimony, and records would help historians learn about our society?
- What if historians were trying to study you? What materials—other than those actually created by you—could they use?

---

3 The idea for this exercise comes from Using the familiar to introduce students to the study of primary and secondary sources. (2002–12). *Designed Instruction.* Retrieved from http://www.designedinstruction.com/learningleads/teacher-support-traces.html. Designed Instruction, LLC provides blackline masters and graphic organizers designed for elementary students. This content is used with permission.

| A trace comes into existence. | The trace is preserved over time. | The trace is found by someone, and deemed to be significant. | The trace is interpreted in the light of other primary and secondary sources. This interpretation turns the trace into evidence. | The evidence is incorporated into a meaningful historical account or narrative. |

Figure 2.5 Walk students through the creation of a flow chart like this one to illustrate the process of transforming a trace of the past into "history." Note that the process is often not as linear as the chart suggests.

ACTIVITY: History Versus the Past

Ask small groups of students to list the differences between "history" and "the past." As a class, discuss the answers and use them to lead toward the following distinctions:

- **The past** is everything—every event, thought, belief, vibrating atom, and tree falling in the forest while no one was there.
- **History** is a necessarily selective interpretation of remains from the past. As Ruth Sandwell puts it, "History is someone's attempt to make sense and order out of the chaos of everything-ness."[4]

With students, construct a flow chart as in Figure 2.5 to demonstrate how the past becomes history.

Teaching Guideposts 1 and 2

Interpretation and asking good questions work together. Asking good questions about a source can lead to reasonable inferences. In turn, making reasonable inferences may lead to more good questions.

The first goal is to move students from a superficial reading of a source (looking for factual information) to making more reasoned and insightful inferences. Prompts such as the following can provide scaffolding:

- This clearly shows that ...
- From [detail] we can infer that ...
- This [detail] suggests that ...
- It doesn't say so, but ... is probably the case, because [detail] ...

PURPOSE

To help students distinguish between "the past" and "history," and to help them see the process by which traces of the past lead to history

DEMONSTRATION OF POWERFUL UNDERSTANDING 1

Student **makes insightful inferences** from primary sources.

DEMONSTRATION OF POWERFUL UNDERSTANDING 2

Student **asks good questions** that turn primary sources into evidence for an inquiry, argument, or account.

4 Sandwell, R. (n.d.). History vs. the past. *Great Unsolved Mysteries in Canadian History*. Retrieved from http://www.canadianmysteries.ca/en/3515.php

Goal	Questions to encourage inferences	Examples for analysis
to analyze a portrait	What does this painting suggest about this person?	• the portrait of the Beothuk woman Demasduit (also known as Mary March) from the Library and Archives Canada portrait gallery[5]
to analyze a written document	What do these diary entries reveal to us?	• the diary of Prime Minister Mackenzie King[6]
to analyze interviews	What can we learn from these testimonials?	• transcripts of interviews with post-war Jewish orphans who immigrated to Canada[7]
to analyze a display of personal possessions	What do these possessions suggest about the owner?	• the panoramic photograph of Charles Darwin's study[8] • the interactive photograph of Anne Frank's room[9] • a list of the belongings of Major Martin, the drowned British officer in Operation Mincemeat, the subterfuge to mislead the Germans about the location of the Allied invasion[10]
to analyze artifacts	What is it? What was it used for?	• Aboriginal artifacts on the McCord Museum website[11] • Acadian artifacts from the Village Acadien[12] • artifacts from the British Museum's "History of the World in 100 Objects"[13]
to analyze images of locations	Where is this?	• photographs of your community in the past, such as those at the History Pin[14] website • historical images of Vancouver[15] or Montréal[16]
to focus on the larger narrative	Tell the story of what might have been happening just before the photograph was taken and just after. What is the larger story behind the image?	• the iconic photograph "Wait for me, Daddy," taken by Claude P. Dettloff in 1940 of a young boy chasing after his soldier father as he marches down Eighth Street in New Westminster and off to war[17]

Figure 2.6 Asking the right questions makes all the difference.[18]

5 Library and Archives Canada. (2008, March 19). Retrieved from http://collectionscanada.gc.ca/pam_archives/index.php?fuseaction=genitem .displayItem&lang=eng&rec_nbr=2837235&rec_nbr_list=2895002,2837235&back_url

6 Library and Archives Canada. (2007). *The diaries of Mackenzie King*. Retrieved from http://www.collectionscanada.gc.ca/databases/king/index-e.html

7 Vancouver Holocaust Education Centre. (2002). Open hearts, closed doors: The war orphans project. *Virtual Museum of Canada*. Retrieved from http://www .virtualmuseum.ca/Exhibitions/orphans/english/

8 Charles Darwin's study. (n.d.). *Wikipedia*. Retrieved from http://upload.wikimedia.org/wikipedia/commons/e/e3/Sal%C3%B3n_Down_House.jpg

9 Anne Frank house. (2010). *The Secret Annex Online*. Retrieved from http://www.annefrank.org/en/Subsites/Home/

10 Operation mincemeat. (2012, June 5) *Wikipedia*. Retrieved from http://en.wikipedia.org/wiki/Operation_Mincemeat

11 Keys to history: Unusual objects. *McCord Museum*. Retrieved from http://www.mccord-museum.qc.ca/en/keys/games/29

12 Photo gallery. (2012). *Village historique acadien*. Retrieved from http://www.villagehistoriqueacadien.com/galeriedephotos_en.cfm?albumID=11

13 British Museum and British Broadcasting Corporation. (2011). *A history of the world in 100 objects*. Retrieved from http://www.bbc.co.uk/ahistoryoftheworld/

14 *History Pin*. (2011). Retrieved from http://www.historypin.com/

15 The Moore panorama digitization project. (2011, March 1). *AuthentiCity*. Retrieved from http://www.vancouverarchives.ca/2011/03/the-moore-panorama-digitization-project/

16 Urban life through two lenses. (2002). *McCord Museum*. Retrieved from http://www.mccord-museum.qc.ca/en/keys/virtualexhibits/twolenses/

17 150 years: British Columbia. (2010–2011). *Vancouver Sun*. Retrieved from http://www2.canada.com/vancouversun/features/bc150ed/war.html

18 These suggested prompts are adapted from Werner, W. (2004). "What does this picture say?" Reading the intertextuality of visual images. *International Journal of Social Education*, (19.1), 64–77.

Students who are new to the interpretation of primary sources and the concept of evidence can begin by interpreting sources from familiar surroundings. They might, for example, consider the contents of a photo album or antique trunk from their family to answer "What was your family like?" Or they could walk down the school hallway to look at graduation photographs or study school annuals to consider "What were these students like?"

Question prompts such as those suggested in Figure 2.6 can continue an exploration of these two powerful understandings. Once students become comfortable making inferences, encourage them to express their degree of certainty about their inferences. The adjective *plausible* is useful to this end, as well as various adverbs such as *probably*, *possibly*, *clearly*, and *definitely*. Using sources well means knowing how certain you are.

Comparing different accounts can also sharpen understanding of the process of interpretation. "Which one of these stories should I believe? Which one is supported best by the evidence?" On a regular basis over the course of the year, students can return to reflect on these questions as well as the broader question, "How do we know what we know?"

ACTIVITY: Hook, Line, and Linker

We can't get to the past without passing through the gates of curiosity. And there are some powerful ways to hook students and entice that curiosity, including well-crafted questions that encourage the making of inferences, powerful inquiry questions that make connections to present-day issues or to students' experiences, puzzles, paradoxes, problems to be solved, and primary sources, especially those that are startling or unusual. Our example here is a drawing, but it could just as well be a written document or object. With a well-chosen source that is tied to a key event or personality and skillful questioning, *hooks* can develop *lines* of inquiry and *links* to the concept of evidence.

Stage 1: Initial Observations

When you introduce a hook—your interesting source—take time to linger at the gates and encourage close observation. Show students the drawing and caption in Figure 2.7 (on page 54 and on the DVD-ROM), ideally by projecting it at the front of the class.

Start by asking students to list what they see in the drawing. Students should list as many details as possible. You may wish to have students work in pairs. Select a few students to point out details on a projected version at the front of the class.

Here are some beginning responses from one student:

- naked people
- a soldier firing a gun
- The soldier has a helmet and fancy clothes.
- canoes
- bows and arrows
- guys dead on the ground
- It might be a fort on the right.

PURPOSE

To analyze a source using increasingly powerful questions

MATERIALS

- an engaging primary source (e.g., Figure 2.7, available on the DVD-ROM)

Figure 2.7 *Deffaite des Yroquois au Lac de Champlain, 1609,* drawn by Samuel de Champlain[19]

Encourage further observation with prompting questions such as these:

1. Describe the arrangement of the people in the picture.
2. What technologies of war are shown?
3. What actions are shown?

Stage 2: Making Inferences

Carefully planned questions that encourage the making of inferences are essential for the *line* and *linker*. Work through the following questions, all of which require students to make inferences.

1. What can you infer about the relationships among the three main groups (the soldier with the gun; the two unclothed groups)? What details enable you to make these inferences?
2. Using both the caption and the picture, identify (infer) who is Champlain and which group is the Haudenosaunee (Iroquois).

---

19 Archives Canada-France. (n.d.). *On French soil in America.* Retrieved from http://www.champlain2004. org/html/11/1102_full_1_e.html There is also a description of this battle written by Champlain in his journal available from New York State Education Office. (n.d.). *Champlain, Hudson, Fulton.* Retrieved from http:// www.p12.nysed.gov/ciai/chf/commtwoworlds/twoworldcommclass.html

3. Based on your observations, where do you think this battle took place?
4. Using everything you have figured out up to this point, who or what do you think (infer) Champlain thought was the most important piece of this picture?
5. Using both the caption and the picture, make an inference about what took place after the moment shown in the picture.

Stage 3: Developing Good Questions for Further Inquiry

The next step is to create, through good questions, a *line* of inquiry connecting the analysis of the source with a lesson or unit to come. These questions and lines of inquiry should meet four criteria:

1. They are based on what we already know (from the source and our inferences), but …
2. … we don't already know the answers, but …
3. … with more investigation they should be answerable, and …
4. … they will lead to larger understandings of the historical situation.

With some classes, it will be enough to suggest with students a few good, big questions that offer such lines of inquiry. Here are a few questions that cannot be answered by analyzing the drawing, but which you can use to spark further inquiry:

1. How important was European technology in the defeat of the Haudenosaunee (Iroquois)?[20]
2. How important was Champlain's alliance with the Wendat (Huron)?
3. What were Champlain's goals? Did he achieve them?
4. What were the goals of the Wendat (Huron)? Did they achieve their goals?
5. What were the unintended consequences of Champlain's actions?

Students can also develop their own questions for further inquiry stemming from the picture, with some guidance, of course. Questions to spark inquiries can be similar to the "What I Want to Know" questions in the KWL reading strategy (What I **K**now/What I **W**ant to Know/What I **L**earned). However, they should follow the criteria given above, especially in that they can probably be answered with some research and that they are worth answering, that is, that they lead us to a more complete understanding of Champlain, the Haudenosaunee (Iroquois), the Wendat (Huron), and the early years of New France. Another simple criterion to guide students in writing good inquiry questions is to request "questions that you can't Google to get the answer but that you can still answer."

Students' early efforts to develop inquiry questions might be superficial or simplistic. Be prepared to take some time to help students develop good inquiry questions, and set aside some time for discussion and feedback in

---

20 See Brook, T. (2008), p. 31.

small groups and as a class. If necessary, give some guidance with prompts such as the following:

- What kind of important questions might you ask about the relations among these three groups before and after this battle?
- What questions would be worth exploring about the technology of war?

Collect students' questions, and compile them to create a wonder wall. With the class, discuss which ones meet the criteria for a good inquiry, or big question. Ask students to choose one or two questions for their personal focus, or decide as a class on a small number for a class focus.

Stage 4: Linking to the Evidence Concept

At different points, your analysis of a primary source can be linked to the concept of evidence. Encourage students to step back to recognize their process of observation and making inferences, as well as the role of good questions. Questions such as the following can help in this reflection:

- How did your thinking change as you studied this source?
- What changed when you read the description?
- What did this source not tell us?
- What are its limitations as a window into the past?
- Why are good questions important?
- What do we need to do next to find the answers to our questions?
- What does this suggest about how historians use evidence to learn about the past?

The example we have used to hook students is an image, but we could use any stimulating source. Make the most of readily available resources such as the class textbook. Most modern textbooks are full of primary sources. In many instances, however, accompanying text explains the source; that is, it does the historical thinking for students. In this case, you may want students to study the source in isolation on a projector screen, and not within the context of the textbook. In a pinch, you can use the textbook but ask students to cover up the explanatory text.

ACTIVITY: Decoding an Image Puzzle

The objectives of this activity are similar to those of the previous activity—to encourage students to observe closely, make inferences, and generate further questions—but this activity adds some intrigue. You reveal the puzzle pieces of an image one by one, asking students to make inferences, ask questions, and make predictions about the missing element(s) as you go. This exercise also illustrates the need for context to interpret sources.

PURPOSE

To encourage students to observe closely and make inferences

MATERIALS

- a photograph suitable for an image puzzle analysis (image in Figure 2.8 available on the DVD-ROM)
- access to PowerPoint or other presentation software to prepare your own image puzzle

1. Show the first puzzle piece. Students list details they observe in this piece of the puzzle and predict what the rest will be. You could ask students to draw the rest of the image.

2. Show the second piece. Students check their predictions, list details from the second puzzle piece, and draw or describe what they think will be the third element.

3. Show the complete image. Students check their predictions. Continue with the same questioning procedure given in the activity **Hook, Line, and Linker** on page 53.

Figure 2.8 The step-by-step revelation of a photograph can be used to encourage students to observe closely and make inferences. This photograph shows children watching armed soldiers protecting police headquarters in Montréal during the October Crisis, October 15, 1970. A puzzle like this can be made using a program such as PowerPoint or by simply cutting up photocopies of the photograph.

Teaching Guideposts 3 and 4

Historical thinking requires more than just reading a website for information or finding pictures to illustrate a story. For the historian, there is no free-floating information. A source is a human creation tied to its creator and its time and place. Therefore, before analyzing the content of a primary source, historians ask questions about the creation of the source, including the author's purpose and perspective—what history educators call **sourcing**—and about the conditions and worldviews existing at the time, which is **contextualizing**. This is what Keith Thor Carlson does in using his knowledge of colonialist attitudes to contextualize Gilbert Sproat's report. These two habits of mind work together, reinforcing each other.

Sourcing: asking questions related to the creation of the source

asking questions about the worldviews of whoever created the source

Contextualizing: asking questions about the conditions and worldviews existing at the time when the source was created

Figure 2.9 When students engage in sourcing and contextualizing various sources, they will find that each process informs the other.

DEMONSTRATION OF POWERFUL UNDERSTANDING 3

To begin analyzing a document or visual, student engages in **sourcing**, that is, asking questions about **when** and **why** the source was created, and by **whom**.

DEMONSTRATION OF POWERFUL UNDERSTANDING 4

Student **contextualizes** sources—he or she keeps in mind the conditions and worldviews prevalent at the time the source was created.

All types of sources—from artifacts to orations—offer particular conventions and challenges for students. The following discussion focuses specifically on the interpretation of historical photographs. Interpretation of other types of sources follows similar but different lines of questioning.

Interpreting Historical Photographs

One challenge in interpreting photographs is that students often consider them to be a trustworthy window on the past, rather than a trace. Students may be willing to believe that a speech or an autobiography is subjective. They are even willing to ask critical questions of a photograph if it appears in an advertisement. But when students encounter an historical photograph, it is often seen as inherently truthful. This is reinforced by textbooks, some of which present images as illustrations and not as historical objects to be interpreted.

Broad inquiry questions about historical photographs can address this challenge directly. "Is a photograph simply a record of a moment in time, or can it also have a message? What can a photograph tell us about the purposes, opinions, and beliefs of the person holding the camera?" This can be followed by an inquiry into specific photographs, such as the photograph of the La Tuque hockey team in the activity that follows.

Sourcing

CONNECTIONS BETWEEN CONCEPTS

Sourcing is connected to historical perspective taking. Taking the historical perspective of an individual from history requires students to use evidence as the basis for their inferences about the person's thoughts and feelings.

The first step when an historian picks up any piece of written or visual evidence is to focus on the source's author or creator. We want to encourage the same habit of sourcing with students: looking at the title or notation that describes the creator of the source and asking

- *Who* made this source?
- *What kind* of source is this?
- *How* was it made?
- *When* and *where* was it created?

The same sorts of questions apply to all sources, whether they are photographs or documents. With some obvious sources, such as propaganda posters, students may be able to infer the answers to these sourcing questions quite readily; however, more often they will need to move to close observation and interpretation. Teach students to observe carefully by scanning the image up and down, left to right, and corner to corner, for about 30 seconds to a minute.

Then, ask students "What can you see?" or ask them to make a list of things they can see. These are open-ended questions to which almost every student will have some answer. (Do not ask "What is happening in the photograph?" This is a question that requires inferences, and quite often students will not have a clue.[21])

At some point, students should begin to consider the decisions of the photographer and how these create a particular feeling or impression. Their

---

21 Card, J. (2008). *History pictures: Using visual sources to build better history lessons* (p. 41). London: Hodder Education.

curiosity should lead them toward more complex and demanding sourcing questions that require students to make inferences, such as the following:

- What decisions has the photographer made in creating this image?
- How does this picture make you feel about...?
- Can you work out what the photographer has done to make you feel this way? What is in the photograph to lead us to feel this way?

Contextualizing

Sources can only be understood, of course, in their historical context. We can help students to make connections between what they see in the source with questions such as these:

- What was going on in this society at the time this picture was taken that might help us interpret the photograph?
- How might the context help us understand what life was like for the people in the photograph?
- From what you know about life at the time, how might someone back then have viewed this event?

Students' prior knowledge, the caption, and surrounding text (e.g., in a news article) may give enough context to allow students to interpret the source thoroughly. In many cases, however, important context such as the techniques or technology of the medium, little known but relevant events at the time, and the social and intellectual milieu in which the source was produced will be outside your students' knowledge. Students may need to do further research, or you may need to supply that context.

To help students grasp the importance of considering context, describe to them an obvious example of misinterpretation stemming from lack of context. SS-Obersturmführer Karl Höcker, the adjutant to the commandant of Auschwitz, kept a photo album. It is full of happy photographs of SS officers enjoying social functions. Ask students, "What impression about SS officers might you be left with if your only piece of evidence about them was this album?" and "What is left out of this album?" What is absent is any clue to the broader context within which the officers are enjoying their social activities: the gas chambers, torture chambers, and treatment of prisoners.[22] This very lack of context makes it a good source for inferring the perspective of its creator, Karl Höcker.

It is important to know whether you can trust a source (and sometimes it is obvious that you cannot). However, some students may be tempted to reject a source such as Höcker's photo album after they label it as "biased." Help students realize that identifying the worldviews and perspectives (or mindset) of a creator can only enrich their understanding of a period of history.

---

22 Auschwitz through the lens of the SS: Photos of Nazi leadership at the camp. (n.d.). *United States Holocaust Memorial Museum*. Retrieved from http://www.ushmm.org/museum/exhibit/online/ssalbum/?content=3

ACTIVITY: Sourcing and Contextualizing a Photograph

PURPOSE

To give students practice sourcing and contextualizing an historical photograph

MATERIALS

- a variety of types of current photographs
- **BLM 2.1: Contextualizing a Hockey Team Photograph** (1 per student)
- projection of Figure 2.12 (optional; available on the DVD-ROM)

If your class has not previously analyzed photographs as evidence, take some time to establish with students the role of interpretation with a few examples. Show students a variety of types of current (i.e., not historical) photographs, such as a family photograph, a sports team photograph, a photograph in an advertisement, a news photograph, and a profile picture on a social networking site. As you display these images, preferably enlarged at the front of the class, include titles and captions if you have them.

In each case, challenge students to get inside the photographer's head, that is, to identify the photographer's purpose and viewpoint beginning with identifying the information in the caption, then moving to close observation, interpretation, and contextualization.

Explain to students that the skills and thinking they showed in your collaborative analysis of these photographs are the same as those that an historian uses when looking at historical photographs: sourcing (asking questions about the creator), close analysis, and contextualizing (using the context to better understand both the subject of the photograph and the photographer's worldview).

Sourcing the Hockey Team Photograph

Now begin a detailed consideration of a particular historic photograph: the La Tuque Residential School's hockey team in 1967. Ideally, project Figure 2.12 and its caption at the front of the classroom (available on the DVD-ROM).[23] If this is not possible, distribute **BLM 2.1: Contextualizing a Hockey Team Photograph**, which includes the photograph. Ask students to delay reading the excerpts provided on the blackline master.

Explain that you are going to follow the same steps you took as a class to analyze the current photographs. Begin by asking a few straightforward sourcing questions:

- When was it taken?
- Where was it taken?
- Who was the photographer?
- What else does the caption tell you?

Making Observations and Inferences

Ask students to examine the photograph slowly for up to a minute. Ask them to share what they see and how these observations help them better understand the meaning of the photograph. Continue with questions such as the following, naming the type of historical thinking from time to time:

---

23 It is important to use good quality photographs for close observation. Many are available at The evidence web. (2008, January 11). *Library and Archives Canada*. Retrieved from http://www.collectionscanada.gc.ca/education/sources

- What are the hockey players wearing on their heads? (observation)
- Why are they wearing feathers if feathers aren't hockey equipment? Who do you think decided that they should all wear feathers? (inferences from context about the purpose of the photograph)
- Do you see any other details that might support your inferences? What is on their hockey sweaters? (observation)
- What are the facial expressions of the boys? (observation)
- What can we infer from this about their feelings? (inference)

Ask students to consider the information they have thus far to infer answers to these more demanding questions:

- What does the photograph suggest about the La Tuque residential school and these students?
- Who may have been the audiences for such a message? (list several)
- What might have been the photographer's purpose in taking the photograph for these audiences?

Contextualizing the Photograph

Now that students have had a chance to observe the photograph in detail, pass out **BLM 2.1: Contextualizing a Hockey Team Photograph**, if you have not done so already. Ask students to read only the two paragraphs below the photograph. As a class, answer the following questions associated with the text. Then, one by one, follow the same process for Excerpts 1 and 2. Note that students may find some contradiction between the photograph and the sources; that is, the boys are smiling, yet the sources speak of dreadful treatment. This is exactly what corroboration should do—confirm inferences in some cases, and challenge them in others.

As you move to teaching Guidepost 5, you will see that students are already well prepared for it if they have successfully completed this exercise on contextualization. Contextualizing with multiple sources involves processes similar to corroboration.

Teaching Guidepost 5

Few of our students become professional historians. But they live in a world overflowing with information, in which it can be hard to distinguish supportable claims from the spurious. The historians' skill in sorting the wheat from the chaff can empower all students to deal with the influx of questionable information in their daily lives.

The process of corroborating a source tests it against other sources of information to give us a better idea of how we should interpret it. Not only do students need to be capable of assessing the credibility of historical sources and to determine gaps in the evidence, but they also need to be aware of the necessity of doing so. The examination of the evidence enables them to develop their own interpretation or to evaluate another's.

DEMONSTRATION OF POWERFUL UNDERSTANDING 5

Student **corroborates** inferences from a single source with information from other sources (primary or secondary), and expresses degrees of certainty about those inferences.

The Questions to Ask

Begin teaching about corroboration—more commonly called crosschecking—by modelling out loud the thinking process of corroboration and assessing certainty. Then, in pairs, students can take turns following your lead, each asking questions and making assertions about a different document.

Before the think aloud, you may wish to post questions such as the following to scaffold student thinking:

- What is similar about these sources? How do they differ?
- Why are they similar or different?
- Does this source confirm what I have already learned?
- Does it extend what I know about the topic?
- Does it challenge what I have already examined?
- Do I have enough evidence on this? Can I move on?

Still other questions can assess the relevance of sources, such as

- Why is this source important?
- What makes this source an important piece of evidence?

Sentence stems for thinking aloud or writing about corroboration include the following:

- Source X supports what I have learned so far because it ...
- Source X goes even further than source Y in showing that ...
- Source X contradicts the evidence of Source Y by suggesting that ...
- These pictures show different effects of ...

Expressing a Degree of Certainty

Closely aligned to corroboration is reflection on degree of certainty. Help students understand that we cannot always find definite answers to our questions in history because there are not always enough sources, they may not tell us all we want to know, or they may disagree with one another. Students will need to use adverbs that express uncertainty, such as *probably*, *likely*, and *possibly*, and verbs such as *suggests* or *implies*.

Sentence stems for thinking aloud or writing about degrees of certainty are

- These sources lead me to believe that ...
- These sources clearly show ...
- It is highly likely (based on the sources) that ...
- These sources clearly show ... but we are still uncertain about ...

At some point in teaching corroboration, ask students to extend their learning by asking questions such as

- How do you think comparing sources might reflect the work that historians do?
- Can you think of other times and places when you might want to compare sources?

Activities that Involve Corroboration

1. **Compare an historical account against sources.** Students can study an account of an historic event and then compare it with evidence from primary sources. Provide students with an inquiry question, such as "What kind of evidence is this based on?" The question could be more provocative: "Is this really how it happened? How can we tell?" The textbook may be the first account to put to the test, but for variety and fun you could also look at online movie trailers or history songs such as the account of the French Revolution sung as a delightful parody of Lady Gaga's "Bad Romance."[24]

2. **Build knowledge from sources first.** This can be done in reverse: Give students a wide variety of primary sources on a specific topic, ask them to interpret the documents to build an understanding of the topic, and then invite them to read and critique the textbook. As a culminating task, students write a letter to the publisher expressing their critique. The challenge for you is to find the primary sources. The extraordinary Begbie Contest Society can meet this need for a variety of Canadian history topics from the blockade of the *Komagata Maru* to the struggle for employment equity.[25]

3. **Compare and rate two accounts using sources.** A third approach is to give students competing accounts and multiple sources, and ask them to decide which is the better account. This is the approach of the activity that follows, about the Battle of Vimy Ridge.

   Another example would be to compare competing accounts on a variety of twentieth-century history topics expressed through anglophone and francophone political cartoons at the McCord Museum web page.[26] Another good option would be to compare songs about the War of 1812: the American "The Battle of New Orleans" and the Canadian "War of 1812."[27]

4. **Use sources to create a new account or interpretation.** Perhaps the gold standard in understanding evidence is an open-ended investigation by which students are required to use a multitude of sources to develop their own accounts. This is the approach in the consolidating activity, **Creating a Classroom Museum** on page 65.

---

24 For a selection of history songs, see History for music lovers by historyteachers. *YouTube.* Retrieved from http://www.youtube.com/user/historyteachers?feature=watch#p/u/8/wXsZbkt0yqo

25 Hou, C. (Ed.). (2004). *The Begbie Canadian history contest: The first ten years.* Vancouver: The Begbie Contest Society. Hou, C. (Ed.). (2008). *The Begbie Canadian history contest: Years eleven to fifteen.* Vancouver: The Begbie Contest Society. Hou, C. (Ed.). (2009). *The Begbie Canadian history contest: The first fifteen years* [CD]. Vancouver: The Begbie Contest Society. Also retrieved from http://www.begbiecontestsociety.org

26 Anglo and Franco perspectives. (2009). *McCord Museum.* Retrieved from http://www.mccord-museum.qc.ca/caricatures/page.php?Lang=1&file=156_2.xml

27 Every song tells a story. (2012). *Public Broadcasting Service (PBS): The War of 1812.* Retrieved from http://www.pbs.org/wned/war-of-1812/classroom/intermediate/every-song-tells-story/

ACTIVITY: Corroborating Two Interpretations of Vimy Ridge

PURPOSE

To compare and rate two interpretations using sources

In this activity, students analyze two respected experts' interpretations of the importance to Canada of the World War I Battle of Vimy Ridge. These are provided on **BLM 2.2: Assessing Two Interpretations of Vimy Ridge**. This blackline master also includes primary sources that students use to decide which interpretation is more credible.

The first step is to model a "think aloud" strategy for corroboration. Following this, students practise corroborating in a cooperative group.

Think Aloud Corroboration

1. Read to the class the two historical interpretations given on **BLM 2.2a: Assessing Two Interpretations of Vimy Ridge**.
2. Show students the following source, either as a handout or projected on a screen or whiteboard:

MATERIALS

- projection or handout of Figure 2.11 (available on the DVD-ROM)
- **BLM 2.2: Assessing Two Interpretations of Vimy Ridge** (1 per student)

Figure 2.10 Excerpt from an interview with E.S. Russenholt: 44th Battalion, Canadian Infantry, by the Canadian Broadcasting Corporation, October 27, 1963

Q. Well, all this [training] did pay off, did it not? When it came to Vimy Ridge?

A. … I suppose that some of the terrible things that happened at the Somme were of some benefit. You know, in turning out the type of army that we had at Vimy. Oh yes, oh my yes. Vimy was, I think, Vimy was the high day for the Canadian Corps…. this was the first great victory….

Q. Your artillery support on this occasion [Vimy] was superb.

A. Superb…. We, during that winter, developed tremendous confidence and reliance on the Lahore division of artillery, because they supported us in the raids that went over, you see, it helped to build up the morale.[28]

---

3. Model sourcing and contextualizing and, above all, corroborating one or another of the interpretations using the testimony of E.S. Russenholt. There is some support here for both. Note the important contextual information that the Lahore division was part of the British Indian Army. You could display some of the sentence prompts from page 62 and refer to them as you think aloud.

Small Group Corroboration

Form student groups of four and distribute the blackline master. Inform students that for this activity, they will be historians. Challenge them to work

---

28 Vimy Ridge. (2010). *Oral histories of the First World War: Veterans 1914–1918.* Retrieved from http://www.collectionscanada.gc.ca/first-world-war/interviews/025015-1220-e.html

together to use the questions provided on **BLM 2.2c** to decide which of the two interpretations on **BLM 2.2a** is best supported by the evidence (the sources) on **BLM 2.2b** and **BLM 2.2c**. Assure them that there is no one right answer, although some answers are better supported by the evidence than others. Students should individually assess one of the sources by answering the provided questions, and then share their individual work with the group. The fifth source can be examined by a student who finishes before the others or discussed by the whole group. Then, ask them to decide together which interpretation is more credible and how they know. You may wish to project the photograph (Figure 2.13, available on the DVD-ROM) to aid analysis.

Consolidating Understanding

An activity involving project-based learning, such as the **Creating a Classroom Museum** activity that follows, is well suited for consolidating understanding of the evidence concept. Before beginning this task, introduce to students the mnemonic device shown in Figure 2.11.

Source: Where does it come from (date/place/author)?
Objective: Why was it written?
Usefulness: How useful is it for what you need?
Reliability: How reliable is it for what you need?
Context: How does what you know fit with this source?
Evidence: How can you use this source as evidence?[29]

Figure 2.11 To help students remember the various types of questions they should ask about virtually any source, provide them with this memory aid.

ACTIVITY: Creating a Classroom Museum

Project-based learning has long been part of history and social studies teaching, although it appears in many different guises, taking the form of class museum displays, Heritage Fair projects, subpages on a classroom website, interactive web posters, and even reproductions of cigar boxes (an inventive approach whereby students research symbols that evoke a period of history via images on a cigar box they make themselves).[30] Projects like these can consolidate powerful understandings about evidence when a *requirement for analysis of primary sources* is built into the assignment. Our activity below is for creating a class museum, but it can be adapted to other research projects.

- **Collect resources.** Before beginning, be sure you have adequate reliable resources to support the area of inquiry you wish to cover. Any primary sources that you present to students should be accessible and age appropriate.

PURPOSE

To put corroboration into practice in a research project

MATERIALS

- adequate sources to support the area of inquiry you wish to cover
- **BLM 2.3: Data Organizer** (1 per student)
- **BLM 2.4: Self-Assessment** (1 per student)

29 Boughey, N. (2003). *GCSE economic and social history source skills booklet*. Self-published. Retrieved from http://www.schoolhistory.co.uk/forum/index.php?showtopic=5845&hl=%20source%20%20skills%20%20booklet&st=75

30 Stephenson, N. (n.d.). The cigar box project. *Thinking in Mind*. Retrieved from http://www.thinkinginmind.com/cigar-box-project/

- **Entry point.** Begin with an imaginative entry point—some puzzling primary source, perhaps, or an engaging museum exhibit, either real or virtual.
- **Introduce the task.** Explain to students that their task is to conduct an historical inquiry using sources, and then create a museum display with the results of their research. Inform students that you are organizing a museum exhibit for the school library. (Alternatively, you may wish to use this lesson to help students create a project for a Heritage Fair[31] or other authentic purpose.)
- **Develop inquiry questions.** You can simply present the class with an inquiry question, but there are many benefits to developing the question with the class, group, or individual students as explained in the activity **Hook, Line, and Linker** (beginning on page 53). Refine these questions so that they are open-ended but focused and doable. They should address a big idea in history.
- **Develop criteria.** Show students examples of similar research projects of varying levels of quality. For example, for a class museum, students should study an exhibit in a professional museum or an online virtual museum. Teach recognition of the qualities of an exhibit of high quality. (You may wish to use **BLM 2.4: Self-Assessment** to help identify these qualities.)
- **Form teams.** If the research project is to be done in teams, insist on some division of labour so that each team member can be held individually accountable. This gives you an opportunity to assess individual thinking and learning. If possible, spend some time to build team cohesion and skills before launching the large project. During a group project, much work should be done in class so you can monitor teamwork.
- **Provide sources.** Students are more likely to work with reliable, relevant sources if you provide at least some of them yourself. Depending on students' ability to research, you may give them more or less free rein to find their own sources.
- **Provide background on sources.** Give students enough background information about the context and origins of sources so that they can make sense of them.
- **Keep the research on track.** Monitor to ensure that student research is systematic. Supporting blackline masters such as **BLM 2.3: Data Organizer** can help students draw out evidence from a source.
- **Keep students focused.** Monitor students to see that their interpretation of sources is directed toward answering the inquiry question. Sometimes this involves careful questioning. For example, if students deem an account to be unreliable, ask them to think about what the source does reveal about, for example, its creator.
- **Reflection.** Provide time for students to reflect on their use of evidence. Provide **BLM 2.4: Self-Assessment** for this purpose.

---

31 Canada's history for kids: Heritage fairs. (2012). *Canada's National History Society.* Retrieved from http://www.canadashistory.ca/Kids/Heritage.aspx

BLM 2.1a Contextualizing a Hockey Team Photograph

Figure 2.12 La Tuque Indian Residential School's hockey team participated in a tournament during the Québec Winter Carnival in February 1967. The photographer was Marcel Laforce.

La Tuque Indian Residential School is about 170 km north of Trois Rivières in Québec, in the town of La Tuque, which has a population of about 12 000 people. The school was run by the Anglican Church until 1969, and then by the federal government, with many of the Anglican teachers remaining. Students were almost all Cree from small villages who lived in residence at the school.

Between 1883 and 1996, many Indian Residential Schools like La Tuque operated in Canada, receiving funding from the federal government but run by various churches. Many schools were underfunded, so food was poor and sometimes in short supply. Clothing was shabby and inadequate in winter. Many of the teachers were untrained. Aboriginal languages were forbidden, cultural practices were discouraged, and the Euro-Canadian culture was praised as superior. Some students graduated with useful skills and happy memories; however, most had negative memories, and many suffered physical, sexual, and mental abuse.

1. What context is provided by this brief history?

2. How does this additional context confirm, extend, or challenge your earlier interpretation of the photograph?

Excerpt 1: Prime Minister Stephen Harper's 2008 Apology

The following official apology from the Government of Canada was given 40 years after the photograph was taken, yet it helps us understand what things were like at the time.

Mr. Speaker, I stand before you today to offer an apology to former students of Indian residential schools…. Today, we recognize that this policy of assimilation was wrong, has caused great harm, and has no place in our country.

BLM 2.1b **Contextualizing a Hockey Team Photograph**

The government now recognizes that the consequences of the Indian residential schools policy were profoundly negative and that this policy has had a lasting and damaging impact on Aboriginal culture, heritage, and language.[32]

3. How does Excerpt 1 confirm, extend, or challenge your interpretation of the photograph?

Excerpt 2: Former Student Matthew Coon Come's Response

Matthew Coon Come is a former national chief of the Assembly of First Nations. Although he is not one of the boys in the photograph, his experience would have been similar to those of the boys pictured. What context does he provide? How does this new context affect your understanding of the photograph?

I was taken away from my parents at a young age to attend La Tuque Indian Residential School, situated in central Québec, approximately 300 miles [483 km] away from my home community of Mistissini, Québec.

I was at the [school] for 10 of the most vulnerable years of my life.… The federal government wanted to take the Indian out of me. It did not succeed. I know that I know who I am. I am eeyou, a human being, son of a great hunter, and member of the Cree Nation.… The federal government wanted our peoples to disappear, because of our title to our lands and resources. It did not succeed. Our peoples are still here to assert our rights. We are still in the way. We are not going away. Church officials slapped me for speaking my language and wanted me to lose my language and traditional ways. They did not succeed. I speak my mother tongue fluently and I and my family are Cree.… I choose to forgive.…

It is time for me to move on. And to continue being Cree, in defiance of everything the federal government intended for me and my people.[33]

4. How does Excerpt 2 confirm, extend, or challenge your interpretation of the photograph?

5. Considering this source along with all of the others, write a short paragraph explaining the various ways that the photograph of the La Tuque Indian Residential School hockey team might have been used in the late 1960s.

---

[32] Harper, S. (2008, June 11). Quoted at Canadian Broadcasting Corporation. Retrieved from http://www.cbc.ca/news/canada/story/2008/06/11/pm-statement.html

[33] Coon Come, M. (2008, June 12). I choose to forgive. *Ottawa Citizen.* Retrieved from http://www.canada.com/ottawacitizen/views/story.html?id=9b0cd1fd-e42e-45e0-b9fb-cd3a0eabbd45

BLM 2.2a Assessing Two Interpretations of Vimy Ridge

Two Historical Interpretations

Following are excerpts from two secondary sources written by two highly regarded professionals about the Battle of Vimy Ridge. They reflect very different conclusions.

First, on the Canadian War Museum's website, historian Tim Cook offers the following comments about Vimy.

Many historians and writers consider the Canadian victory at Vimy a defining moment for Canada, when the country emerged from under the shadow of Britain and felt capable of greatness. Canadian troops also earned a reputation as formidable, effective troops because of the stunning success.[34]

Second, in *The Globe and Mail* on April 7, 2007, journalist Michael Valpy wrote of the same battle, as follows.

It [Vimy Ridge] had a negligible effect on the war's outcome. The Canadians had equal casualties and more strategic successes in other battles, such as Amiens and Passchendaele. If French or British rather than Canadian troops had driven the German enemy off Vimy Ridge, history probably would have forgotten about it. As it is, over the years, Canadian propaganda—and there is no other word for it—has airbrushed out the participation of British officers, tacticians, and artillery, and even supporting British infantry.[35]

The Corroboration

If you were an historian trying to figure out which interpretation is closer to the truth, you would have to consult primary sources, such as those provided for you on BLM 2.2b and BLM 2.2c.

1. In your group, read aloud the two interpretations above and discuss how they differ.

2. Be an historian. Choose one of the sources on BLM 2.2b and BLM 2.2c and use the Questions for Assessing Sources on BLM 2.2c to analyze it. (Each member of the group chooses a different source.) Your individual goal is to use your source to help your group decide which of the above interpretations is more credible.

3. When everyone has finished writing their answers, read your source aloud to your group and share what you have written.

---

34 Cook, T. (2004, updated 2012). The Battle of Vimy Ridge (April 9–12, 1917). *Canadian War Museum*. Retrieved from http://www.civilization.ca/cwm/exhibitions/vimy/index_e.shtml

35 Valpy, M. (2007, April 7). Vimy Ridge: The making of a myth. *The Globe and Mail*. Retrieved from http://www.theglobeandmail.com/archives/article751295.ece

---

BLM 2.2b Assessing Two Interpretations of Vimy Ridge

4. When all group members have shared their assessment of their source, as a group decide on a consensus answer to these questions: Which of these two interpretations is more credible? How do we know? How certain are we?

5. Do you have enough evidence to reach a conclusion? If not, identify what other kinds of sources you need to be more certain of your answer.

Be prepared to share your group's conclusions with the class.

Sources

A. *... the most thrilling letter I have ever written you.... I hope you will find it the same. The greatest victory of the war has been gained, and I had a small part in it.* (Letter from Lieut. Clifford Wells [Canadian] to his mother, April 20, 1917)[36]

B. *I would not want to have the impression left that Vimy was our greatest battlefield.* (General Arthur Currie, senior Canadian officer in World War I)[37]

C. *A more desolate scene than this battlefield could scarcely be imagined. Every foot of earth had been up heaved time and time again during the furious bombardments from both sides, until the very bowels of the Ridge had been hurled on high and spread abroad.... Amid this flood ... lay the half-submerged bodies of the dead, whose blood had coloured to rusty red the stagnant water lapping around them.* (War Diary, No. 11 Canadian Field Ambulance, 4th Division)[38]

D. *The fierce battle over Vimy Ridge was fought to a standstill. To be able to call oneself a Vimy fighter, was from then on a high honour!... In the hearts of the fighters and their loved ones, who restlessly, with deep yearning lived through it all in the Homeland [Germany]; the memory of the days of heroic glory and deepest sorrow glows indelibly at the Battle of Vimy Ridge, that patch of earth sanctified by the rivers of noble blood and uncountable heroic graves.* (Generalleutnant Alfred Dieterich, The German 79th Reserve Infantry Division in the Battle of Vimy Ridge, April, 1917).[39]

36 Wells, C. (1917). *From Montreal to Vimy Ridge and beyond: The correspondence of Lieut. Clifford Almon Wells, B.A., of the 8th battalion, Canadians, B. E. F., November, 1915–April, 1917.* Toronto: McClelland and Stewart. Retrieved from http://www.archive.org/stream/frommontrealtovi00welluoft/frommontrealtovi00welluoft_djvu.txt

37 Currie, Gen. A. Quoted in Michael Valpy, "Vimy Ridge: The making of a myth."

38 Cited in Moran, H. (2007). The Canadian Army Medical Corps at Vimy Ridge. In G. Hayes, A. Iarocci, & M. Bechthold (Eds.), *Vimy Ridge: A Canadian Reassessment* (p. 142). Waterloo, ON: Laurier Centre for Military Strategic and Disarmament Studies and Wilfred Laurier University Press.

39 Cited in Godefroy, A. (2007). The German Army at Vimy Ridge. In Hayes, Iarocci, & Bechthold (Eds.), *op cit*, 234.

E. *Canadian soldiers returning from Vimy Ridge, May 1917.* (Photographer: William Ivor Castle. Library and Archives Canada).[40]

Figure 2.13 Canadian soldiers pictured after the Battle of Vimy Ridge.

Questions for Assessing Sources

1. Who wrote (or made) this source, and when, where, and why was it made (if you can tell from the information provided)?

2. Which—if either—of the historical interpretations does it help to support? How?

3. Does this source confirm what you already know? If so, how? If not, does it challenge what you think you know about the Battle of Vimy Ridge? How?

4. How does this source extend your understanding and tell you something new?

40 Castle, W.I. (1917). Dept. of National Defence / Library and Archives Canada / PA-001332. Retrieved from http://collectionscanada .gc.ca/pam_archives/index.php?fuseaction=genitem.displayItem&lang=eng&rec_nbr=3194757&back_url=%28%29

BLM 2.3 Data Organizer

Name: _____ Date: _____

Inquiry Question
Sample question: What is the story of X?
Source
Sample questions: What type of source is this? Who created it? When and where was it produced?
Context
Sample questions: What other events or developments were happening at the time the source was created? How might they have influenced this source?
Description
Sample questions: What do you notice that's important about this source? What do you notice that's interesting? What can't you explain?
Inferences about the perspective of the creator
Sample questions: To what groups might the creator have belonged? Why do you think he or she made this source? Who do you think was the audience for this? What do you think the audience wanted to hear or see? How might the background of the creator and the audience have influenced this source?
Inferences to answer inquiry question
Sample questions: What can you learn from examining this source? How does this source help you answer your inquiry question? Does it confirm, extend, or contradict what you know? What does it not tell you? What further questions do you have?

BLM 2.4 Self-Assessment[41]

Name: _____ Date: _____

Criteria	Always	Mostly	Sometimes	Rarely
Research Questions				
I understood my inquiry question before beginning my project, and tried to answer it as I did my research.				
Research				
I identified sources that helped answer my inquiry.				
I recognized where I needed more information and looked for sources to find it.				
I recorded the sources of my information.				
Analysis of Sources				
I described all of the key details from my sources.				
I analyzed the possible purpose and values of the creator(s) of the sources (author, photographer, etc.).				
I drew conclusions about how the sources answered my questions and what they did not tell me.				
I wrote notes in my own words and did not copy directly unless I quoted the source.				
Conclusions				
I drew thoughtful conclusions about my inquiry based on a review of my research findings.				
Content and Organization				
My exhibit title communicates the big ideas of my exhibit and captures attention.				
My interpretation of the primary sources is written in short paragraphs organized around a topic sentence.				
Each of my paragraphs draws the attention of viewers to key elements of the source and helps them understand the big ideas of my exhibit.				
Writing				
My text engages viewers because it relates to their personal experience, asks a provocative question, or includes a quotation that draws them into the content.				
The writing is grammatically correct.				
Presentation				
The exhibit attracts viewers, holds their attention, and helps them understand big ideas.				

41 Adapted from D'Acquisto, L. (2006). *Learning on display: Student-created museums that build understanding* (pp. 92–93). Alexandria, VA: Association for Supervision and Curriculum Development.

The Big Six Historical Thinking Concepts

Chapter 3

CONTINUITY AND CHANGE

How can we make sense of the complex flows of history?

Guideposts to Continuity and Change

> **Guidepost 1**

Continuity and change are **interwoven**: both can exist together. **Chronologies**—the sequencing of events—can be a good starting point.

> **Guidepost 2**

Change is a **process**, with varying paces and patterns. **Turning points** are moments when the process of change shifts in direction or pace.

> **Guidepost 3**

Progress and decline are broad evaluations of change over time. Depending on the impacts of change, progress for one people may be decline for another.

> **Guidepost 4**

Periodization helps us organize our thinking about continuity and change. It is a process of interpretation, by which we decide which events or developments constitute a period of history.

74 The Big Six Historical Thinking Concepts

NEL

Figure 3.1 Sometimes the best way to hook a student's interest is to display a photograph that sparks curiosity. Why are the military officers in this photograph standing on the furniture? They are trying to catch a glimpse of the actual signing of the Treaty of Versailles on June 28, 1919. They believe this to be a great moment in history—a turning point that will conclude what was then known as the Great War and also change the world. Did it? That is one of the questions Margaret MacMillan (2003) tackles in her history *Paris 1919: Six Months That Changed the World.* As we shall explore, the historian found a complex mix of continuity as well as change in those turbulent days.

Thinking about CONTINUITY AND CHANGE

Understanding and communicating what happened in the huge, infinite past—across regions, across populations, and across centuries—requires vast simplification. The chronicle, a simple list of events in the chronological order in which they happened, is a starting point in making sense of the past. But it serves that function at the risk of conveying a notion of history as a series of discrete, even disconnected events or changes. It cannot illustrate change as a process that varies in both pace and direction. It fails to acknowledge the vast and multiple continuities that underlie change, and which contribute equally to the fabric of human experience.

Before the introduction of historical thinking to a classroom, students may go no further in thinking about historical change than to ask "When did it happen?" so they can memorize the date for the unavoidable test. By teaching students how to think like an historian, we enable them to see change as a process that speeds up, slows down, and sometimes takes a turn. We encourage them to peek underneath examples of change to see the continuities that contribute just as much to the course of human history.

How One Historian Approaches Continuity and Change

As we begin to think about how to teach the twinned concept of continuity and change, let us consider what we can learn from the award-winning *Paris 1919: Six Months That Changed the World*.[1] The author is Toronto native Margaret MacMillan, a renowned professor of history and Officer of the Order of Canada who is now the fifth Warden of St Antony's College at Oxford University. MacMillan's riveting choice for a book title suggests a singular moment of dramatic change: something happened in a particular year (1919), in a particular place (Paris), and within a particular time frame (six months), and then the whole world was changed forever! As we begin to read MacMillan's text, however, it soon becomes apparent that the historian is subtly exploring continuity and change occurring over hundreds of years.

Continuity Propelling Change: A Long Time Coming; A Staggering Result

MacMillan examines the efforts of Woodrow Wilson, Georges Clemenceau, and David Lloyd George, as well as a whole cast of lesser known characters, to achieve closure for the participants in World War I and to set the stage for a new world order. The work of these three powerful men, MacMillan argues, had ramifications that spilled out over the course of the rest of the twentieth century. Her juxtaposition of the small-scale, close-range details of individuals' daily lives in Paris with the large-scale, long-range impact of the decisions made there creates a powerful narrative.

MacMillan does not contend that the changes wrought by the signing of the Treaty of Versailles happened overnight, at the end of six months of negotiations. Instead, she shows how change had been occurring over the course of the days, lifetimes, centuries, and eons leading up to the signing, as well as in the decades that followed. Empires and ideologies that had evolved over many centuries tumbled over the precipice of the summer of 1914 and demanded a reordering on a new basis by the leaders who met in Paris in 1919. As MacMillan explains to her readers, ages-old continuities played a major role.

> We know something of what it is to live at the end of a great war. The voices of 1919 were very like the voices of the present. When the Cold War ended in 1989 and Soviet Marxism vanished into the dustbin of history, older forces, religion and nationalism, came out of their deep freeze. Bosnia and Rwanda have reminded us of how strong those forces can be. (p. xxvii)

1 MacMillan, M. (2003). *Paris 1919: Six months that changed the world.* Toronto: Random House. This book has also been published under the titles *Peacemakers: The Paris Peace Conference of 1919 and Its Attempt to End War* and *Peacemakers: Six months that changed the world.*

KEY TERMS

change: an alteration; possibly evolutionary erosion or sudden collapse, gradual building, or revolutionary upheaval

chronicle: a list of events; a timeline

continuity: staying the same; an uninterrupted succession or flow

decline: the erosion of conditions

periodization: the process of using themes to divide history into chunks of time with beginning and end dates

progress: the betterment of conditions

Were the three world leaders in any position to affect the course of change? They would try. The Paris of 1919, MacMillan writes, "housed a virtual world government" (p. 57). If there was any time to change the world order, this was it. American president Woodrow Wilson argued for national self-determination: all nations should have the power to control their own affairs. Wilson got his way: the League of Nations was formed for the purpose of protecting national self-determination and world peace. But European nations had spent the previous century amassing global colonial empires, a continuity that had propelled a devastating industrial war, and could not help but precipitate dramatic change far beyond the control of the leaders in Paris. Woodrow Wilson's principle of national self-determination did not turn out to be a clear blueprint for the shape of world peace. It unleashed competing claims, nasty conflicts, and unwieldy compromises. As MacMillan observes, to the question of where boundaries should be drawn, "every competing nationality had a different answer" (p. 58).

> Whether historians find continuity, change, or both in the past will depend on where they look and what questions they ask.

Whether historians find continuity, change, or both in the past will depend on where they look and what questions they ask. Everywhere MacMillan turns her gaze, she is compelled to ask questions of continuity and change. Was the new Soviet regime in Russia the harbinger of a new world order (i.e., change) or simply a murderous despotism in new clothing (i.e., continuity)? The League of Nations set up a Mandate System, whereby former colonies in the Arab world, as well as those in the Pacific and Africa, were placed under the control of others. MacMillan asks, "Was it merely a bit of window dressing, as cynics thought, to describe old-fashioned land grabbing [continuity], or was it a new departure in international relations [change]?" (p. 99).

Cultural Identity: A Powerful Continuity

Cultural continuity—the long-standing sense of identity held by a whole people—is just as central to this story as is change. MacMillan reveals compelling examples of cultural continuity coexisting with change and playing a role in driving the events of history.

The first example of the coexistence of continuity and change in MacMillan's book can be found immediately after the table of contents. Here the author provides a note on place names: "L'viv [in present-day Ukraine] is variously Léopol, Lemberg, Lwów or Lvov" (p. xv). Borders shifted back and forth, regimes changed, and so did the name of this little spot on the globe. Yet the community remained much the same throughout this process—its population, most of whom saw themselves as Ukrainians, evolved culturally at a much slower pace than did the city's name.

A series of maps on the pages that follow MacMillan's note on names further illustrates cultural identity as a historical continuity. The maps of Europe in 1914, Europe in 1920, East Central Europe in 1923, and the Middle East in 1916 and 1923 tell similar stories of political transformations of regions in which people defined their ongoing identities in quite different ways. Political borders may have been changing, but the cultural identities within

Europe and the Middle East were evolving much more slowly. Thus, before MacMillan's text even begins, we can see two examples of change existing alongside continuity.

The interplay between continuity and change continues to be visible throughout the story that MacMillan tells. In the Balkans, claims of continuous (but largely forgotten) national histories were used to bolster campaigns for radical change. "All over the Balkans, teachers, artists and historians were at work, reviving memories, polishing national myths, spreading a new sort of consciousness" (p. 112). If they had not actually been maintained by communities over time, now national memories were purposefully reconstructed, updated, and paraded for political ends. Not only Serbians but also Greeks, Croats, Montenegrins, Bosnians, and Slovenes, along with Albanians, Bulgarians, and Romanians all sought new recognition, claiming that the events of history had interrupted their continuity as nations.

Figure 3.2 At any one moment in time, continuity and change exist alongside each other. Sometimes change will seem more prominent (the French Revolution), while continuities appear to take a backseat (the French language and culture). At other times, continuity will seem prominent (celebrations marking the 2012 Diamond Jubilee of Queen Elizabeth), while change appears to take a backseat (calls for an end to the monarchy quiet to a whisper).

The Evaluative Question: Progress or Decline?

At the centre of MacMillan's story of continuity and change is the evaluative question: Was the world a better place after 1919? Change can be a story of progress, stasis, or decline. Indeed, the same events generally represent progress for some and decline for others. For the Japanese delegation, Woodrow Wilson's principle of self-determination was of little interest, as their national identity and their borders were secure. Instead, their interest lay in another area: they proposed a racial equality clause for inclusion in the League of Nations charter. Woodrow Wilson, born in Virginia (where racism, a legacy of slavery, still had a hold) was not enthusiastic. Even if the British had supported this clause, they would have voted against it out of regard for their Australian and New Zealand dominions, which were vehemently opposed—these dominions wished to retain their race-based immigration policies. American foreign policy advisor Edward M. House remarked to Wilson, "The trouble is that if this Commission should pass it, it would surely raise the race issue throughout the world" (p. 320).

TEACHING TIP

Students may have a hard time deciding whether an event represents progress or decline because it may represent progress from one group's perspective but decline from the perspective of another. Encourage students to remark on all perspectives. See the activity **Sequencing the Story of Work** on page 93 for a classroom activity on this topic.

Wilson vetoed the Japanese amendment, even though the majority on a commission charged with the task of establishing the League of Nations had voted in its favour. In this episode, we can see a further intertwining of continuity and change. In this case, the threat of profound change led directly to a continuation of the nineteenth-century racial order. We can also see in this case how perspectives may differ on whether a change represents progress or decline. Wilson would have seen ending the legitimacy of racial discrimination as a decline, whereas the Japanese delegates (and African Americans, had they been at the conference) would definitely have viewed it as progress. This example illustrates how perspectives on progress and decline can vary from group to group. The reader can also see that these perspectives may change over time.

At the same time, Wilson's campaign to create the League of Nations, and the hope of a more secure world in which national self-determination was a basic principle, surely represented a vision of progress. A vision of progress, however, does not necessarily lead to progress. The League of Nations became a toothless organization, with no power to control the actions of countries disposed toward violence. The leaders at the Paris Conference cannot be held responsible. Nonetheless, MacMillan's examination allows us to see the flaws in the vision and the visionaries' feet of clay, both of which contributed to this failure. MacMillan invites us to begin to assess the consequences, considering whose lives improved and whose did not.

Like many historians, MacMillan reserves her most explicit judgments for the final chapter of her book.

> They took pains over the borders in Europe, even if they did not draw them to everyone's satisfaction, but in Africa they carried on the old practice of handing out territory to suit the imperialist powers. In the Middle East, they threw together people ... who still have not managed to cohere into a civil society. If they could have done better, they certainly could have done much worse. (p. 493)

Examining the Claim of the Title

Ironically, after being immersed in MacMillan's detailed study and reading about so many continuities side by side with so many changes, the reader is not necessarily convinced that "six months" in 1919 "changed the world" any more than any other six-month time period. Through her focused attention, MacMillan opens the door to a refutation of the assertion in her own title. She shows her readers how the world worked in 1919, but leaves them doubtful that 1919 was really the beginning of a new era. Perhaps that new era should be marked by "ten days that shook the world" (the 1917 October Revolution in Russia), or "the guns of August" (August 1914—the first month of World War I), or simply the beginning of the twentieth century?

The decision about where to start or end a period of history—periodization—is ultimately an interpretation. Where historians choose to place the divider that organizes history into an "old" chapter and a "new" chapter depends on the questions they ask. Do the questions MacMillan asks lead her to a well-supported conclusion? According to historian Tony Judt, they do. In his *New York Times* review of *Paris 1919: Six Months That Changed the World*, he examines various historical flashpoints and then concludes that "Paris in the spring of 1919 is still the best starting point for anyone wishing to understand today's world."[2]

MacMillan finishes her volume with the questions that shaped the plot of *Paris 1919*: "How can the irrational passions of nationalism or religion be contained before they do more damage? How can we outlaw war?" And she ends, despite her theme of *change*, by remarking on a striking *continuity*: "We are still asking those questions" (p. 494).

We have been examining MacMillan's consideration of the events of 1919 because they demonstrate the intertwining of continuity and change. She identifies a turning point in history, the signing of the Treaty of Versailles, only to open up important questions about the extent to which continuities survived through the cataclysm of World War I and six months of decision-making in Paris. Her ability to encounter these big questions is exactly what we wish to engender in our students.

Let us investigate the ways we can encourage students to question continuity and change in history by examining four guideposts about this twinned concept and how we can bring those big ideas into the classroom.

The Simultaneity of Continuity and Change

Putting events in chronological order has long been a staple of school history. One could not understand the story of World War I without being able to sequence accurately the assassination of Franz Ferdinand, the entry into the war of the United States, the exit of Russia, and the Treaty of Versailles. Dates are the key means by which we are able to order multiple events—to see which are prior, which subsequent, and which simultaneous. So the chronology—especially in its expression as the timeline—has a warranted place in the classroom.

A problem arises, however, when easily tested dates become the *ends* rather than the *means* for the study of history—a situation we can recognize when memorization parades as historical knowledge. The problem disappears and timelines become more useful when we make use of their potential; a well-constructed timeline that includes elements of both continuity and

Continuity and Change

 Guidepost 1

Continuity and change are **interwoven**: both can exist together. **Chronologies**—the sequencing of events—can be a good starting point.

2 Judt, T. (2002, December 1). We'll always have Paris. *New York Times*. Retrieved from http://www.nytimes.com/2002/12/01/books/we-ll-always-have-paris.html?pagewanted=4&src=pm

change can help students see that the two can coexist and affect each other. An indicator of sophisticated historical thinking is the predisposition to seek out continuities running concurrent to obvious change, and, vice versa, to seek out change where continuity has been assumed. Questions of continuity and change also become important tools for linking the present to the past by comparing similarities and differences between the status, conditions, and practices of specific peoples today with those at a given moment in the past.

Change: A Process

It is unlikely that young people think of their everyday life as a sequence of dated events unless they are prompted to do so. Rather, they tend to realize that they are part of ongoing processes that occur at various rates. For example, the intensity of study at school increases during the last days before exams and then decreases after the last paper is submitted. Students probably carry around a generally unarticulated but accurate sense of the pace and profundity of contemporary change.

The question for history educators to consider is whether young people conceptualize *historical* change in the same way that they view *contemporary* change, or if they view history differently, as a series of events and dates. Although literature from Britain advocates the teaching of continuity and change, there has been scant empirical study of students' understandings in this area.[3] Do teenagers who have lived in Canada all their lives, and who have grown up with the continual invention of new consumer technologies over the course of their short lives (change), assume that change has *always* been rapid, profound, and ongoing? Do those who have lived their lives in a stable and safe democratic state (continuity) find it difficult to conceive of catastrophic political upheaval? Do they understand their own immersion in cultural shifts, such as the widespread acceptance of same-sex marriage, that are profound indicators of the possibilities of future change, or do they tend to assume that today's beliefs are the same as yesterday's beliefs and will eventually become tomorrow's beliefs?

Students who see continuity and change in their own lives can be encouraged to transfer that understanding to the past. By realizing that they are part of history themselves, they can better see that the past operated the same way. Understanding change as a process will help them leave behind the idea of history as a mere series of events. Indicators of sophisticated historical thinking about the process of change include facility in using vocabulary that describes the pace of change, and a propensity to ask questions about the pace and depth of change.

Continuity and Change

> **Guidepost 2**

Change is a **process**, with varying paces and patterns. **Turning points** are moments when the process of change shifts in direction or pace.

---

3 See Change and continuity. (n.d.). *The Historical Association.* Retrieved August 4, 2011 from http://www.history.org.uk/resources/secondary_resource_2594_61.html

Figure 3.3 This time-lapse photograph of a total eclipse of the Moon was taken in Buenos Aires, Argentina, in 2010. Although mainly of interest to astronomers, it can also be of interest to history teachers as a metaphor for change. An eclipse is something that most people think of as an event that occurs at a particular point in time. The time-lapse photograph illustrates the opposite: an eclipse happens over time, as a gradual process. Similarly, societal change sometimes happens gradually over months, years, or eons. Incremental change can be hard to notice at first, but can nonetheless lead to dramatic transformation.

Progress and Decline: Relative Descriptors

Change has not only a pace but also a direction, toward better or worse conditions. Changes can create greater opportunity, security, equality, and well-being, and generally improve people's lives, or they can signal hardship, injustice, oppression, and destruction. Judgments of progress and decline indicate evaluations of change over time. We have seen that the racial equality clause proposed by the Japanese at the Commission of the League of Nations was viewed as progress by the Japanese, but as decline by those countries that valued their discriminatory immigration policies.

Present students with a contemporary example of change affecting several groups with clear indicators of progress for one group and decline for another; for example, defeat of one political party by another in an election, or a

Continuity and Change

> **Guidepost 3**
> **Progress and decline** are broad evaluations of change over time. Depending on the impacts of change, progress for one people may be decline for another.

Figure 3.4 In the 1830s, the artist Thomas Cole created "The Course of Empire," a series of five paintings showing the same location at five points of time. At left are the third and fourth paintings in the series: *The Consummation of Empire* (top) and *Destruction* (bottom). Analysis of these images reveals striking continuities over time, a plethora of symbols representing a civilization benefiting from great material progress, and symbols representing decline.[4] In Cole's own description of *Destruction*, he says, "Ages may have passed since the scene of glory—though the decline of nations is generally more rapid than their rise. Luxury has weakened and debased." What warning might Cole have been sending through this series of paintings?

decrease in the tax rate for the most wealthy at the cost of a social program for the middle class. Similarly, many of the changes of history can be judged as beneficial to one group of people and harmful to the interests of another. This makes determinations of progress and decline inherently dependent on perspective.

Periodization: Placing Order on the Past

All historical periods—the Elizabethan Era, the Cold War, the Industrial Revolution—have a beginning, an ending, and a name, all given to them by an historian or group of historians. By choosing a chunk of time that is set off from what preceded and followed it and giving it a name, the historian defines a period of history. Just as the geographer decides the size and extent of a geographic region, so does the historian—or textbook author or teacher—decide how large an historical period is and where its boundaries lie. This is a task of interpretation, as evidenced by the heated discussions among historians about just when various periods of history began or ended.

Organizing history into periods for students helps them make sense of the past. Teaching them that periodization is an interpretive accomplishment of the historian and that it varies according to themes, perspectives, and questions provides the next level of challenge. Outside of Canada, is 1867 likely to provide the period boundary separating one history course from another? Students can be encouraged to grasp periodization as interpretation through a discussion of when the "modern era" began. It is the rare student who would say that it extends back to the Enlightenment and French Revolution. Instead, they might put the starting point at the end of World War II, the 1960s with rock and roll, or merely the day they were born. If students come up with different individual answers, these are not necessarily wrong. Students' answers will differ according to the criteria they use for modernity.

Continuity and Change

> **Guidepost 4**

Periodization helps us organize our thinking about continuity and change. It is a process of interpretation, by which we decide which events or developments constitute a period of history.

---

4 An interactive exploration of these symbols is available at the *Explore Thomas Cole* website, at http://www.explorethomascole.org/tour/items/67/decode

---

Generating Powerful Understandings
of Continuity and Change

Use the lessons and activities in the second half of this chapter to enable your students to move from limited to powerful understandings of the ideas embodied in the guideposts.

> **Guidepost 1** Continuity and change are **interwoven**: both can exist together. **Chronologies**— the sequencing of events—can be a good starting point.

DEMONSTRATION OF LIMITED UNDERSTANDING	DEMONSTRATION OF POWERFUL UNDERSTANDING
Student does not grasp that continuity and change can happen simultaneously.	Student uses the conventions and vocabulary of **chronology** to demonstrate how continuity and change are **interwoven**.

> **Guidepost 2** Change is a **process**, with varying paces and patterns. **Turning points** are moments when the process of change shifts in direction or pace.

DEMONSTRATION OF LIMITED UNDERSTANDING	DEMONSTRATION OF POWERFUL UNDERSTANDING
Student sees change in the past as a series of events.	Student describes the varying pace and direction of change and identifies **turning points**.

> **Guidepost 3** **Progress and decline** are broad evaluations of change over time. Depending on the impacts of change, progress for one people may be decline for another.

DEMONSTRATION OF LIMITED UNDERSTANDING	DEMONSTRATION OF POWERFUL UNDERSTANDING
Student sees change as either progress or decline for all.	Student describes **progress and decline**, noting that progress for one people may be decline for another.

> **Guidepost 4** **Periodization** helps us organize our thinking about continuity and change. It is a process of interpretation, by which we decide which events or developments constitute a period of history.

DEMONSTRATION OF LIMITED UNDERSTANDING	DEMONSTRATION OF POWERFUL UNDERSTANDING
Student thinks of historical periods as fixed.	Student uses criteria to define a **period of history**, and explains why alternative definitions might be plausible.

Working with CONTINUITY AND CHANGE

Introducing Continuity and Change

"Come on, Bart. History can be fun. It's like an amusement park except instead of rides, you get to memorize dates."

> —Marge Simpson in "Margical History Tour," an episode of
> *The Simpsons* that aired on December 22, 2004

That history is just "memorizing dates" is the stereotypical bad rap history always gets. So a good first step in introducing continuity and change is to assure students that these concepts are not necessarily about memorizing dates of events, but instead are about riding the roller coaster of history. It speeds up, it slows down, it hurtles over a precipice. (Although unlike a roller coaster, history doesn't stop.) A good second step is the following introductory activity, which you can use to get students thinking about change as not just an event on a particular date, but a process that happens alongside continuity.

ACTIVITY: Sparking Curiosity about Continuity and Change

This thought-provoking guessing game can be fun (even more fun than memorizing dates!), as well as a stimulus to curiosity. The answers are usually contrary to what students expect, so they will be perplexed, wondering how their expectations could be so wrong. Reflecting on the reasons for the discrepancy offers you an entry point to all of the powerful understandings for this concept: continuity mixed with change, change as process rather than a series of events, the varied impact of change, and periodization.

- Distribute **BLM 3.1: Guess the Country** and direct students to complete both Round 1 and Round 2.
- The country described by both sets of clues is Canada. Most students are able to correctly identify Canada in Round 1, but few do so in Round 2. Ask students what clues led them to their answers. The elements of continuity—system of government, demography, economics—make Round 1 easier. The stark changes since 1867 make Round 2 harder.
- Use this opportunity to introduce some of the elements of continuity and change and related vocabulary by asking the following questions:
  - How would you describe things that have stayed the same since 1867?

PURPOSE

To start students thinking about how and why change happens, and why some things stay the same

MATERIALS

- BLM 3.1: Guess the Country (one per student)

- How would you describe the changes? Were they widespread or patchy? Would they have happened suddenly or slowly?
- Did the changes improve Canada (i.e., progress), or did they make it worse (i.e., decline)?
- What might explain why certain elements have stayed the same and why others have changed?
- Did some event provoke the changes, or were they part of a long process?
- What does this game suggest to you about Canada and what it means to be a Canadian?
- What does this game tell you about history? (For example, some things change at the same time as others stay the same; change is not necessarily linked to a single event; national identity is not something fixed.)

Alternatives

Another good starting point for exploring the questions above is to have students construct an individual timeline of their own lives. This activity is a good opportunity for introducing vocabulary such as *decade* and *turning point*. Students can also reflect on the history of their school using the hallway photographs of graduates as sources.

Teaching Guideposts 1 and 2

Although our goal is to help students understand the qualities of continuity and change, we need to be sure that this understanding is grounded in a familiarity with chronology. This includes relevant vocabulary, an awareness of the scale of time, and a sense of the order of events and periods. We cannot expect that students will learn the conventions of chronology naturally and spontaneously. Depending on the grade level, you will need to teach these with tools such as timelines and the frequent use of relevant vocabulary.

Beware the timeline, however, as it does have pitfalls. Traditional uniform and linear timelines that emphasize discrete events encourage students to assume that historical change follows a uniform and linear pattern. In a study by Keith Barton, American students assumed that immigrants came to North America, lived in small cabins, and then built cities en masse. Students were confused by evidence of "pioneer" life in the west well after the establishment of cities in the eastern United States. Barton emphasizes how important it is for teachers to provide opportunities for students to understand the wide range of lifestyles and experiences in any given historical period.[5]

Following are terms and phrases useful while talking about continuity and change:

- **general historical terms:** decade, century

DEMONSTRATION OF POWERFUL UNDERSTANDING 1

Student uses the conventions and vocabulary of **chronology** to demonstrate how continuity and change are **interwoven**.

DEMONSTRATION OF POWERFUL UNDERSTANDING 2

Student describes the varying pace and direction of change and identifies **turning points**.

---

5 Barton, K.C. (1996). Narrative simplifications in elementary students' historical thinking. In J. Brophy (Ed.), *Advances in research on teaching* (vol. 6, p. 74). Greenwich, CT: JAI Press. Cited by von Heyking, A. (2011). Historical thinking in elementary education: A review of research. In P. Clark, *New possibilities for the past: Shaping history education in Canada* (p. 185). Vancouver: UBC Press.

- **the names of particular periods relevant to your course:** Great Depression, Cold War
- **terms for describing duration:** short-term, long-term
- **terms for describing pace and pattern:** turning point, abrupt, choppy, jerky, explosive, gradual, gentle, drawn-out, sluggish

Asking the Right Questions

To dispel the false impressions left by the unexamined timeline, engage students with inquiry questions that get them thinking about change in different ways. The most fundamental question for a lesson on change would be, "How did X change during this time and how did it stay the same?" The following examples show how it can be tweaked, however, to become more engaging:

- Has our (school, city, entertainment, work, food, or family lifestyle) really changed in the last 100 years?
- What would a time traveller coming to Canada from 100 years ago find the most similar? The most different?

Other questions can focus on the pace and pattern of change:

- What kind of a change was the settlement of the Prairies?
- How quiet was the Quiet Revolution?
- How revolutionary was the Quiet Revolution?

Still other questions help students develop an understanding of terms such as *turning point*:

- Was the Treaty of Versailles a turning point?
- What were the turning points in the history of labour in Canada?

Finally, include questions that help students see that continuity and change are interwoven:

- In this time of radical change after World War I, what stayed more or less the same?
- *The more things change, the more they stay the same.* How true is this for weapons technology during World War II?

ACTIVITY: Enhanced Timelines

Students should construct their own timelines as much as possible and not just copy them from a textbook or wall poster. Many excellent software and online programs exist for constructing timelines, but students can make them just as well with butcher paper, coloured felt, photocopies, and any bric-a-brac that enlivens the product.

Encourage students to use visuals. According to Linda Levstik and Keith Barton, timelines "typically connect one thing that students don't know much about—dates—with something else they don't know much about—wars

PURPOSE

To encourage students to see how change can vary in pace and direction, and how continuity and change can coexist

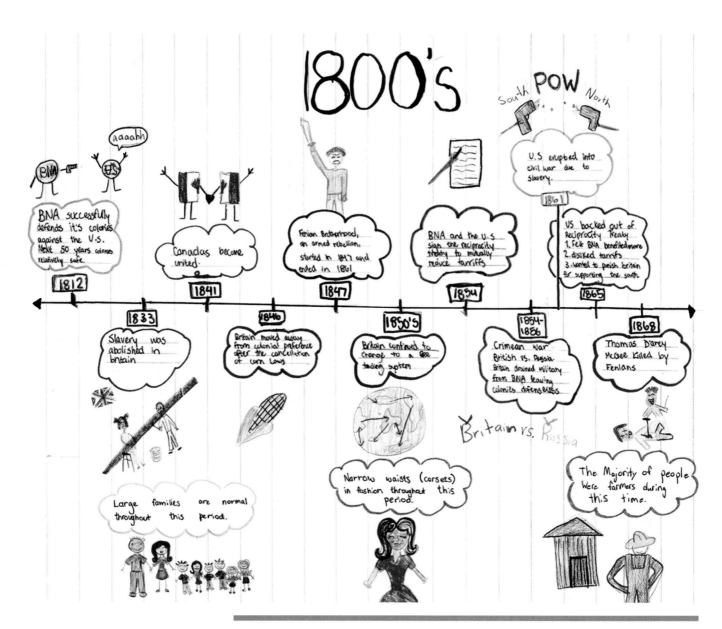

Figure 3.5 Illustrations, graphic elements, and data all raise a timeline to a different level. Students should try to incorporate "what else" was happening elsewhere in the world, and to ask "What was staying the same this whole time?" The four Grade 8 students who created this timeline of Canada in the mid-1800s showed three continuities along the very bottom of the page, and included another continuity right on the line for the 1850s.

MATERIALS
- poster paper (optional)
- kraft or white paper on a roll (optional)
- coloured paper and coloured markers
- paper, scissors, etc.

and politics."[6] In their guide for elementary and middle school students, Levstik and Barton advocate posting drawings or photographs of how people dressed and what machines they had alongside the usual timeline labels for wars, politics, and dates. Using images to layer one topic on another on a timeline offers opportunities for including examples of continuities alongside examples of change. Alternatively, continuities could be incorporated above the line, and changes below the line.

6 Levstik, L., & Barton, K. (1997). *Doing history: Investigating with children in elementary and middle schools* (p. 75). Mahwah, NJ : Lawrence Erlbaum Associates.

Students can keep an ongoing individual timeline, which they can add to periodically, or you can make it a group activity. A timeline on the classroom wall, however, has the advantage of providing a constant visual reminder of previous learning as you work through a unit of study.

Creating a Class Timeline

- Put up a large piece of kraft paper, leaving plenty of room to extend the timeline as needed. Place the timeline on the wall in full view so that it is readily available for reference and for making ongoing additions.
- Draw the basic timeline using coloured markers to distinguish elements such as centuries, decades, and historical periods.
- Throughout a course of study, conclude each lesson by asking students which events, people, or primary sources should be placed on the line. Students will often suggest discrete events with fixed dates. Encourage the inclusion of elements of continuity or slow change. Further, encourage elements for comparison: you can show what life was like for a variety of people at a given time from, for example, different regions, ethnic groups, and social classes.
- Either add the class-approved entries right away or assign small groups to research and plan each entry for the timeline.
- Encourage students to add relevant personal connections to the timeline. The Bringing History Home project suggests "If a student finds something at home that relates to history, invite them to add it to the line. A dynamic, messy, full-to-the-brim timeline is a sign of a class that's engaged in history full-tilt."[7]
- After the timeline reaches an acceptable size, use it to tell the "story" of the period of history you are studying. This will help students make sense of the various elements and see the big picture. To make this happen, give each student a placard with an event, person, or trend that is present on the timeline. Get students to organize themselves in a line in the correct sequence. Then, in order, each student can tell their portion of the story.
- Allow time to discuss what the timeline reveals about the process of change, using questions such as those suggested by Christine Counsell of Cambridge University:

    What story does your timeline show? Why did you choose that event? Why haven't you included...? Don't you think this time line really shows...? When I see your timeline I see.... But that bunching up at that bit suggests speed! But the clustering up suggests things happened more quickly!! Should you really end the timeline there?

    A timeline should never be boring,... it should be a REVELATION.[8]

---

7 Fillpot, E. (2010). Constructing timelines: The BHH five processes. *Bringing History Home.* Retrieved February 14, 2012, from http://www.bringinghistoryhome.org/assets/bringinghistoryhome/timelines.pdf

8 Counsell, C. (2008). Making meaning out of change, continuity and diversity. Teaching about historical change and continuity. *Schools History Project.* Retrieved from http://www.schoolshistoryproject.org.uk/ResourceBase/issues/CounsellChangeContinuity.htm

---

Teaching Guidepost 3

It is common for students, especially in North America, to equate change with constant progress. Linked to this is a second idea, often strongly held, that people of the past were not as smart as we are. This notion seems to stem from the past's lack of access to contemporary science and technology, as revealed in this interview with two British Grade 4 students:

> *Teacher: Could we learn anything from the Brendan story that it's not trying to tell us?*
> *Carly: They weren't very clever.*
> *Teacher: Why?*
> *Carly: 'Cos they couldn't make oars, to row the boat.*
> *Jeff: They did use oars, in the picture.*
> *Carly: Oh, did they? [finds picture] Oh yeah!*
> *Teacher: What do you think then, do you think people then were not as clever as us, or about the same, or cleverer, or what?*
> *Jeff: They can't figure out about volcanoes, and icebergs, and that.*
> *Teacher: So they're not as clever as us?*
> *Jeff: No.*[9]

As you plan lessons to consider progress and decline, consider beginning with inquiry questions that lead students to describe progress and decline with greater sophistication:

- In what ways has the automobile made life in North America better or worse? When and how did things get better? When and how did things get worse?
- How big a step forward was medicare, or was it a series of big and little steps? Were there any steps backwards?
- To what extent did Canada become a fair and free society in the period from 1900 to 1950? from 1950 to 2000? In what decades was change like a speeding train? Like a horse and buggy? Like a car in reverse?

Other inquiry questions can help students explore different impacts:

- What changed for mainland Canadians when Newfoundland and Labrador joined Confederation? What changed for Newfoundlanders and Labradorians?
- Was the fur trade a rip-off? How did the lives of First Nations change during this period? How did it change for Europeans?
- Was the Great Depression all that depressing? Who suffered the most during the 1930s? Who was hardly affected?
- Did women or men gain the most from the 1982 Canadian Charter of Rights and Freedoms?

---

9 Ashby, R., Lee, P.J., & Shemilt, D. (2005). Putting principles into practice: Teaching and planning. *How students learn: History, mathematics, and science in the classroom* (p. 154). National Academies Press. Retrieved from http://www.nap.edu/catalog/10126.html

Certain vocabulary can be useful for describing features of change, for example:

- **for describing the quality of change:** sustainable, planned, or intended versus unintended or chaotic; progressive versus regressive; contested or resisted versus welcomed or popular; revolutionary versus reactionary
- **for describing types of change:** economic, environmental, political, technological, social, or cultural
- **for describing the impact of change on different peoples:** widespread, extensive, broad-based, deep, radical, or transformative versus narrow, superficial, shallow, or modest

ACTIVITY: **Sequencing the Story of Work**[10]

Sequencing unrelated events (the discovery of insulin, King–Byng Affair, stock market crash, etc.) is unlikely to help students develop a mental map of the past. However, if students build a sequence or timeline around a common theme, such as work, they can use the story structure and their knowledge of the theme to help them develop a mental map and at the same time identify patterns of continuity and change, such as progress and decline. In this sample activity, students sequence and discuss patterns related to the history of work in Canada.

PURPOSE

To identify patterns of progress and decline

MATERIALS

- BLM 3.2: Episodes in the History of Work in Canada (1 per student group)

- Prepare a series of cards that describe elements in an important narrative, such as the story of work in Canada in the example on **BLM 3.2: Episodes in the History of Work in Canada**. (Note that every card is assigned a letter so you can easily report the correct order of the cards to students at the conclusion of the activity. On the blackline master, the cards are arranged in chronological order left to right, top to bottom, but the lettering is random.)
- Distribute the cards to students in small groups, and ask them to put the cards in chronological order.
- You may wish to ask students to conduct independent research to identify dates for each event, thereby confirming their chosen order. This step is not absolutely necessary.
- The events on the sample cards on the blackline master continue up to about 1970, so at some point either you or your students will need to add new cards to bring the narrative up to date.
- Write the names of the events in order on an enlarged timeline on the wall, drawing on student ideas as you do so. Alternatively, ask students to create individual timelines in their notebook.
- Ask students to describe the nature of the change they see on the timeline. For example, "What has changed the most? What has changed the least? What were the turning points? Which events show progress or decline?" You may also wish to preview the next understanding by asking how the story could be divided into periods.

---

10 This activity was inspired by an idea from Ian Dawson. Dawson, I. (2007). Time for chronology? Ideas for developing chronological understanding at secondary level. *Thinking History* (p. 10). Retrieved from http://www.thinkinghistory.co.uk/Issues/IssueChronologyTime.html

---

- Consider the different viewpoints of change. For example, "What events would be most important for an historian of women's history? Of Aboriginal history? Of technology?" Ask students to use the timeline to tell the story from these different perspectives.
- Add reference points, that is, ask about what other events were happening in the country or the world at the same time, and who was alive at this time.

Teaching Guidepost 4

The main inquiry questions for this understanding are, "Why do historians divide up the past into periods?" and "What are the advantages and disadvantages of doing this?" These are very abstract questions, however, and it would be best to return to these only after providing questions on specific periods, such as the following:

- When were the 1960s? (Did this famous decade really begin in 1960 and end in 1970?)
- When did British Columbia become British?
- When was the fall of New France: 1759 or 1763?
- What might an historian who specializes in Vietnamese immigration to Canada choose for historical periods of the last 200 years?
- What would a timeline for technological change in Canada look like? What would be the turning points? What would be the historical periods?
- What would a timeline of the last 20 years look like? What periods? What turning points? To what extent would it be a time of progress or decline?

Christine Counsell offers a variety of astute questions—almost "mini-inquiries"—for thinking about timelines. She advocates that teachers challenge students to question their beginnings and endings, and the labels that beginnings and endings enshrine:

> *Is this the end of the story of Muslim Spain? Or was the end in 1235? Or did it end earlier? Or did it really end in 1495? Or did it really end then at all? What is the 'end'? For whom was it an end? Was it an 'end' for some and not for others? ... What shall we call 'Middle Ages'? (It deserves a name other than 'middle'!)*[11]

ACTIVITY: Living Graphs

The term *living graph* is used by Ian Dawson to describe a two-dimensional timeline.[12] The horizontal (*x*) axis consists of an ordinary timeline. The vertical (*y*) axis adds a component of judgment in relation to a chosen criterion.

DEMONSTRATION OF POWERFUL UNDERSTANDING 4

Student uses criteria to define a **period of history**, and explains why alternative definitions might be plausible.

PURPOSE

To help students see change as a process and see periodization as interpretation

MATERIALS

- materials for making graphs, either individually or as a class

11 Counsell, C. (2008). Making meaning out of change, continuity and diversity. Teaching about historical change and continuity. *Schools History Project*. Retrieved from http://www.schoolshistoryproject.org.uk/ResourceBase/issues/CounsellChangeContinuity.htm

12 Dawson, I. (n.d.) Timelines and living graphs. *Thinking History*. Retrieved February 20, 2011, from http://www.thinkinghistory.co.uk/ActivityModel/ActModTimeline.html

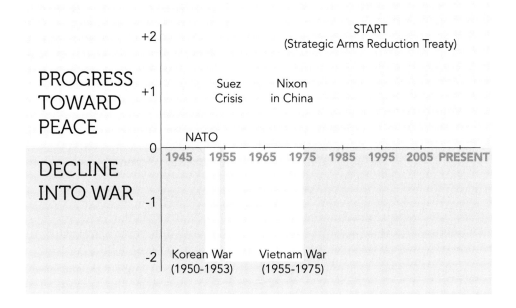

PROGRESS
TOWARD
PEACE

DECLINE
INTO WAR

+2

+1

0

-1

-2

START
(Strategic Arms Reduction Treaty)

Suez
Crisis

Nixon
in China

NATO

1945 1955 1965 1975 1985 1995 2005 PRESENT

Korean War
(1950-1953)

Vietnam War
(1955-1975)

Figure 3.6 On a living graph, students begin by deciding where an entry should be according to its date on the horizontal axis. They then decide where an entry should be according to the extent to which it meets a particular criterion on the vertical axis. This graph shows just a few of the events that might be recorded to explore the development of peace after World War II.

For example, the graph in Figure 3.6 plots events according to the date of the event and according to the event's contribution to world peace. It is the requirement for judgment that gives this graph "life." After showing students a living graph, review the phrase *turning point* and show how turning points on a living graph can help you identify the start and end points of a period of history (for example, when instances of worldwide cooperation started to become more common).

The creation of a living graph begins when you provide students with a number of items—events, people, inventions, and the like—and a criterion. The degree to which the criterion is met forms the vertical axis. Students decide where that item should be ranked between two extremes: not meeting the criterion at all and meeting it completely. Students often prefer if you provide a numeric rating scale such as −10 to +10 or −2 to +2, as on the example in Figure 3.6.

Because living graphs are all about interpretation and debate, Dawson calls them "timelines with attitude."[13] The first opportunity for student debate is when you work toward consensus on the placement of events along the vertical axis. The second opportunity for debate comes when you ask interpretation questions to determine what periods of history are illustrated by the graph, and when they start and end. Use both opportunities in the following living graph activity.

---

13 Dawson, I. (n.d.) Timelines and living graphs. *Thinking History.* Retrieved February 20, 2011, from http://www.thinkinghistory.co.uk/ActivityModel/ActModTimeline.html

---

Periodization Using a Class Living Graph

- To create a living graph as a class, first choose a topic related to your curriculum. For example, ask students: Did we "give peace a chance" as John Lennon and Yoko Ono asked the world to do in 1969?[14] How well did the world powers and United Nations fulfill the promise of peace after World War II?
- Next, provide students with a number of relevant significant events or trends that could be posted on the graph. To keep the exercise manageable, you may wish to restrict the events or trends to those related to the Cold War.
- Ask students to post the events on the graph at what they consider to be the right place according to both axes. Some rankings will be obvious. In the example of a world peace graph, the placement of the Korean War would not be difficult, but more debate may be generated over the placement of the creation of NATO—in some ways it contributed to peace, but in other ways it did the opposite. Even events that were clearly positive or clearly negative can generate debate. For example, the establishment of a UN peacekeeping force to resolve the Suez Crisis is clearly an example of progress toward peace, but students may disagree about how positive a step it was toward peace and therefore where it should be placed vertically. (It only kept the peace for 10 years, until Egypt ordered the United Nations to leave.)
- After students have reached consensus on placement of the events and trends on the vertical axis, they can use that interpretation to decide how this span of time could be divided into periods:
  - Are there any periods of time when there seem to be more examples of peaceful actions (e.g., détente during the 1970s or the Gorbachev reform period of the 1980s)?
  - What is the starting point for that period? The end point?
  - What marks the end of the Cold War?
  - Did it start a new era of peace?

Students could divide history into periods according to a wide number of themes: discoveries and inventions, immigration trends, steps toward responsible government, the rise and fall of the Spanish Empire, the French Revolution, or the history of work, such as in the activity **Sequencing the Story of Work** on page 93. A research project at Simon Fraser University, for example, asked students to investigate the question, "Has Canada become a more compassionate country over the past 100 years?" in relation to immigration, rights and freedoms, and the social safety net.[15] All of these themes could be charted on a living graph and divided into periods. These could then be compared with the time periods that appear in the textbook being used in class or with other sources.

---

14 This lesson works well with the YouTube video of John Lennon and Yoko Ono at their bed-in in Montréal singing "Give Peace a Chance." Retrieved April 11, 2012, from http://www.youtube.com/watch?v=acb15JsCGSk

15 O'Neill, K., et al. (2008). *Compassionate Canada?* Burnaby, B.C.: Simon Fraser University. Retrieved February 20, 2011, from http://www.sfu.ca/compassionatecanada/index.html

For units that extend over weeks or months, a living graph could be charted on the wall with items added and rated as the unit evolves. Students could pause from time to time to decide together when various periods began and ended.

Consolidating Understanding

By creating their own metaphor for change, students consolidate and express their understandings about the process of change using a specific example. An appropriate metaphor can help students recognize and demonstrate the levels of change, as well as the variety in direction, pace, and type of change. The opportunity to work creatively in a different medium can also be engaging.

For example, the late Anishinabe elder Art Solomon used the metaphor of a fire to talk about the power of traditional knowledge to heal First Nations communities after the residential school years. As Solomon described it, the fire of traditional knowledge was almost snuffed out during that harsh time. Only embers were left in the firepit, though they stayed alight, glowing. As First Nations now reclaim their traditional knowledge as part of their healing process, the fire is growing, giving warmth to families and communities. Similarly, Margaret MacMillan uses a fire metaphor in *Paris 1919* (2003) when she asks if the general strikes after World War I were isolated outbreaks or "flames from a vast underground fire" (p. xxix).

In contrast, the French historians of the Annales School[16] used metaphors of water in the ocean. They described spectacular events—the Battle of Québec, the assassination at Sarajevo, the decisions of Gandhi or Hitler—as mere crests of foam on the back of history's waves; in the view of the Annales School, the deep tides and currents far beneath the surface were far more important.

Both fire and water have two key characteristics of a good metaphor: (1) broad application, that is, several points of comparison to the change process, and (2) the potential for developing important insights. For our purposes, we have chosen a metaphor with these qualities, but one that is also close to students' direct experience and personal interest: a car journey.

ACTIVITY: History as a Car Trip

History teacher Rachel Foster found the car trip could serve as an excellent metaphor for the unfolding of change through an historic period. It was particularly accessible and appealing to her students, who were working on a unit on the American Civil Rights movement.

I began the activity by asking pupils to brainstorm as many factors as they could think of that would slow down or speed up a car journey. The class quickly filled the board with ideas, with some of the boys in particular

PURPOSE

To consolidate and express understandings about continuity and change

MATERIALS

- coloured markers
- chart paper

---

16 The Annales School was a hugely influential group of French historians, including Fernand Braudel, Georges Duby, and Emmanuel Le Roy Ladurie.

---

relishing the opportunity to show off how vastly superior their knowledge of cars and driving was to mine. After [I began] wondering aloud how the civil rights movement was a bit like a car journey, pupils were asked to take each factor that affected the speed, rate, nature and direction of change (for example, violence, federal government intervention, media attention, leadership, non-violent tactics) and see if they could match it to one of the ideas on the board.[17]

A car trip involves both continuity, such as geography or long highways, and change, such as stoplights or the temptations of a coffee shop. Changes in direction, speed, and quality of the ride have rich possibilities.

- Consider the change and continuity of the school year, and ask students, "Is it more like a waltz or moshing?" Like a game of checkers or a game of basketball? Explain that these are all metaphors for the pace of school life.
- Spend some time exploring with the class the idea of a metaphor and what makes a good one: similarity with the change process that is the subject of the metaphor (e.g., cars travel at a variety of speeds, just as social change happens at variable rates), insight, creativity, clarity, and accuracy (metaphors can mislead as easily as lead to insight).
- Introduce the metaphor for the project—a car trip as a metaphor for the change and continuity in a period of history they are studying—and outline the project in broad terms. Explain to students that they may tell about the car trip, combining writing and visuals, in an annotated map, as is the case in our example.
- Ask students, as Rachel Foster did, what factors might make a car trip go slowly or quickly. Also ask what might influence the quality of the trip, such as making it a smooth or bumpy ride, and what might change a car's direction. Record students' answers for all to see.
- Next, walk students through Figure 3.7.
- Ask students to create a similar chart for the unit you are currently studying, continuing to use the metaphor of a car trip. You may wish to provide students with the question in the top left cell, which can guide their metaphor.
- Present students with the requirements and criteria for the project, as well as materials for creating visual representations such as a metaphor map (chart paper and markers). A checklist such as the one in Figure 3.8 could be useful for self- and peer assessment.
- Allow students time to create their maps. Students may need help in laying out their maps so that they don't run out of room.

---

17 Foster, R. (2008, June). Speed cameras, dead ends, drivers, and diversions. *Teaching History, 131*(5). Retrieved February 17, 2012, from www.history.org.uk/file_download.php?ts=1217426087&id=1516

What are factors in the history of work that affected the direction, speed, or nature of change?	What is comparable in your metaphor?	How are the two similar in direction, speed, or nature of change?
Technology	Cars	New engines and factories can increase speed; new technologies can be flexible in speed and direction; but both have limits such as geography.
	Roads	Technology can sometimes lead to dead ends, just as roads can; potholes and new machines both cause disruptions; in both cases, choices must be made about routes to follow.
	Turns, traffic lights	Both of these can alter the direction and speed of change.
Unions	Public transit	Unions and buses both try to provide benefits for people.
	Speed cameras	Unions and speed cameras both watch for violations of laws.
Laws	Speed limit signs, traffic lanes, highway patrols	Directions and laws contribute to the safety of drivers and workers.
Economic crisis	Traffic jam, running out of gas, detours	Change may slow down, stop, or take an alternative route.

Figure 3.7 To help students understand the assignment in the activity **History as a Car Trip**, you may wish to walk them through this example, which is based on the information in the activity **Sequencing the Story of Work** on page 93.

METAPHOR MAP CHECKLIST

Interpretation of metaphor
☐ Central metaphor is easily understood
☐ Map includes many points of similarity that extend and support the metaphor

Insights
☐ Map reveals ideas that may not have been obvious

Explanation
☐ Adequate explanation is given to support the comparisons convincingly
☐ Supporting details are clear and accurate

Visual presentation
☐ Map is laid out in an interesting and colourful way
☐ Text is legible and neat

Figure 3.8 This checklist can be expanded into a chart so that students decide whether each criterion "needs work," "meets requirements," or "exceeds requirements." Provide students with a checklist like this at the beginning of the task, so they know how they will be assessed.

BLM 3.1 **Guess the Country**[18]

Round 1: *The year is 1867. Use the clues below to guess what country is being described.*

1. This newly independent country is a democracy based on the parliamentary system.

2. Much of the country's economy depends on primary industry such as forestry, fishing, and agriculture. Transportation systems crisscross the country.

3. The population and economy are growing rapidly. In the previous 10 years, the population had increased by one third, mainly because of immigration.

4. The majority of the population is English speaking, with a large French-speaking minority and many First Nations and Métis.

5. Winter sports are popular. So is a summer game, lacrosse, which is the national sport.

6. This country has a powerful neighbour to the south that has a large army.

Round 2: *Play the game again with a different set of clues. The year is still 1867. Use the clues below to guess what country is being described.*

1. Child labour is common in this country, with children as young as 8 years old working to help support their families, especially in the clothing and footwear industries.

2. There is widespread discrimination toward racial minorities and toward women. For example, women and some minorities cannot vote.

3. Violence is common, especially at election time. Under the law, a man has the right to beat his wife and children if he does not use excessive force.

4. The distribution of wealth is extremely unequal in this country. A study of one major city found that the poorest 40 percent of the population earn only 1 percent of the income.

5. Life expectancy of this country's citizens is less than 50 years. Infant mortality (the death of children before the age of 1 year) is 20 percent. Epidemics are common.

6. City streets stink. They are filled with decaying garbage and the excrement of thousands of horses, cows, and pigs. Outdoor toilets are in most backyards, along with chickens, pigs, and even cattle.

7. Alcohol consumption is high: an average of 27 litres of liquor and beer for every man, woman, and child per year.

8. Forty percent of the children in this country do not go to school, although most citizens do learn to read, either at home or at work.

9. The average number of children in a family is seven.

---

18 All data is from Conrad, M., Finkel, A., & Jaenen, C. (1993). *History of the Canadian people, 2 vols.* Toronto: Copp, Clark, Pitman.

E Many First Nations in the St. Lawrence Valley and near the Great Lakes were farmers. They also hunted, fished, or gathered food. They made medicines and manufactured homes, boats, and other technologies. Some First Nations lived in towns of up to 2000 people.	**D** Europeans adopted First Nations technologies, especially for transportation and clothing. In turn, First Nations adopted metal goods such as axes and muskets. Although fish were the first resource that attracted the newcomers, they soon began trading with First Nations for furs.	**G** Newcomers from France came to farm the St. Lawrence Lowlands and the lands surrounding the Bay of Fundy. Most of these newcomers were farmers or labourers, while others were landowners (called seigneurs), priests and nuns, merchants, and tradespeople.
B New France expanded its fur trade through much of North America. The military and agriculture also provided jobs. There was some shipbuilding and ironworks.	**A** The conquest of New France did not greatly affect the daily working lives of the *canadiens* and First Nations. Control of the fur trade, however, changed to the British-controlled Hudson's Bay Company and the Northwest Company.	**F** New immigrants opened up farmland in Upper Canada (southern Ontario). Women made most of the household goods, such as soap, candles, and clothing, while the men cleared and farmed the land.
C People began to move to the rapidly growing towns to work in industries such as shoe manufacturing and breweries in Eastern Canada.	**K** Increasing numbers of immigrants came to farm the Prairies and grow wheat. Others came to British Columbia to work in forestry, mining, and fishing. First Nations and Métis people also worked in the new industries.	**L** Men, women, and children worked long hours for low wages in dangerous conditions in factories. Unions started to organize workers and demand better wages and working conditions.
I Governments began to pass laws that reduced working hours, improved working conditions, and controlled child labour.	**J** Governments began to provide programs to support the general well-being of workers, such as pensions, social assistance, unemployment insurance, and medicare.	**H** Most workers began to work in service jobs. More people worked in cities and fewer on farms. Just as many women as men were now in the workforce.

19 Based on information from Conrad, M., Finkel, A., & Jaenen, C. (1993). *History of the Canadian people, 2 vols.* Toronto: Copp, Clark, Pitman.

Chapter 4

CAUSE AND CONSEQUENCE

Why do events happen, and what are their impacts?

Guideposts to Cause and Consequence

> ### Guidepost 1
> Change is driven by **multiple causes**, and results in **multiple consequences**. These create a complex web of interrelated short-term and long-term causes and consequences.

> ### Guidepost 2
> The **causes** that lead to a particular historical event **vary in their influence**, with some being more important than others.

> ### Guidepost 3
> Events result from the interplay of two types of factors: (1) **historical actors**, who are people (individuals or groups) who take actions that cause historical events, and (2) the social, political, economic, and cultural **conditions** within which the actors operate.

> ### Guidepost 4
> Historical actors cannot always predict the effect of conditions, opposing actions, and unforeseen reactions. These have the effect of generating **unintended consequences**.

> ### Guidepost 5
> The events of history were **not inevitable**, any more than those of the future are. Alter a single action or condition, and an event might have turned out differently.

Figure 4.1 In 1900, H.L. Blake pans for gold in Buster Creek, Alaska, on his gold claim. This photograph graces the cover of Charlotte Gray's history of the Klondike Gold Rush, *Gold Diggers: Striking It Rich in the Klondike* (2010). In her book, Gray documents the experiences of six adventurers who, like H.L. Blake, made their way through mountain passes and snowy blizzards to what is now Yukon. What could have caused so many people to make this trek? What happened as a result of their exploits?

Thinking about
CAUSE AND CONSEQUENCE

The simplest models of cause and consequence come from the physical world: a cue ball rolls along the green felt of a billiard table, grazes the eight ball off-centre, and the black sphere drops neatly into the side pocket. Aha! The white ball caused the black one to drop into the pocket. But that is only the ending. Without the flat surface and the motion of the chalked cue, the event would not have happened. And, behind the table and the cue are human actors—the most complicating and, in history, the most central elements of all. First we see the two players, with their different skill levels, applying their different strategies. Further back in time, we see a manufacturer producing a billiard table, the inventors deciding on the rules of the game itself, an economy that makes billiard playing affordable, and a society that welcomes a new and different leisure activity.

Before the introduction of historical thinking in a classroom, students may limit their thinking of the causes of historical events to the immediate causes—the cue balls of history. By introducing students to historical thinking, we teach them to think beyond the immediate, to consider the interplay of causal factors ranging from the focused influence of the choices made by historical actors to the broad influence of prevailing social, political, cultural, and economic conditions. Further, students can go on to consider the ways in which conditions, opposition, and unforeseen reactions can thwart the actors' intentions, resulting in unintended consequences.

How One Historian Approaches Cause and Consequence

As we begin to think about how to teach students about cause and consequence, let us consider what we can learn from the experience of historian Charlotte Gray. One of Canada's most popular authors of biography and literary nonfiction, Gray focuses her award-winning work on Canadian historical characters and Canadian experiences. In her book *Gold Diggers: Striking It Rich in the Klondike*,[1] Gray shines a light on six individuals whose lives intersected in Yukon during the three-year gold rush of the late 1890s. Not only does Gray tell an intriguing tale of the hopes, dreams, and ambitions of these historical actors, but she also tells about the social, economic, political, and cultural conditions that both inspired the actors' decisions and influenced the consequences that resulted. Charlotte Gray grounds *Gold Diggers: Striking It Rich in the Klondike* in the close detail of lived experience. She begins by describing the resolute nature of her six protagonists.

KEY TERMS

agency: the power to act

cause: an action or condition that contributes to a result

condition: a broad societal, political, economic, or cultural circumstance

consequence: an outcome that results from actions or conditions

structure: another word for condition; specifically, the societal, political, economic, and cultural conditions within which actions play out

unintended consequence: a result that is unexpected and never planned for

Figure 4.2 Cha Yu-Ram of South Korea takes a shot in the women's 8-ball Pool Singles quarterfinals in the 2010 Asian Games in Guangzhou, China. What events led to this moment? What social, economic, political, and cultural conditions made it possible?

---

1 Gray, C. (2010). *Gold diggers: striking it rich in the Klondike.* Toronto: HarperCollins.

They arrived [in 1896] with their shovels, gold pans, and picks, eager to make their fortunes. There were other lures, too—the chance to conquer unknown territories, live on the frontier, escape the rules and regulations of more ordered societies. Wild-eyed and leather-skinned, muscular and pugnacious, they clung to their dreams like warriors on a crusade... (p. 6)

Gray goes on to paint a rich picture of the ways in which her six protagonists confronted challenges foreign to most North Americans living in the consumption-dominated early twenty-first century. By staying primarily at the level of individual experience, she aims to achieve a psychological depth in her portrayals that would be more difficult to achieve had she written a broad overview of the events. All of Gray's characters left memoirs and written accounts of their exploits, published or unpublished, which provided the author with a rich trove from which to assemble their stories.

Humanity and Conditions: Effecting History

Individually and collectively, the six individuals at the centre of Gray's story were trying, indeed scrambling, against time and competition to fulfill obligations and expectations, desires and dreams. Human beings are at the core of history, because they act with intent. Historians virtually all subscribe to this idea, which prevails even in the new environmental histories wherein historians consciously examine humans in the context of the larger ecological systems that they inhabit—in relation to animals, plants, and Earth's natural cycles.[2] People are at the centre of history because of all creatures, we alone imagine possible futures and take actions intending to bring about favourable outcomes and to avoid disastrous ones.

> People are at the centre of history because of all creatures, we alone imagine possible futures...

Charlotte Gray's characters certainly took actions to bring about favourable outcomes and to avoid disastrous ones. Bill Haskell, for example, took actions to get rich: he set out for Yukon as an individual, joined with a partner, and became part of the 300 000-strong human tide that swept into the lands of the Tutchone, Tlingit, Inuit, Hän, and Tagish, close to the Arctic Circle. It was Gray's fascination with actions like these that propelled her to research and write her book.

A student might, understandably, assume that the charismatic, risk-taking, inspiring characters of history are the drivers of history. Gray would have been under no such illusions. Her Yukon characters all undertook substantial risks with the intention of achieving ambitious goals. But did they create the history into which they walked? To understand *causes* we need to examine more than just the motivations and actions of individuals and even large groups—we need to examine the broader conditions.

---

2 See Cronon, W. (1992). A place for stories: Nature, history, and narrative. *Journal of American History*, 78(4), 1347–1376. The Annales School of historians comprises the most significant counter-example to this generalization. See page 97 for more on the Annales School.

Figure 4.3 One can imagine the steps that may have led to seeds sprouting as they are in this photograph of a farmer's field in French River, Prince Edward Island. Here are a few: (1) 7000 years ago, the Aymara and Quechua people find and cultivate the potato in the Andes Mountains, (2) in 1570, the Spanish bring the potato to Europe, and (3) by 1780, it finally gains popularity as a food staple. Then we speed ahead to recent years: (4) a young couple buys a farm, (5) they plow the land, and (6) they plant potato eyes. If any of those steps (and many more) did not take place, the field would not look the same. Similarly, the conditions have to be right, for example, (1) an economy that makes potato farming viable, (2) enough sunlight, (3) enough water, and (4) an absence of harmful pests.

The gold diggers' dreams and desires were shaped by the time period, places, and cultures into which they were born and in which they lived. Some of these conditions (e.g., the prevailing mood of "gold fever") presented opportunities for their actions. Some conditions (e.g., difficult access to Yukon) constrained the possibilities. In turn, the actions of Gray's six characters—along with those of thousands of other gold seekers—reshaped the constraints and opportunities available for others. For an understanding of historical causation, it is thus critical to look beyond the individuals to the *conditions* in which people act. As Karl Marx put it, "Men make their own history, but ... they do not make it under circumstances chosen by themselves."[3]

Consider the economic conditions prevalent in the years leading up to the Klondike gold rush. North America had been experiencing its worst depression ever—times would not be so bad again until the Great Depression took hold in the 1930s. Jobs were scarce, and people were hungry for opportunities. In this desperate time of few jobs and struggling businesses, news of gold found in the Klondike was bright news indeed. The value of the gold that the men and women sought was stable only because of the larger economic system of currency and exchange into which it would flow.[4]

As Charlotte Gray tells us, Bill Haskell heard the news after taking the recently constructed transcontinental railroad west to Colorado. Here he heard fabulous stories of gold in Yukon from a more seasoned adventurer,

---

3 Marx, K. (2008). *The eighteenth Brumaire of Louis Bonaparte* (p. 15). Rockville, MD: Wildside Press. (Original work published in German in 1852).

4 Morse, K.T. (2003). *The nature of gold: An environmental history of the Klondike gold rush.* Seattle: University of Washington Press.

Joe Meeker, with whom he teamed up. Despite the remoteness of the fabled gold in northern Canada, Haskell and Meeker would pursue it all the way. Thus, numerous conditions came together to set the course of Haskell's life: the economic hard times, the value a culture placed on a yellow rock, the expanding transportation network that brought Haskell to Colorado, and finally the "gold fever" he caught along with 300 000 others. This last point highlights a condition that is often overlooked: a climate of opinion, or worldview, prevalent in a society. "Gold fever" was the lens through which Haskell's ideas about his future were focused and narrowed.[5]

The Best Laid Schemes

The consequences of human actions are never exactly what we intend them to be: people encounter opposition, conditions change. As Robbie Burns wrote, "The best laid schemes o' mice an' men gang aft agley." (The best laid schemes of mice and men often go astray.) Gray's book ends at the level of scrutiny where it begins, telling about the experiences of her six adventurers. She shifts her focus, however, to the *consequences* of the northern sojourn. Were those consequences the ones that Bill Haskell and Joe Meeker would have expected when they first put their plans together back in Colorado? Probably not. The partners decided to cash out as the winter of 1897 set in. On the way to the coast, Meeker lost his footing on an ice shelf over the raging Yukon River, and drowned. Haskell continued on without his partner but somehow got turned around. "Haskell found himself drawn back to Dawson: he appears on a town registry in 1901. Then he vanishes" (p. 371).

CONNECTIONS BETWEEN CONCEPTS

The ethical dimension of history is often engaged alongside consideration of whether particular consequences were intended. If the 300 000 adventurers did not intend to bring poverty to the Tr'ondëk Hwëch'in First Nation, should we nevertheless hold them accountable?

Although Gray does not explore the broader consequences of the Klondike gold rush, there were many. But did the 300 000 dreamers who attempted the journey to Yukon intend all of those consequences? Tonnes of gold were infused into the North American economy, buoying monetary circulation. The environment of Yukon was overwrought by the massive, though brief, population explosion. The Tr'ondëk Hwëch'in First Nation was shunted aside, their traditional economy ruined, and the people reduced to poverty. As Chief Isaac, who led the Tr'ondëk Hwëch'in First Nation through these difficult times, described it, "White man kills all moose and caribou near Dawson, which is owned by Moosehide [the Tr'ondëk Hwëch'in First Nation].... Moosehides hunt up Klondike, up Sixtymile, up Twentymile, but game is all gone. White man kill all."[6] It is unlikely that the 300 000 dreamers ever considered—much less cared about—such an outcome.

Making Things Happen: Agency versus Prevailing Conditions

Recall the billiard game that introduces this chapter. The example makes it clear that a whole parade of individuals and groups made decisions and took actions

---

5 See Becker, C. (1932). *The heavenly city of the eighteenth-century philosophers.* New Haven, CT: Yale University Press.

6 Chief Isaac. (1911, December 15). Quoted in Dawson Daily News. Historical accounts, the Klondike goldrush. *Chief Isaac's People of the River.* Retrieved from http://www.chiefisaac.com/historical_accounts .html#The_Klondike_Gold_Rush

that, when put together, led to the eight ball dropping into the pocket. So the idea of agency—the power to act—is essential in understanding causes and consequences in history. As we have seen, however, conditions also play a role—the ball would not have dropped into the pocket in a society that did not permit leisure activities. Social theorists call these conditions *structure*. A question many historians have wrestled with is how much influence each of these causal factors have *on one another*—and therefore on the course of history.

Social theorists have suggested a dichotomy between agency and structure. On the one hand is the exercise of human agency and autonomy; on the other hand are the social structures and constraints within which actions are conceived and played out. How much autonomy do we have? To what degree do the social, institutional, and cultural structures into which we were born constrain the exercise of agency? Are we bound, ultimately, by an "iron cage" of the conditions in which we find ourselves? Social theorists have dealt persuasively with this dichotomy by emphasizing the dependence of each on the other. Collective human agency is, itself, what produces and reproduces social structures, which in turn act as constraints to human agency in the future[7]—a chicken and egg scenario, if there ever was one.

Historians also differ in their opinions of whether conditions or human actions have more influence on the course of history. Their opinions are reflected in the explanations they construct about how and why the events of the past turned out as they did. Those historians who view conditions as more influential may end up with more deterministic histories, wherein the large, ongoing, and underlying forces dwarf the actions of human individuals and collectivities. Then there are those historians who focus more on individual and collective agency. Authors like Charlotte Gray, who write for the general public, tend toward this end of the spectrum. Gray purposefully set out to "humanize" the history of the gold rush. As Gray explains in the preface to her book, "Individual stories have a psychological depth too often missing from the grand narratives of the past, where crowds are faceless" (p. xiii).

In a balanced history, conditions would not be left to serve as mere stage sets for the actions of their protagonists. Nor would underlying forces dominate. Perhaps the most effective histories are those in which historians have woven the two ends of this polarity together to show the influence of human agency on conditions and vice versa.

Figure 4.4 Social theorists are not interested so much in the question of whether human agency or prevailing conditions have more influence on events. Instead, they are interested in how each, in turn, affects the other.

7 Sztompka, P. (Ed.). (1994). *Agency and structure: Reorienting social theory*. Yverdon, Switzerland: Gordon & Breach; Giddens, A. (1984). *The constitution of society: Outline of the theory of structuration*. Berkeley and Los Angeles, CA: University of California Press.

Chapter 4: Cause and Consequence **109**

How can our discussion of Charlotte Gray's history of the gold rush in the Klondike help us teach about cause and consequence? Primarily, it demonstrates that causes and consequences of an event are not a simple walk from point A to point B. Instead, we would be better to picture a web of interrelated causes and consequences, each with various influences. Let us investigate this web further by examining five guideposts for cause and consequence, and how we can bring those big ideas into the classroom.

The Multiplicity of Cause and Consequence

As Charlotte Gray demonstrated in her history of the Klondike gold rush, there was no single cause for the gold rush, nor for each individual's choices and actions. Instead, there were multiple causes, both short-term and long-term, that led the events of the past to play out as they did. Similarly, the gold rush led to innumerable short-term and long-term consequences, at both individual and societal levels. Virtually every change in history, be it individual or societal, has had many causes and will have many consequences. Just as changes have causes and consequences, so do continuities. For example, before 1939, successive Canadian governments refused to admit certain groups of immigrants into the country. This exclusionary policy—this continuity—was designed to prevent change and it had profound consequences.

To lead students toward an understanding of the complexity of cause and consequence, you might begin with an example such as the billiards game described at the opening of this chapter. Students will begin by identifying the immediate causes (the cue ball grazes the eight ball), but with the right questioning you can help them grasp that many causal factors worked together to create the event and that a whole variety of consequences may result.

Varying Levels of Influence

Most students will acknowledge as a given that the influence of their peers varies. When a classmate urges a student to attend the school dance, he or she might feel somewhat willing to attend. But when the hippest kid in class says everyone should go, the decision is made. Even if the scenario does not exactly match the reality in your classroom, you can use it to get students thinking: they will get the point that different causes (which, in this case, take the form of sources of encouragement) can have varying levels of influence, some having a major or minor influence, some having no influence, and some having a constraining influence ("Don't go!" says another classmate).

Getting students to acknowledge that levels of influence can vary is a first step. Your goal should be to encourage students to weigh the various causes of the historical events or changes that they are studying. An accomplished student of historical thinking is able to analyze the set of causes, describe how they influence one another, and rank them from most to least influential.

Cause and Consequence

> **Guidepost 1**

Change is driven by **multiple causes**, and results in **multiple consequences**. These create a complex web of interrelated short-term and long-term causes and consequences.

Cause and Consequence

> **Guidepost 2**

The **causes** that lead to a particular historical event **vary in their influence**, with some being more important than others.

Causes of Two Kinds

Since the 1980s, a number of researchers in Europe, the United Kingdom, and North America have conducted empirical studies on how young people understand historical causation. Working in high school classrooms in Sweden, Ola Halldén found pervasive evidence of what he defined as *personalization*. By that, he means that students tend to seek "explanations of historical events ... in the actions, reactions, and intentions of individual persons."[8] It appears that many students lay the responsibility for the course of history squarely on the shoulders of individuals who have taken actions resulting in change. Halldén's studies support the notion that history teachers should help students move beyond such personalization to consider causal conditions.

Along the same lines, in a summary of British research, American researcher Avishag Reisman identifies a second common misconception among students. She says that "... adolescents tend to give disproportionate causal weight to the immediate antecedent of an historical event, rather than consider context and contextual causes."[9] Reisman's working assumption is that "contextual causation is ... the mark of expert historical reasoning."[10] So, Halldén and Reisman both advocate for teaching that would help students move *beyond* the focus on immediate, short-range causes and toward consideration of larger contexts and more abstract conceptions of cause, or in other words, conditions.

> ## Cause and Consequence
>
> ### ▷ Guidepost 3
> Events result from the interplay of two types of factors: (1) **historical actors**, who are people (individuals or groups) who take actions that cause historical events, and (2) the social, political, economic, and cultural **conditions** within which the actors operate.

Figure 4.5 This set of statues, unveiled June 18, 2010, at the Manitoba Legislature in Winnipeg shows the Famous Five. Honouring individuals by creating statues of them can leave the impression that these individuals created change in isolation. What causes besides individual action may have led to the success of the Famous Five in the Person's Case? What conditions may have set the stage? How might the efforts of the Famous Five have interplayed with the conditions of the time to generate change? What does the collectivity of five statues suggest about how these women worked together?

---

8 Halldén, O. (1998). Personalization in historical descriptions and explanations. *Learning and Instruction, 8*(2), 132.

9 Reisman, A. (2009). Teaching the historical principle of contextual causation: A study of transfer in historical reading. In M. Martens, U. Hartmann, M. Sauer, & M. Hasselhom (Eds.), *Interpersonal understanding in historical context* (p. 46). Rotterdam: Sense Publishers.

10 Reisman. (2009). Teaching the historical principle of contextual causation, p. 55.

This is not to say that historical actors or the immediate antecedents of an historical event do not play a role in causing change. As Denis Shemilt says in his earlier work, "People make History, and motivated action is the mainspring of that production."[11] Omission of people's intentional actions as causal factors would be a mistake.[12] So, in the balanced approach that we encourage for the classroom, educators should promote consideration of the actions of historical actors, the conditions in which they operated, and the interplay between the two.

As you introduce the cause and consequence concept to your classroom, guide students toward an understanding that both of these are contested and fluid. Historians often disagree on what constitute the causes and consequences for particular events or the relative importance or weight of particular causes or consequences. Further, their conclusions change as they consider new questions, arguments, and evidence.

Figure 4.6 Actions and conditions combine to cause an event.

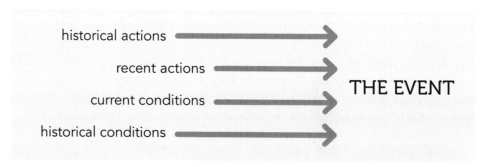

The Surprises of History

Cause and Consequence

Guidepost 4

Historical actors cannot always predict the effect of conditions, opposing actions, and unforeseen reactions. These have the effect of generating **unintended consequences**.

When students mistakenly explain the causes of events as human action alone, they are more likely to have difficulty recognizing that actions have unintended consequences. It is the obstacles—often in the form of prevailing conditions—that historical actors run into that throw their intentions to the winds. The broader societal, political, economic, and cultural conditions all play a role in thwarting the best laid plans. Similarly, historical actors may run into unexpected opposition, such as a spirited defence of a city the actor is attacking, or unforeseen reactions, such as unexpected massive public support for a bill.

Encourage students to consider personal plans that have not turned out as intended. Sometimes the unexpected consequence can be a welcome turn of events, such as a surprise scientific discovery. In other cases, it can be a disaster. Consider the following:

- Bill Haskell, in Charlotte Gray's history, most likely did not expect that his actions, in concert with those of all the other would-be miners, would someday lead to a booming tourism industry in Dawson City.

---

11 Shemilt, D. (1980). *History 13–16: Evaluation study.* Edinburgh: Holmes McDougall.

12 James Voss advocates the more balanced approach suggested by Shemilt in Voss, J.F. et al. (1994). The collapse of the Soviet Union: A case study in causal reasoning. In M. Carretero & J.F. Voss (Eds.), *Cognitive and instructional processes in history and the social sciences* (pp. 403–430). Hillsdale, NJ: Lawrence Erlbaum Associates.

Figure 4.7 When the RMS *Titanic* sank in 1912, many people drowned because the ship did not have enough lifeboats to accommodate all its passengers. The world was shocked, and shipping companies were soon required to carry sufficient lifeboats. Three years later, the SS *Eastland* flipped over while docked in the Chicago River. In this photograph, taken on July 24, 1915, you can see survivors standing on the side of the sunken ship. In all, 844 people were drowned in this disaster. The cause for the ship's instability was, in part, the added weight of so many lifeboats. Ironically, the deaths were an unintended consequence of efforts to increase the safety of seagoing passengers.

- In one of the most famous cases of unintended consequences, Thomas Midgley, Jr., invented air conditioning in the 1920s. Society embraced this great invention. It was only much later that scientists realized that the chlorofluorocarbons (CFCs) used in the process Midgley designed were eating a hole in the ozone layer. So scientific reality had brought on a world-changing consequence that Midgley could not have intended.
- In 2011, the dictators of three Arab countries—Tunisia, Egypt, and Libya—tried to retain their control of countries they had long ruled. A Tunisian street vendor named Mohamed Bouazizi, 26, was fed up with government corruption that made it impossible for him to make a living. So he set himself on fire. His protest sparked a popular

uprising that spread to other countries, threw the autocrats out of power, and led to upheaval throughout the region in what became known as the Arab Spring.

Never Inevitable

Cause and Consequence

Guidepost 5

The events of history were **not inevitable**, any more than those of the future are. Alter a single action or condition, and an event might have turned out differently.

Many students view the past as almost preordained: it was inevitable that Europeans would populate North America; it was inevitable that Canadians would be a nation of primarily English speakers; it was destiny that the Allied nations would win World War II.

Students who grasp that causal factors for an event invariably include multiple conditions and actions can be encouraged to take the next step: to realize that events occurred as they did *because* of the unique set of causal factors at play at the time. But change just one condition or action, and it could alter the way the event played out. As Thomas Andrews and Flannery Burke state, "Change a single prior condition, and any historical outcome could have turned out differently."[13] Consider, for example, biologist Alexander Fleming's "mistake" of failing to clean up his workstation before going on vacation. When he came back, a strange fungus was growing—it was penicillin. Fleming had unwittingly created the world's first antibiotic. Penicillin has since saved millions of people, affecting the course of history. Chance or accidents, therefore, can also cause change.

Counterfactuals are questions that ask what the world would be like if history had taken a different turn. Whether answered in classroom discussions or in novels, counterfactuals can help students grasp that the events of the past were never inevitable. Here are a few "what if ... " questions you might share with your students.

- What if prospectors had not found gold in Yukon? Would the gold rush still have happened? Would a rush have happened if the economic conditions had not been so bad in North America?
- What if the United States had sent its huge army into the Canadian west after its civil war ended in 1865? How would Canada's borders be different today?
- What if French reinforcements had arrived at Québec in September 1759? Would General Montcalm have been able to repel the British, leaving Québec in the hands of France? Would Canada have become a nation of French speakers?

13 Andrews, T., & Burke, F. (2007). What does it mean to think historically? *Perspectives 45*(1). Retrieved from http://www.historians.org/Perspectives/issues/2007/0701/0701tea2.cfm

Generating Powerful Understandings of Cause and Consequence

Use the lessons and activities in the second half of this chapter to enable your students to move from limited to powerful understandings of the ideas embodied in the guideposts.

> **Guidepost 1** Change is driven by **multiple causes**, and results in **multiple consequences**. These create a complex web of interrelated short-term and long-term causes and consequences.

DEMONSTRATION OF LIMITED UNDERSTANDING
Student attributes events to a single cause, often a short-term one. Alternatively, student lists causes and consequences provided by others, without understanding the causal relationships.

DEMONSTRATION OF POWERFUL UNDERSTANDING
Student identifies **multiple short-term and long-term causes and consequences** of an historical event and recognizes their complex interrelationship.

> **Guidepost 2** The **causes** that lead to a particular historical event **vary in their influence**, with some being more important than others.

DEMONSTRATION OF LIMITED UNDERSTANDING
Student does not differentiate between the influence of various causes.

DEMONSTRATION OF POWERFUL UNDERSTANDING
Student analyzes the **causes** of a particular historical event, **ranking** them according to their influence.

> **Guidepost 3** Events result from the interplay of two types of factors: (1) **historical actors**, who are people (individuals or groups) who take actions that cause historical events, and (2) the social, political, economic, and cultural **conditions** within which the actors operate.

DEMONSTRATION OF LIMITED UNDERSTANDING
Student personalizes all historical causes, either as "great leaders" or as abstractions with human attributes, whose intentions cause events to take place.

DEMONSTRATION OF POWERFUL UNDERSTANDING
Student identifies the interplay between the actions of **historical actors** and the **conditions** at the time.

> **Guidepost 4** Historical actors cannot always predict the effect of conditions, opposing actions, and unforeseen reactions. These have the effect of generating **unintended consequences**.

DEMONSTRATION OF LIMITED UNDERSTANDING
Student thinks of past events as expected results of plans and actions.

DEMONSTRATION OF POWERFUL UNDERSTANDING
Student differentiates between intended and **unintended consequences**.

> **Guidepost 5** The events of history were **not inevitable**, any more than those of the future are. Alter a single action or condition, and an event might have turned out differently.

DEMONSTRATION OF LIMITED UNDERSTANDING
Student thinks of past events as inevitable, through failure to consider human choice, intention, and decision making.

DEMONSTRATION OF POWERFUL UNDERSTANDING
Student demonstrates that an event of history was **not inevitable**.

Working with
CAUSE AND CONSEQUENCE

According to Tim Lomas, history teaching works best when it is a mixture of the detective story and the soap opera.[14] Students become engaged by both the puzzling questions in history and the interesting personalities involved. The analogy of a detective using clues to investigate crimes is apt for describing an historian or student interpreting evidence. It is especially suitable for describing a classroom inquiry about cause and consequence because the key questions we ask about the causes and consequences of history are *why* and *how*—exactly the questions a detective tries to answer.

Introducing Cause and Consequence

To introduce students to the various aspects of cause and consequence, we suggest a generic activity that will engage students by having them analyze causes and consequences in relation to their personal experience.

ACTIVITY: How I Got Here

In this activity, students consider events in their lives that have contributed to their arrival at the current situation in this exact moment. Further, they reflect on the consequences of being in this current place and time.

- Explain that the task is to create a personal timeline to explore why things happen in life.
- Ask students to make an *X* in the centre of a blank piece of paper, and label it "Present."
- Encourage students to suggest various decisions or actions that they took to arrive at this present place and time. They may need prompting to consider immediate causes, for example, the causes that triggered them to come to class, such as the bell ringing; short-term causes, such as their timetable; and long-term causes or conditions, such as them passing last year's history class or moving to the neighbourhood. Have students record these in their notebook, to the left of the X.
- Ask students for some underlying causes or influences that shaped their decisions or actions along the way. For example, Canadian laws require all school-aged children to attend school. They should record these on their timelines.

PURPOSE

To help students understand that there are short-term and long-term causes and consequences of events

MATERIALS

- 1 blank sheet of paper per student

---

14 Cited in Brown, G. & Wrenn, A. (2005). It's like they've gone up a year! Gauging the impact of a history transition unit on teachers of primary and secondary history. *Teaching History 121*, 7.

- Now ask students to imagine the consequences of being in class. Again, they might need prompting. For example, "You are here in class today, and what might that lead to? Are you likely to be sent to the principal's office for skipping class? No? So making the decision to be here has consequences." Ask students to complete a few short-term and long-term possibilities, and record these on their timelines to the right of the X.
- Prompt students to reflect on how causes and consequences interact with history, using specific examples from their own timelines. Encourage students to expand the discussion to include examples from the world around them. Depending on the level of the class and your learning goals, introduce key terms such as *underlying and immediate causes*, *conditions*, *triggers*, *agency*, *consequences*, and *human choice*.

Teaching Guidepost 1

As you recall from previous chapters, using a powerful inquiry question to jump-start a lesson, unit, or project will ignite students' curiosity as well as guide their historical thinking along productive channels.

You may wish to simply rephrase the demonstrations of powerful understandings as questions, such as "What were the short-term and long-term causes of Confederation?" or "What were the consequences of the Klondike gold rush?" However, while these questions are a serviceable means to encourage an exploration of multiple causes and consequences, questions with some added intrigue and personality are more likely to spark students' interest:

- Was it really the Fathers of Confederation who gave birth to Canada?
- What difference did Skookum Jim and George Carmack make to Yukon?

Some other possible question templates for inquiries on multiple causes are

- What lay behind X?
- How did X make a difference? (could be framed for investigating either cause or consequence)
- What kind of a difference did X make to Y? (could be framed for investigating either cause or consequence)

Some question templates for inquiries on multiple consequences are

- Was X a success? In what ways?
- How did X make a difference?
- Did X make any difference for Y?
- What kind of a difference did X make to Y?
- Whose lives were changed by X?
- What was the impact of X on our local area?

The following are possible question templates about different explanations of cause and consequence:

- How do these two explanations of X differ? Why do they differ? Which explanation of X is better?

> **DEMONSTRATION OF POWERFUL UNDERSTANDING 1**
>
> Student identifies **multiple short-term and long-term causes and consequences** of an historical event and recognizes their complex interrelationship.

Causes have many shapes and sizes. Students will better understand the nuances of the causal relationship if we give them tools—a variety of words for describing change in different ways. Introduce students to vocabulary so they can better articulate their analysis of the causal process.[15] The teaching of vocabulary need not be dictionary focused nor teacher directed. Begin by providing an explanation, description, or example of the new term (such as *underlying, long-term, short-term, trigger, immediate*). Ask students to write their own explanation of the word, and to use it properly in a sentence. Then, ask students to construct a picture, pictograph, or symbolic representation of the term. Periodically review and reflect on how the words are used in context.[16]

The sentence prompts below, and the consolidating activity **Concept Map about the Disappearance of the Bison** on page 127, help you explore the variety of causes and consequences with students.

Prompts for causes:

- The underlying causes were …
- A contributing factor was …
- The problems were exacerbated by …
- Ultimately, the trigger was …

Prompts for consequences:

- The immediate result was …
- A long-term effect was …
- An unintended consequence was …
- Although X had planned for Y, the end result was …

ACTIVITY: Champlain and Change

Focusing on consequences at the beginning of a unit can help establish the importance of the topic and provide an overview. A possible line of inquiry for this activity might be "How did Champlain change the New World? Does he alone deserve to be called the founder of New France?"

- Distribute **BLM 4.1: Champlain and Change** to pairs or small groups of students. Ask them to cut out a set of cards.
- Explain to students that the cards include (1) actions or conditions that are causes, and (2) consequences linked to the causes. Point out that there is considerable overlap of the two because a consequence of some causes may in turn be a cause of some other consequence. Tell students that, as a result, they should expect to have differences of opinion about identifying some of these causes and consequences.
- Use the cards to connect causes and consequences and thereby demonstrate how events might be linked. For example, show the two cards on the left in Figure 4.8 and point out that the founding of Port Royal is identified as a cause, or at least one cause, and Acadia as a consequence.

---

15 Woodcock, J. (2005). Does the linguistic release the conceptual? Helping year 10 to improve their causal reasoning. *Teaching History, 119*, 6–7.

16 Adapted from Marzano, R. (2001). *A handbook for classroom instruction that works* (pp. 293–295). Alexandria, VA: Association for Supervision and Curriculum Development.

CAUSE		CONSEQUENCE		CONSEQUENCE
Champlain, with the Sieur de Monts, founded Port Royal in 1605 on the Bay of Fundy, the first permanent French settlement in Canada.	*... was an action that led to...*	Port Royal was the beginning of the French colony of Acadia in what is now Nova Scotia and New Brunswick. There are about 100 000 Acadiens who live in Canada today.	*... and ...*	Initially, First Nations were not forced by Europeans to change their way of life. They traded for goods, such as iron axes and pots, which at the time seemed to be useful and to fit well with their traditional culture.

Figure 4.8 A cause and two of its consequences

- Continue by suggesting that the fur trade, described on the card on the right in Figure 4.8, could be another possible consequence that followed the cause, the settlement of Port Royal.
- After a few more examples, ask students to group the remaining cards into possible causes and related consequences. Ask questions such as the following to make explicit, and explore students' understanding of, the idea of multiple causes and consequences:
  - Which consequence cards seem to have more than one cause?
  - Which actions of Champlain resulted in several consequences?
  - Which cards are hard to classify? (These cards can be the best choices for a class discussion.)
  - Which ones do not seem related? (You could introduce the idea of antecedent events.)
- Direct students to do one or more tasks to extend their understanding of multiple consequences, as follows:
  - **Analysis Strategy 1:** Students can classify the cards into categories that reflect various types of consequences. If students develop categories on their own, you may wish to limit the number of categories to four or five to encourage some generalization and comparison. Alternatively, you can provide students with suggested categories, such as environmental and socio-cultural consequences.
  - **Analysis Strategy 2:** Students can classify the cards into short-term and long-term consequences. However, terms like *short-term* and *long-term*, though useful, are vague. Encourage students to define exactly what they mean by these terms before continuing the activity.
  - **Analysis Strategy 3:** To appreciate the interconnection of consequences and causes, that is, the ripple effect, students can link the consequence cards into series of direct and indirect consequences.

– **Analysis Strategy 4:** Students can arrange the cards in three piles: consequences that are clearly a result of Champlain's actions; consequences that are partly a result of Champlain's actions; and consequences that were only indirectly linked to Champlain.

In all of the strategies above, allow students the option of putting cards in more than one grouping and of having an "Uncertain" pile. Depending on the time allowed and context, it is very likely that several of the cards will elicit differences of opinion from students.

Teaching Guidepost 2

E. H. Carr wrote that "historians feel a professional compulsion ... to establish some hierarchy of causes."[17] This is because the causes that lead to a particular historical change vary in their influence, with some being more important than others. It is necessary to identify which causes are more influential. However, establishing the relative importance of causes is a sophisticated thought process, and there is no easy template or algorithm to give students the right answer. Students, therefore, need ample opportunities to consider and weigh multiple underlying forces, and collective and individual agents of change. (Note that another activity that explores this process is **Counterfactuals in the Classroom** on page 126.)

A simple way to have students think critically about relative importance is to ask them to rank a list. For example, "What are the three most important consequences of...?" or "Rank these causes in order of importance." This is the form of inquiry of one of the MysteryQuests of the *Great Unsolved Mysteries in Canadian History*; it begins with the question, "What was the biggest impact of the Klondike Gold Rush?"[18]

Some possible question templates for inquiries about causal webs are

- Why was X so shocking? (or surprising, horrible, popular, etc.)
- Why did X happen in year Y?
- Why did X happen so quickly? (or slowly, peacefully, violently, etc.)

The following are some possible question templates for inquiries about relationships or relative weights of causes and consequences:

- Did X make Y happen or did X just make Y more likely?
- What was the real cause of X?
- Was it only X to blame for Y?
- Which person/event/development did most to shape people's lives in the twentieth century?

---

17 Carr, E.H. (1987). *What is history?* (2nd ed.) (p. 89). Toronto: Penguin Books Canada.

18 Woytuck, W. Impact of the gold rush. *Great Unsolved Mysteries in Canadian History: MysteryQuest24.* http://www.mysteryquests.ca/quests/24/indexen.html

Introduce students to verbs such as the following for describing cause and consequence:

- **verbs to express short-term causes or catalysts**: incited, kindled, triggered, sparked
- **verbs to express long-term causes or underlying conditions**: led to, contributed to, made possible, resulted in, encouraged, blocked, prevented
- **verbs to express relationships among causes and consequences**: made worse, accelerated, exacerbated, strengthened, reinforced, increased, weakened, blocked

ACTIVITY: Weighing Causes of the Oka Crisis

Any number of graphic representations can be used to show causal webs and the relative importance of causes. In this activity, students use a "relevance square" to rank the relative importance of causes and then justify their rankings and ratings.[19]

- Distribute **BLM 4.2: Oka Crisis Causal Factors** and a large sheet of paper to each small group of students. The blackline master provides 12 causes of the Oka crisis. Ask students to cut these out to create 12 cards, and then distribute the cards equally within the group.
- Ask students to draw a square in the centre of the large sheet of paper, writing in it the words *Oka Crisis*.
- Students consider the question, What caused the Oka Crisis? They review the causes noted on their cards and decide which are the most important and which are the least relevant. They take turns placing a card on the paper. If the cause is important, they place it in the square. The greater the importance of the cause, the closer to the centre they place the card. If students determine a card is not relevant at all, they place it outside the square. As students place a card, they explain the reasoning behind their choice to their group. The group discusses the placement until it reaches a consensus.
- When the groups are finished, they defend the placement of their cards to other groups.

(Note that the Oka crisis is still controversial. There is no common consensus on the factors involved, and the list of factors included on the blackline master is not comprehensive. For example, it omits the women of the longhouse, the activities of the Mohawk Warrior Society, and the tactics of the Canadian Army. As a result, you may wish to include additional causes.)

PURPOSE

To help students understand and assess the varying importance of causes

MATERIALS

- **BLM 4.2: Oka Crisis Causal Factors** (1 per group of students)
- 1 large sheet of paper per student group
- scissors (1 per student or per student group)

---

[19] Thanks to John Myers, Curriculum Instructor, OISE, University of Toronto, for the "Relevance Square" format.

Teaching Guidepost 3

DEMONSTRATION OF POWERFUL UNDERSTANDING 3

Student identifies the interplay between the actions of **historical actors** and the **conditions** at the time.

Investigating the interplay of causal factors, including both conditions and the actions of historical actors, requires that students play the detective. Sometimes the causes are not so obvious. To start students thinking about this interplay, pose questions such as these:

- Was Nellie McClung the main reason why women got the vote?
- What conditions helped her make a difference?
- Who helped her make that difference?
- What or who made it harder to make a difference?

Emphasize to students that individuals in history are not solely responsible for the events of history. Some students may believe that humans alone make history. There have certainly been agents of great change—individuals who have altered the course of events. John A. Macdonald, for example, was the architect of Canadian Confederation; similarly, Mahatma Gandhi led the Indian independence movement. Examples like these illustrate that individuals can make an important difference.

Yet even these great people did not make events happen all on their own. They needed the support of many other people: advisers and allies, fighters and firebrands. Even their opponents affected how history played out. It is important to clarify with students that people have an effect on history not only as individuals, but also as members of groups. Political parties, social organizations, peace activist groups, workers' unions, temperance societies, and parents' associations—all of these are examples of groups through which people can effect change by working toward a mutual goal.

Students easily grasp that a single event can trigger another; for example, a change in the law can result in independence for colonies such as Canada or India. The more difficult causal factors for students to recognize are prevailing conditions that indirectly affect the actions of historical actors. Consider the economics of the reciprocity treaty with the United States, which had a huge influence on Macdonald's drive for Confederation, or the economics of the textile industry and the salt tax, which in part inspired Gandhi's efforts to gain independence for India. Without prompts from you or scaffolding, such as the history triangle on **BLM 4.3: Harriet Tubman: History Maker?**, students are liable to give these conditions much less weight than historians would.

Once you have introduced the influence of underlying conditions, students may wonder to what extent people do effect change. Are they in control, or are they mostly controlled by outside forces? Are we kings and queens or just pawns in the game of history?

As is often the case in history, there is no simple answer. Some events will be largely influenced by one individual's actions, while other events will seem to be almost inevitable because of prevailing conditions. The important point is to consider both. To help students explore this interplay, use the **Who or What Makes Historical Change?** activity on page 123. It can be used with inquiry questions to investigate the interplay of conditions and players for virtually any historical event.

Beforehand, introduce students to words that can help them describe the two kinds of causes:

- **verbs to describe human intentions**: intend, decide, expect, foresee, predict
- **verbs to describe the influence of conditions**: block, slow, strengthen, accelerate, exacerbate, transform

ACTIVITY: Who or What Makes Historical Change?

Invite students to consider the question of human agency in history by exploring the influence of one individual. Our example is Harriet Tubman, a key player in the Underground Railroad.

- Ask student pairs to use **BLM 4.3: Harriet Tubman: History Maker?** to weigh the influence of Tubman against the influence of groups and conditions on two events associated with Tubman, and to consider how one might have affected the other.
- After pairs have completed their work, call randomly on them to report on their decisions and reasons. You may wish to post a large version of the triangle at the front of the class so students can show the placements they chose.

    If students do not refer to the full range of factors that they have studied, prompt them to consider what might be less obvious factors, such as (1) religion (e.g., the inspirational story of Moses, who led the Jews out of slavery in Egypt), (2) politics (e.g., the founding of the Republican Party), and (3) the legal system (e.g., the abolition of slavery in Canada, and the *Fugitive Slave Act* of 1850 in the United States).

    It is an axiom of this book that history is about interpretation and debate. Students are likely to disagree on the weight of the effects of individual action, group action, and underlying conditions, or how one affected another. Ask students to comment on why there might be different interpretations. (Students might take different factors into account, or they might see the influence of various factors in a different light. For example, one pair might view religion as an external societal condition, whereas another pair might view it as internal inspiration.)

- Ask your class to consider the inquiry question that makes up the title of this activity: "Who or what makes historical change?" Extend the discussion to consider history as an act of interpretation using these questions:
    - If two historians were to look at the same sources about Harriet Tubman and the end of slavery, would they be likely to come up with the same conclusion or would they disagree as our class did?
    - What did we learn about historical thinking from this activity?

To give students a chance to investigate the interplay among individuals, groups, and conditions, which together effect change

- **BLM 4.3: Harriet Tubman: History Maker?** (1 per pair of students)

Alternative

One variation for reporting to the class would be to make a big triangle on the classroom floor with masking tape and label the vertices "Individual," "Groups," and "Social Forces." For each event, instead of simply asking for oral reports, ask a few students to stand in the triangle at the spot where they and their partner had placed the event and to explain their reasoning.

Teaching Guidepost 4

Students tend to think that things happened in the past because people—especially powerful people—wanted them to happen. The more these people wanted something to happen, the more likely it was to happen.

Related to this is the illusion that historical change is rational. Students tend to assume that people "figured out" how to do things correctly (or how to think correctly), and change occurred as a result. For example, students tend to assume that women gained equal rights because men finally "figured out" that women were equal. They believe that Martin Luther King, Jr., gave a speech that helped Caucasians "figure out" that they shouldn't be prejudiced.

According to Barton and Levstik, students expect history to be composed of causal links, and they expect those links to be "quick, clean, and obvious."[20] The exercise below is intended to help students see that history is much messier, with both intended and unintended consequences.

ACTIVITY: Comparing the Promise and Reality of Striking It Rich

The actors of history are all of us, some having more influence than others. The four people who discovered the gold that started the Klondike gold rush were not powerful people. Yet their decision to mine a claim had extensive consequences on their personal lives, caused an influx of hundreds of thousands of people into the region, and even buoyed the North American economy with an infusion of gold bullion.

In this activity, using **BLM 4.4: Gold! And Then What?**, students predict what the foursome who found the gold might reasonably have expected would be the consequences of their decision to mine a claim. Then, students compare their predictions against what really happened.

An inquiry question to use to frame this activity would be, "What was the promise and what was the reality of striking it rich?" Students will have had experience facing realities that contradict their hopes. You could build on their intuitive knowledge by presenting them with a challenge: "Tell us about a time when you did something with a pretty clear idea of what was going to happen and then you were surprised that things turned out differently."

---

20 Barton, K., & Levstik, L. (2004). *Teaching history for the common good* (p. 135). Mahwah, NJ: Lawrence Erlbaum Associates.

Teaching Guidepost 5

In popular culture, contingency is most well known by the anecdote of the butterfly effect: a small change in circumstances can cause a large change in outcome as, hypothetically, the beating of a butterfly's wings might alter the path of a tornado. "What if … ?" questions, or counterfactuals, are the basis of the activity suggested here for exploring contingency.

According to a 15-year-old student, World War II necessarily followed Hitler's invasion of Poland because "the war could not have been caused by something else." In a subsequent interview, he made it clear that "it was just meant to happen and it did."[21]

For this student, like many others, school history is "given": it is an inevitable series of events with no dead ends, no might-have-beens. When a student thinks that World War II *had* to happen, that these events were destined to occur, they are ignoring what Shemilt calls causal possibilities,[22] or contingency. Counterfactuals are a way to counter this tendency and to consider how historic events and trends were not preordained but rather resulted from a variety of factors coming together.

Counterfactual questions, or "thought experiments," can also help students explore the relative importance of causes. In addition, in their appeal to imagination—albeit based in evidence—counterfactuals are fun.

Counterfactuals take the form of "what if" questions in history. For example, "What if Archduke Franz Ferdinand returned alive from his visit to Sarajevo?" The assassination was, after all, a near thing. Gavrilo Princip's accomplice missed the royals en route to city hall. Princip was lamenting his failure when the touring car carrying Franz Ferdinand and his wife came to a stop directly in front of him to allow the cars at the head of the procession to back up because they had made a wrong turn.

Historians have used counterfactuals for centuries, but they fell out of favour for a time and into the embrace of Hollywood and science fiction. They became popular again among historians and the general public with the publication of *Virtual History* (Picador, 1997), edited by Niall Ferguson; *What If?* (American Historical Publications, 1999); and *What If? 2* (2001), edited by Robert Cowley. The contributors to these books imagined an Aztec empire that Cortés never conquered, an America that lost its revolution, a world war that Hitler's armies won, and other fascinating causal possibilities.

The following are some question templates to spark inquiries about human choice and contingency:

- What if…?
- Would X (imagined event) have changed the outcome of Y?

---

21 Cited in Shemilt, D. (2000). The caliph's coin: The currency of narrative frameworks in history teaching. In Peter Stearns et al. (Eds.), *Knowing, teaching, and learning history: National and international perspectives* (p. 89). New York: New York University Press.

22 Shemilt. (2000). The caliph's coin, p. 89.

- What would have been the impact if X had happened?
- What alternatives did X have, and what might have happened if he/she did Y?

The following activity, **Counterfactuals in the Classroom** can assist students in exploring the concept of the "non-inevitability" of history.

ACTIVITY: Counterfactuals in the Classroom

If you wish to spend time on a counterfactual, the question should prompt students to consider a scenario that is probable, that is, one based on decisions or events that could have easily happened differently. For example, "What if William had failed to conquer England?" or "What if Martin Luther had been burned at the stake?"[23]

If you wish to use a substantial counterfactual to guide a unit, introduce the question at the beginning of the unit as you would any inquiry question. Students suggest a brief answer early on, although they should recognize their understanding is limited. For any extended answer, students need to have a sound understanding of the historical events and of the relationships among causes. They need to include criteria such as plausibility (Is the answer supported by a realistic consideration of the factors?) and comprehensiveness (Are all important factors, groups, and individuals considered?), and to use evidence and sound reasoning.[24]

Alternatively, to use counterfactuals as the basis of a major assignment, first pose the counterfactual question. Students then answer the question by creating a project such as a work of historical fiction or an alternative time-line. A counterfactual scenario can also be the beginning of a role-play. Give students the context and perspectives of certain historical actors, and then encourage them to imagine how they might act, remaining within the limits of plausibility. For example, on a few occasions, history teacher Charles Hou, well known in British Columbia for his retrials of Louis Riel, put Sir John A. Macdonald in the classroom dock, rather than Riel, and accused him of causing the North-West Resistance. The situation was not probable, but it certainly engaged students, inspiring them to reflect on the causes of the conflict in new ways, and reminding them that history is not inevitable.

Consolidating Understanding

Word webs, mind maps, and concept maps are common ways of expressing the connections among a variety of factors. Colours, images, symbols, as well as words and connecting lines can help express various causal factors, weights, and relationships. The key element for historical thinking about cause and

---

23 Cowley, R. (Ed.). (1999). *The collected what if?: Eminent historians imagine what might have been.* New York: American Historical Publications.

24 For some teaching suggestions on counterfactuals, see Gini-Newman, G. (2004). Counterfactual history: Good teaching, bad history? part 2. *Rapport*, Winter, p. 16. Retrieved from http://ohassta.org/adobefiles/rap_Counterfactual%20HistoryRapport%20Article%20Part%202.pdf

consequence is the use of linking verbs, and a concept map is a format that makes linking verbs a central feature. The activity for consolidating students' understanding features these useful tools.

ACTIVITY: Concept Map about the Disappearance of the Bison

As students create a concept map, linking the words and phrases on **BLM 4.5: The Disappearance of the Bison**, they consolidate their understanding of cause and consequence. Our example focuses on a specific historical event, the disappearance of the bison, but, of course, you can create your own blackline master and apply this activity structure to any significant historical consequence that you are currently exploring with students.

Depending on students' understanding of the main concept (disappearance of the bison), they will require more or less scaffolding. Our example provides students with the suggested topics and linking words, but further scaffolding could include giving the possible causes—technology, government, economics, population pressure, and environment—around which the topics could be organized. The number of topics could also be reduced. On the other hand, students who show a greater ability to reason about causation could complete the map without the linking words or the topics.

Perhaps the most important way to support student thinking is to take time at various points in the exercise to verify, clarify, and extend the understanding of the relationships and relative importance of the causal factors. You could begin with an example, such as "The **professional hunters** *used* **long-range rifles** *to support* (feed) **railway crews**. The **professional hunters** *led to* the *disappearance of the bison*." Along the way, note good examples of students' connections, and have a "pause for a cause" to present them to the class.

The blackline master instructs each student to use a different-coloured marker; this is to make it easier for you to monitor what each group member is contributing. The linking verbs reflect relationships of causation, but students may use other words.

Extensions

You do not need to limit your use of the concept map to a consolidating activity on causation. It can be an ongoing activity (a method for assessing learning) in which students assemble the web little by little as a lesson or unit unfolds. A large concept map can be drawn on the classroom wall, or students can create one electronically during or after a lesson using brainstorming and mind-mapping software (e.g., XMind[25]).

Concept maps can also be used as pre-writing for an essay. Students label the linked concepts that fall under the category of political causes, environmental causes, and so on, and use them to write sentences and paragraphs about those causes.

PURPOSE

To help students consolidate their understanding of cause and consequence by creating a concept map

MATERIALS

- **BLM 4.5: The Disappearance of the Bison** (1 per group)
- large piece of paper (1 per group)
- a different coloured marker for each member of each group

25 XMind: Collaborative minds [Computer software]. XMind Ltd. Available at http://www.xmind.net/

BLM 4.1a **Champlain and Change**[26]

In 1611, Ochasteguin and other chiefs of the Huron Confederacy agreed to an alliance with the French and gave Champlain a wampum belt, a form of contract. The Algonquin, Mi'kmaq, and Montagnais (Innu) also allied with the French.	During the 1649 attack on the Wendat (Huron), the Haudenosaunee (Iroquois) tortured and executed Jesuit missionaries, such as Jean de Brébeuf, who were living among the Wendat.
The French would only trade guns to First Nations people who had become Christian.	Jean de Brébeuf became a martyr for Catholics and in 1930 he was canonized, that is, he was recognized as a saint. He is one of the patron saints of Canada.
From 1647 to 1649 the Haudenosaunee (Iroquois) massacred the Wendat (Huron) in a series of attacks. Surviving Huron fled their territory of Wendake (Huronia).	Many of the First Nations people died of European diseases, including smallpox. This was especially true of those people, such as the Wendat (Huron), who had close contact with the newcomers.
Champlain's exploration and trade later developed into a vast French fur-trading network across North America. At one point, French traders reached the mouth of the Mississippi in the south and the Rocky Mountains in the west.	Under pressure from France, Champlain sent out Christian missionaries to spread the Catholic faith among the First Nations.
Champlain explored and made accurate maps of the Great Lakes and present-day New York State and Ontario.	Champlain encouraged intermarriage between the French and First Nations saying, "Our sons shall marry your daughters and together we shall form one people."
At first the First Nations people were uninterested in changing religion, but over time many converted to Christianity and abandoned many of their traditional beliefs.	From intermarriage of French and First Nations people during the fur trade, the Métis Nation emerged and flourished.
Champlain sent out young French men called *coureurs de bois* to live among the Wendat (Huron). He urged them to learn the Wendat language and learn how to travel and live in the new land.	After 1609, the Haudenosaunee (Iroquois) became the enemies of the French. They began a war against the French that lasted off and on for 150 years.

26 Based on information from Fischer, D.H. (2008). *Champlain's dream*. New York: Simon and Schuster; Conrad, M., Finkel, A., & Jaenen, C. (1993). *History of the Canadian people* (Vol. 1). Toronto: Copp, Clark, Pitman.

BLM 4.1b Champlain and Change

In 1609, Champlain accompanied a Wendat (Huron) war party against the Haudenosaunee (Iroquois). Champlain and two French companions fired their harquebuses at the Iroquois, who had never seen guns before. The French killed two chiefs, and the warriors panicked and fled.	Initially, First Nations were not forced by Europeans to change their way of life. They traded for goods, such as iron axes and pots, which at the time seemed to be useful and to fit well with their traditional culture.
Before the arrival of the French, there had been ongoing wars between the Haudenosaunee (Iroquois) and the Wendat (Huron).	After many years of trading, First Nations became dependent on European goods and stopped making their own traditional goods.
Champlain dreamed of finding a passage by sea to China, and explored to the west of the St. Lawrence River to find it. However, there was no inland waterway to the Pacific Ocean.	In 1608, Champlain founded a fort at what is now the city of Québec. When he died in 1635, it had a population of about 150.
At Port Royal Champlain established the Order of Good Cheer. The Order organized festivals and produced the first play in Canada, *The Theatre of Neptune in New France*.	Champlain, with the Sieur de Monts, founded Port Royal in 1605 on the Bay of Fundy, the first permanent French settlement in Canada.
Fur-bearing animals, killed in large numbers for trading, became hard to find. Many First Nations people moved to live near French settlements where they began to eat unfamiliar food, such as bread and peas.	Champlain published four books, including a treatise on seamanship and leadership. His leadership principles included respect and honesty. His books also described in detail the geography, wildlife, and First Nations of early Canada.
The fort at Québec was the beginning of New France. It grew to 70 000 Canadiens by 1760, when the British conquered it.	Port Royal was the beginning of the French colony of Acadia in what is now Nova Scotia and New Brunswick. There are about 100 000 Acadiens who live in Canada today.
New France evolved to become the province of Québec.	Port Royal developed into the village of Annapolis Royal with a population of about 500.

BLM 4.2 **Oka Crisis Causal Factors**[27]

1 The town council of Oka decided to expand its golf course and build luxury housing on land that was traditionally used by the Mohawk and contained a burial ground of their ancestors.	**7** When the police moved to dismantle the blockade, a gunfight started. During the battle, someone shot and killed Corporal Marcel Lemay of the Québec police.
2 The Mohawks of Kanesatake had been challenging the loss of their lands in the courts ever since 1868, but their claims had been rejected.	**8** After the gun battle, the police withdrew, leaving behind their bulldozer and six police cruisers.
3 The Kanesatake Mohawk set up a blockade to stop construction of the golf course.	**9** After a month of confrontation, Premier Bourassa called on the army for support.
4 On July 11, 1990, the Québec police tried to remove the blockade with a bulldozer, while using tear gas and concussion grenades to disperse the Mohawk.	**10** The Mohawk Warrior Society, a controversial group inside Kanesatake, led the resistance to the police and army.
5 Few Canadians paid attention to the Mohawk land claims before 1990.	**11** Two elderly Mohawks died from medical conditions exacerbated by the crisis.
6 Unemployment was high in Kanesatake at this time and living standards were in decline.	**12** The Royal 22e Régiment of the Canadian Army took over from the police and surrounded Kanesatake for a month.

---

[27] Based on the following sources: The Oka crisis. *CBC Digital Archives*. Retrieved from http://www.cbc.ca/archives/categories/politics/civil-unrest/the-oka-crisis-1/oka-stare-off.html; Aboriginal people in the news. *Media Awareness Network*. Retrieved from http://medi-asmarts.ca/diversity-media/aboriginal-people/aboriginal-people-news; Lackenbauer, P.W. (2008). Carrying the burden of peace: The Mohawks, the Canadian Forces, and the Oka crisis. *Journal of Military and Strategic Studies 10*(2).

BLM 4.3 Harriet Tubman: History Maker?

Individuals affect the course of history. So do groups of people. In the background are the conditions that set the stage for events to happen. Which of these three has the most influence on the course of history? How does each affect the others?

Consider the example of Harriet Tubman, known in her lifetime as "Moses." (She was referred to as Moses, after the biblical figure who led the Jews out of slavery in Egypt.) To what extent did her actions make history happen or was it the Underground Railroad and other groups of people that had the most influence? What about the larger social forces at play, such as the economy, war, laws, and religion? Did conditions affect Tubman's actions? Did Tubman's actions affect conditions?

The answer will vary depending on the event you're thinking about. For example, assume you were doing an analysis of **Event 1**: Tubman's own escape from slavery. You decide that this historical event occurred as a combination of her own efforts and those of a small group of people helping her. To show your answer, write **1** somewhere between the "Individual" and "Groups" corners. If you think Tubman was the main causal factor, place **1** closer to the "Individual" corner.

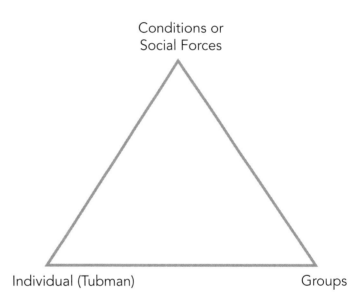

Now examine two other historical events associated with Harriet Tubman:

> **Event 2:** The increased number of slaves escaping to Canada after 1850
> **Event 3:** The abolition of slavery in the United States

1. With a partner, study these two historical events, paying close attention to causal factors.

2. Decide to what extent each event was the result of Tubman's efforts or a group effort, or the effect of conditions. Decide if conditions affect people's actions, and vice versa. Place a **2** and **3** on the diagram to show the combination of factors that you believe fits each event. Write down your reasons next to the triangle. Be ready to explain your reasoning to your partner and to the class.

BLM 4.4a Gold! And Then What?

On August 16, 1896, an American prospector named George Carmack, his Tagish wife Kate Carmack (Shaaw Tláa), her brother Skookum Jim (Keish), and their nephew Tagish Charlie (Káa Goox) were travelling through the area south of the Klondike River in Yukon. Resting by the side of a creek, one of them noticed a glitter in the water. They had found gold, lying thick between slabs of rock like cheese slices in a sub sandwich. After dancing for joy, they made a mutual decision: they would make a claim to the land and mine it.

Task 1

After reading the above paragraph, generate a list of consequences that the foursome probably intended and expected to happen as a result of their decision. Think about the following:

- **short-term consequences**: What would they have likely intended and expected to happen to them personally immediately after they laid the claim?

- **medium-term consequences**: What would they have intended and expected to happen in the months after they got the mine going?

- **long-term consequences**: What would they have intended and expected to happen in the years to come?

Then, read the following history of what really happened.

Consequences of the Klondike Discovery[28]

George Carmack, Kate Carmack, Skookum Jim, and Tagish Charlie measured out four mining claims and the next day registered these with the police: two claims for George Carmack and one each for Skookum Jim and Tagish Charlie. They were expecting to be wealthy soon, but, for the moment, they had no money. So the men spent the winter sinking shafts in the bedrock, while Kate sewed furs into mittens and moccasins and baked bread to sell to other miners.

Meanwhile, reports of the gold and the successful miners had exploded across the front pages of newspapers. Thousands of men and a few women left their jobs and made their way to the Klondike. About 40 000 made it to Yukon.

---

28 Based on Gray, C. (2010). *Gold diggers: Striking it rich in the Klondike*. Toronto: HarperCollins; Berton, P. (1972). *Klondike: The last great gold rush 1896–1899*. Toronto: Anchor Canada; Porsild, C. (2000). Shaaw Tláa (Kate Carmack). *Canadian Dictionary of Biography Online*. Retrieved from http://www.biographi.ca/009004-119.01-e.php?BioId=41820; Porsild, C. (2000). Keish (Skookum Jim, James Mason). *Canadian Dictionary of Biography Online*. Retrieved from http://www.biographi.ca/009004-119.01-e.php?BioId=41611; Culture and religion. *Chief Isaac's People of the River*. (n.d.). Retrieved from http://www.chiefisaac.com/culture_and_religion

BLM 4.4b Gold! And Then What?

Boomtowns sprang up along the routes to the gold fields. Dawson City exploded from a population of 500 in 1896 to 30 000 in 1898. The landscape changed as well. For example, as Dawson City grew, the surrounding trees fell, because newcomers required timber to make houses, to build sluice boxes for mining, and for firewood.

The earliest inhabitants of the area, the First Nations peoples, were affected profoundly by the arrival of the miners. Many died after being exposed to contagious diseases, such as diphtheria and typhoid, brought into the region by the miners. This included people of the Tr'ondëk Hwëch'in First Nation, who had lived along the Klondike long before the discovery of gold. When the prospectors began to arrive in large numbers, their leader, Chief Isaac, foreseeing an increased disruption of his people, moved the community out of Dawson City to a traditional camp, called Moosehide, downriver to make way for the prospectors. He also sent Tr'ondëk Hwëch'in songs and the dance stick, known as the Gunhawk, to the Tr'ondëk Hwëch'in's cousins in Alaska. He entrusted these cousins to hold onto these songs until a time when the Tr'ondëk Hwëch'in were able to relearn the songs and bring the dance stick back to their homeland. Today, the people are in the process of learning these songs once again.

And what happened to the first four prospectors? Their first winter was difficult, but then, over the next few years, the three men divided up the work on the four claims—and the money started pouring in. They shared close to $1 million in gold. Jim built a big house for his wife and daughter at Carcross (about 600 km south of Dawson City) in 1898. Beautifully furnished, it was the grandest in the village. Shortly afterwards, in 1904, Skookum Jim sold his claim. At his death in 1916, after a lengthy illness, he left a generous gift to the First Nations people of Yukon.

And George Carmack? In 1900, after he and Kate had moved to California to live with George's sister, he abandoned Kate there, leaving her almost penniless. Subsequently, she returned to Carcross, where her brother Jim built her a cabin. She lived there until her death from influenza in 1920. George Carmack married a woman from Dawson City and moved to Seattle. Advised by his new wife, he invested in real estate and became very rich. He died in 1922.

The gold claims had made Tagish Charlie, who became known as "Dawson Charlie," a wealthy man. Then in 1903, still prospecting, he found more gold, this time in the Kluane region. This started another gold rush that lasted for several years. Tragically, heading home one night in 1908, Tagish Charlie fell off the White Pass and Yukon Route bridge at Carcross, went through the ice, and drowned.

Many of the prospectors, especially the earliest to arrive, became quite wealthy. They didn't hide the fact, spending extravagantly and basically living it up. Other prospectors, however, were unable to make a living, and they soon left the Klondike and headed home.

Within a very few years, it was difficult for any individuals to get rich by simply panning for gold and working their claims by hand. Gold was getting harder to find. Large machines were needed to wash the gold out of creeks and hills with high-powered hoses, dredges were needed to chew up creek beds, and big money was required to purchase and bring in the machinery. Gold mining became an industry run by corporations. By 1900, the main Klondike gold rush was over, and by 1903, gold production was falling.

Today, the population of Dawson City is less than 1400. However, the town is a national historic site. Its buildings have been restored, and it receives more than 50 000 tourists each year.

Task 2

1. Review your list of consequences.

    • Put a check mark beside every intended consequence that actually did happen.

    • Put an X beside every intended consequence that did not happen.

    • If you do not know if an intended consequence happened, put a question mark beside it.

2. Return to the "Consequences of the Klondike Discovery" section above. Cross out any consequences that you predicted the foursome both intended and expected. Underline consequences that you believe were not intended or expected at all.

3. Reflect on the inquiry question you considered at the beginning of class:

    • What was the promise and what was the reality of striking it rich?

    • How has your thinking changed?

BLM 4.5 The Disappearance of the Bison

Goal: You and your team members make a concept map about the disappearance of the bison herds from the Prairies in the nineteenth century.

1. Read over the list of topics below, which are all related in some way to the disappearance of the bison herds. Read the linking verbs.

2. One member of your team writes the central topic—Disappearance of the Bison—at the top or in the middle of a large piece of paper. Write the other topics randomly around this central concept. Leave lots of space between topics.

3. Each of you chooses a coloured marker and uses it to draw a line between topics that you think are connected. Next to these lines, write a linking verb to explain how these topics are related. (You can also use verbs that do not appear on this sheet.) All team members contribute and write at the same time, but it is a good idea to ask questions and discuss your decisions with one another as you work.

Topics:

American government	Canadian government	long-range rifles
professional hunters	Laws of the St. Laurent	railway	railway crews
First Nations	Métis	pemmican	drought	reservations
Northwest Uprising, 1885	grassland	cattle	Canadian army
commercial leather	farmland	newcomers	American army
Gabriel Dumont	Louis Riel	John A. Macdonald
food and shelter	market	treaties	disappearance of the bison

Suggested linking verbs:

led (to)   caused   was an underlying cause of   resisted

was a factor in   resulted in   contributed to   aided   defeated

was made worse by   supported   opposed   negotiated

encouraged   attracted   fought   controlled

used   put pressure on   made it easier to

Chapter 5

HISTORICAL PERSPECTIVES

How can we better understand the people of the past?

Guideposts to Historical Perspectives

> **Guidepost 1**

An ocean of **difference** can lie between current **worldviews** (beliefs, values, and motivations) and those of earlier periods of history.

> **Guidepost 2**

It is important to avoid **presentism**—the imposition of present ideas on actors in the past. Nonetheless, cautious reference to universal human experience can help us relate to the experiences of historical actors.

> **Guidepost 3**

The perspectives of historical actors are best understood by considering their **historical context**.

> **Guidepost 4**

Taking the perspective of historical actors means inferring how people felt and thought in the past. It does not mean identifying with those actors. Valid inferences are those based on evidence.

> **Guidepost 5**

Different historical actors have **diverse perspectives** on the events in which they are involved. Exploring these is key to understanding historical events.

Figure 5.1 This movie still shows actress Émilie Leclerc-Côté portraying Esther Wheelwright in the documentary film *Captive: The Story of Esther* (2005). Leclerc-Côté's challenge was to infer how the real Esther thought and felt several centuries ago—what we call taking an historical perspective. Journalist Julie Wheelwright faced this same challenge when writing her biography *Esther: The Remarkable True Story of Esther Wheelwright: Puritan Child, Native Daughter, Mother Superior* (2011). How did the actor and the journalist know what it was like to be the real Esther? On what would their success at depicting the "real" Esther depend?

Thinking about
HISTORICAL PERSPECTIVES

Taking an historical perspective means attempting to see through the eyes of people who lived in times and circumstances sometimes far removed from our present-day lives. It means considering the different "things" that made up their everyday living—technologies, clothing, housing, food—as well as the landscapes of their communities and settlements; the larger social, economic, and political orders (and the disorder) that shaped their world; and, most difficult of all, the customs, ideas, and belief systems through which they made sense of it all. In short, what was it like to be them?

Before the introduction of historical thinking in a classroom, students may think they can simply imagine the thoughts, feelings, hopes, dreams, and fears of historical actors. After all, everyone has feelings. It's easy for students to put themselves in the shoes of a World War II Japanese kamikaze pilot, or Montezuma meeting Cortés for the first time, right? Not necessarily. While it is true that basic human feelings are similar, there are decades of difference between the worldviews of these individuals and our own. To imagine without consulting any evidence, as students are wont to do, is to guess—a practice that is foreign to the historian and which should be foreign in the history classroom.

By teaching students how to take an historical perspective, we enable them to use evidence to make evidence-based inferences about the thoughts and feelings of the characters of history. Students learn to take historical context into account when making inferences, and to seek out multiple perspectives when trying to understand the events of history. They will better understand, for example, why Confederation took the form it did when they can "hear" the thinking of the decision makers in the 1860s.

How One Historian Approaches Historical Perspectives

As we begin to think about how to bring historical perspectives into the classroom, let us consider what we can learn from the journey taken by historian and journalist Julie Wheelwright as she researched and wrote *Esther: The Remarkable True Story of Esther Wheelwright: Puritan Child, Native Daughter, Mother Superior*.[1] Although she now lives in London, England, Julie Wheelwright grew up in British Columbia. The subject of *Esther* is Wheelwright's own Canadian ancestor: a girl who got caught up in the religious tensions of eighteenth-century North America. In part because of Esther's origins in an important New England family (her great-grandfather, John Wheelwright, was a relative of Anne Hutchison, founder of Rhode Island; her brother was Boston's major banker in the mid-eighteenth century), and in part because she became the Mother Superior of a central Québec institution, unusually rich documentary records of Esther's life have survived the centuries.

Esther Wheelwright's story begins in the small Puritan village of Wells, Maine. Abenaki warriors kidnapped seven-year-old Esther from her home there in 1703 and took her to an Abenaki village in the woods of New France, where a family adopted her. A Catholic priest brought her to Québec City, where she entered the Ursuline convent at the age of 14, and where she spent most of her adult life. Of interest to us is the author's struggle to truly know the thoughts, feelings, and loyalties of Esther when no documentary evidence actually stated what those were. Julie Wheelwright's dauntless efforts to take the historical perspective of her ancestor, and her transparency about the challenges she faced in doing so, can help us understand the challenges and benefits of bringing historical perspectives into the history classroom.

The Big Puzzle

In Julie Wheelwright's estimation, Esther largely thrived through two difficult transitions across three utterly different belief systems and ways of living. First, she was raised within the harsh Puritanism of her family of origin, with strict punishments and constant threats of raids by First Nations enemies. Next, she was plunged into a First Nations culture that was, as described in Wheelwright's account, "full of love, challenge, and satisfaction ... " (p. 55), at least after her initiation rites. Finally, Esther entered the world of the Québec Catholic cloister with its strict vows of poverty and obedience. The people in these three worlds spoke three different languages and would have seen only one another's differences: they warred with one another, believing the "other" to be an eternal enemy. But there were many areas of overlap: they traded with one another, intermarried, and shared the experience of living

1 Wheelwright, J. (2011). *Esther: The remarkable true story of Esther Wheelwright: Puritan child, native daughter, mother superior.* Toronto: HarperCollins Ltd. The Wheelwright story runs parallel to that told by Bancroft Prize–winning American historian John Demos in *The Unredeemed Captive: A family story from early America* (New York: Knopf, 1994), about seven-year-old Eunice Williams, taken hostage by Mohawks from Deerfield, Massachusetts, in 1704.

KEY TERMS

anachronism: a practice or technology represented outside of the time period in which it existed

diverse perspectives: the different ways that various people can view an historic event

historical actor: a person who existed in the past

historical perspective: the viewpoint of an historical actor

making inferences: developing evidence-based estimations of the thoughts and feelings of historical actors

presentism: imposing the thoughts, beliefs, and values of today onto historical actors

taking an historical perspective: using evidence and historical context to infer the thoughts and feelings of an historical actor

in a harsh environment. In many ways, these three worlds, all coexisting in eastern North America, were closer to one another than we, in the twenty-first century, are to any of them.

For Julie Wheelwright, the big puzzle underlying the entire narrative is the question of Esther's conflicting loyalties. Did Esther retain loyalty to her Protestant family of origin, from which she was kidnapped in a violent raid, and from which she was further separated by her Catholic vows? How did she feel among the Abenaki? How did she come to terms with the world of Catholic New France, at a time when people on both sides of the religious divide thought that straying from orthodoxy meant eternal damnation? Did she view her vows as a rejection of her Puritan roots? A route to a safe haven? A religious commitment?

The difficulty in knowing Esther's thoughts and feelings stems not only from the lack of documentation from Esther on this topic, but also from the fact that Esther moved from one society to another. Normally, in the absence of contradictory documentation, an historian can make certain assumptions about an historical actor by considering the context of the society in which he or she lived. Julie Wheelwright does not have that option. She cannot assume that Esther kept the Puritans' disdain for the Catholics, for example, because Esther was immersed in two other societies that did not feature this world-view. Nor could Julie assume that Esther embraced the Catholics' disdain for the Puritans, because she had Puritan family members whom she may have loved and mourned. Historians often have the benefit of making inferences about how historical actors thought and felt by drawing from the evidence of the social milieu in which the actors lived. For Julie Wheelwright, it was more complex because, by the age of 14, Esther had lived in not one world but three.

Navigating the Barriers to the Past

In her book, Julie Wheelwright tells us about the ceremony of Esther's entry to the Ursuline convent, so we, the readers, know the words Esther would have spoken. But somehow, knowing what was said and done during the ceremony is not enough to convey what was going on in the mind of the 14-year-old girl. As Julie Wheelwright writes, "If there was such a thing as individual choice for Esther, an eighteenth-century captive English girl living among the most powerful and charismatic Catholics in New France, I need to know if she exercised it" (p. 92). In her attempts to find out, Julie employed a mix of psychological common sense (i.e., assumptions of timeless human experience) and sensitivity to historical and cultural differences over time.

Julie Wheelwright interweaves chapters describing her own research process with chapters telling the narrative of Esther's life. This method allows her to better negotiate the distance between present and past, placing herself in Esther's shoes. In the following passage, she explains her own mental processes as she ponders Esther's entry into the convent as a nun:

I remember my own awkwardness at fourteen and wonder what it meant for Esther to encase her body in a full-length habit of heavy black serge; she would never run or swim again, never have another set of eyes upon her naked limbs, never give or receive an intimate caress. (p. 112)

Thus, the author shares with the reader her questions about what Esther was thinking and feeling. These questions, however, reveal what might concern Julie Wheelwright in the same situation, and may not be a fair estimation of what was on Esther's mind. Can Julie Wheelwright reasonably extrapolate from her own experience at age 14, or is she too invested in her twenty-first-century sensibilities?

In her search to understand Esther's apparent choice to remain in Catholic New France, away from her Puritan family of birth, the author regrets the lack of evidence:

Esther left no record of her story, so I am feeling my way through it, relying on my emotional connection to her to fill in the blanks where the black hole of documentation gapes wide. (p. 137)

The author herself understands the limitations of using her own life experience as a guide to Esther's feelings. She admits to "stumble[ing] over this idea of such extreme sacrifice" (p. 136), an experience she finds foreign:

I was raised a lukewarm low Anglican, and my intellect can't quite grasp what it means to love God so deeply that you are willing to give up your family, love, sexual passion and children to spend a lifetime in prayer. (pp. 134–135)

Julie Wheelwright looks back from a multicultural, feminist, secular, liberal, First Nations–sensitive contemporary Canada. She—and we—have the benefits of hindsight and a wealth of historiographic forerunners whose missteps we can take care to avoid. And yet the very conceptual and interpretive lenses through which we must look are necessarily foreign to the totemic, superstitious, and religious sensibilities of the peoples of three centuries ago.

> ... the very conceptual and interpretive lenses through which we must look are necessarily foreign to the totemic, superstitious, and religious sensibilities of the peoples of three centuries ago.

As Julie Wheelwright herself points out, feminism drove her generation to search for "individual identity" (p. 136). In contrast, "Esther was taught that every concession to the self had to be regarded as impure, and therefore that she had to extinguish any thought or desire not focused exclusively on God" (pp. 149–150). The divide between present and past appears to defeat the author, and in the end she acknowledges that she does not fully understand the motives that drove Esther in the foreign country of the eighteenth century.

Figure 5.2 Can we make valid inferences about the thoughts and feelings of people who lived long ago in a world quite different from our own? Some human experiences are universal—we can connect with and empathize with others because we share similar emotional experiences. Most every adult has taken joy in a baby, been torn with grief, or fallen in love, as have the two teenagers shown in *Romeo and Juliet*, the 1871 painting by British artist Ford Madox Brown. Danger lurks, however, in depending on our commonalities with the people of the past—we so easily slip into making unfounded assumptions. We cannot assume, for example, that all societies experience romantic love in exactly the same way.

Reading between the Lines

If Julie cannot know Esther's motives, she does learn much about her by means of meticulous research. Esther's personal letters, in particular, provide ample indication of Esther's frame of mind at various stages of her life. Esther does not always say exactly what she is thinking, but Julie is able to extrapolate, or read between the lines. Consider, on page 143, Julie's comment on a letter Esther wrote to her superiors when she was in the position of Mother Superior.

A letter to the Mother House ... reveals her loneliness. "We are not lacking in debts and some pretty large ones," she wrote. "Nobody but me, however, knows about them and I am in no hurry to acquaint the Community with the fact, for fear of distressing them." (pp. 251–252)

Esther's letter does not say outright that Esther is lonely. Instead, Julie, the historian, draws this information from Esther's statements. Esther was in charge of a convent deeply in debt, and yet she could share this information with no one in the convent community. Julie posits that this burden must have brought great loneliness. Herein lies a powerful tool for interpreting documentation from the past: the making of inferences.

Another Way of Understanding the Past

Julie Wheelwright never fully understands her ancestor. Not fully understanding, however, is not bad history. Inferences need not be thrown out because we are not quite sure if they are true. After all, it is impossible to know for absolute certain what other people are thinking, even in the present. The act of acknowledging the limitations to what we can know about the past is a sign of healthy historical thinking. The acknowledgment allows historians to make inferences, without which we would be unable to understand history. Julie Wheelwright explains the rewards of making inferences.

My research into Esther's life has opened my eyes and my ears to another way of understanding the past. Now I can see better what lies beneath official documents and obscuring institutional histories, can see better how to interpret the subtle, symbolic meaning of silver spoons, false family crests, and painful silences. There is always a subtext that suggests the enduring power of a story, our yearning to know what came before us and our desire to understand where the past might lead us. (p. 271)

We have been examining Wheelwright's biography of an ancestor because the author's transparency about the challenges she faced allows us insights into the process of taking an historical perspective. One virtue of *Esther: The Remarkable True Story of Esther Wheelwright* is its openness in laying out the difficulties inherent in interpreting the experiences of people living in the eighteenth century from the vantage point of our own. Julie Wheelwright shows us how to arrive at plausible, evidence-based claims, even while we maintain vigilance for pitfalls and humility about our conclusions.

> **CONNECTIONS BETWEEN CONCEPTS**
>
> Evidence is a dependable route to understanding why the people of the past experienced the world differently than we do today. Hard statistics, such as birth and death rates, ages of marriage, literacy rates, and family size, for example, can all help us make inferences about people's experiences, thoughts, and feelings.

Now consider the ways we can encourage students to make plausible inferences based on historical context and evidence, drawing on "universal" human emotions and ideas while maintaining a keen awareness of the vast differences that can lie between now and the past.

Now and Then: An Ocean of Difference

Separating us from the past is not just time but also scientific discoveries and intellectual upheavals, industrial and political revolutions, the separation of church and state and the rise of secularism, the recognition of civil rights, and the digitization of the world. As Julie Wheelwright points out, there is a massive chasm between her world and that of Esther.

Many students are unaware of the ways worldview affects virtually every aspect of their lives, including how they deal with problems, handle relationships, and view social obligations. Perhaps the best approach to enlightening students on this front is to present them with a contrast involving something of particular significance to many of them. For example, most teenagers today view music as a highly accessible commodity, to be downloaded, viewed on television channels, or heard through ear buds. Take students back to a time before music could be recorded—to a time when music was always a live performance. How might people in the past relate to music differently because of the way they heard it?

The Minefield of Using Universals

To put oneself in the position of a person from the past requires a difficult empathetic leap. To infer how people thought and felt, we must inescapably assume some measure of commonality between them and us. If a person, long ago, was burned at the stake, we can imagine that they felt intense pain, just as we would in a similar situation. If two people, centuries ago, fell in love, we can see a parallel to our own ideas of love, and imagine the heady mix of excitement, desire, promise, and commitment that "falling in love" implies today. Without assuming some commonality, we are stymied in our attempts to understand how the world looked and felt to people in the distant past.

Yet, every time we assume such commonalities, we risk imposing ideas and emotions distinctive to *our* times on a world in which people experienced things in profoundly different ways. Thus, deep religious belief may have enabled a martyr to experience the pain of burning flesh in a way that is foreign to people in the modern, secular West. Similarly, some aspects of our notion of romantic love are particular to our historical era. Did lovers centuries ago need constant communication, as do today's texting sweethearts? Even the vocabulary we use today to describe both the contemporary world and the historical, with words like *religion*, *state*, and *human rights*, are often impositions of our own sensibilities on the world of the past.

The first challenge, then, lies in picking apart the human universal from the historically specific. The two dangers of drawing on our experience of universal human experience are anachronism and presentism, both of which you will want to help students avoid. Anachronism can be illustrated by showing students movie stills, paintings, and plays that show aspects out of place in the period of history being depicted. Artwork is commonly littered with "mistakes." In Shakespeare's *Julius Caesar*, Cassius announces "The clock has stricken three," although clocks were not invented until the Middle Ages.

Presentism is anachronism of the mind: instead of mistakenly placing not-yet-invented technology into the past, we mistakenly imbue the people of the past with thoughts and feelings that more properly belong to the present. For example, students might infer that a mother in eighteenth-century Canada would be shocked to find out that her 10-year-old child was drinking beer at lunch. Drinking beer, or ale, however, was actually the norm for men, women, and children in that period of history because milk was considered unhealthy and water often carried communicable diseases.

Context Is Crucial

Historical context can help historians and students understand the perspectives of people in the past. We can better appreciate Esther Wheelwright's decision to become an Ursuline nun if we take into account the central role of religion to people in the era in which she lived. Students will better understand the perspective of a Ukrainian Canadian child writing a letter to her imprisoned father if they realize that thousands of Ukrainian Canadian men were taken away during World War I, not because they had committed crimes, but because they were considered to be enemy aliens.

Historical Perspectives

> **Guidepost 3**
The perspectives of historical actors are best understood by considering their **historical context**.

Figure 5.3 How can historical context help us understand the events of history? In an historic clash between Prime Minister Lester B. Pearson and French president Charles de Gaulle during a state visit to Canada in 1967, Pearson gave a strongly worded speech rebuking the state visitor on public radio. De Gaulle responded by cutting his visit short. Why would a prime minister be so rude so publicly? Consider the immediate context: de Gaulle had concluded a public speech in Montréal the previous day with the rousing phrase *Vive le Québec libre!* (Long live a free Québec!) The photograph at left shows his stance as he shouts this phrase, which was the rallying cry of Québec separatists during a period of intense Québec nationalism. This context helps us understand Pearson's outrage.

Historical Perspectives

> **Guidepost 4**

Taking the perspective of historical actors means inferring how people felt and thought in the past. It does not mean identifying with those actors. Valid inferences are those based on evidence.

Keeping Inferences Grounded

Taking an historical perspective does not entail identifying with or experiencing the feelings of an historical actor, as you would if you were empathizing with that person. Instead, it means making inferences to *achieve valid understanding* of what the historical actor's thoughts and feelings likely were. We cannot achieve this by simply imagining the past. All inferences about the thoughts and feelings of historical actors must be grounded in textual, visual, oral, or artifactual evidence. Otherwise, it's all guesswork. This is the scenario that historiographer Keith Jenkins mocks in his fictional school exercise whereby the teacher asks students to "pretend to be a fox, a snowflake, an angry king."[2] How does it feel? No answer, of course, would be out of bounds without the supporting evidence requirement.

A dilemma in trying to make inferences from evidence is that evidence rarely speaks directly to the questions we ask. Assume that we ask, "Was Cleopatra feeling courageous?" Most historical actors will not document explicitly that they were feeling courageous. Even if Cleopatra *had* declared "I feel courageous," we would have to question if this was a true representation of her feelings. After all, bravado can be a cover for terror.

Therefore, historians do not expect to find "the true testimony." Instead, they seek knowledge by reading between the lines: they make inferences. This act of interpretation works only if it is based on evidence. Consider, for example, how Julie Wheelwright ascertained the likely opinion of John Wheelwright (Esther's father) about his daughter's education.

John Wheelwright, who had paid for his children's education and ensured that his eldest son was taught French, must surely have appreciated his daughter's accomplishments as a schoolmistress. (p. 177)

Julie clearly did not have a letter or journal entry in which John Wheelwright stated that he was proud of his daughter's accomplishments. She did, however, have evidence that John Wheelwright had invested in his children's education—from which Julie inferred that he respected education generally. Julie did not guess John's opinion about Esther's profession. She made an inference based on evidence. Use examples such as the one described here to demonstrate to students the importance of using evidence as the basis for making inferences.

From Both Sides Now

"What really happened" in history can be hard to pin down because every participant in history sees through the lenses of his or her own experience and worldview. Father Bigot was the priest responsible for taking Esther

Historical Perspectives

> **Guidepost 5**

Different historical actors have **diverse perspectives** on the events in which they are involved. Exploring these is key to understanding historical events.

---

2 Jenkins, K. (1991). *Rethinking history* (p. 42). London, UK: Routledge.

away from her Abenaki family and bringing her to the Ursuline convent. As Wheelwright tells us, "it pained Father Bigot to see the white daughter of an important English family so dirty, underfed and poorly clothed, and living among 'savages'"[3] (p. 77). The Abenaki who had cared for Esther as a member of their family for five years would not have viewed her circumstance in the same light. They would see the family ties with Esther to which Father Bigot would not have had access.

People tend to have different perspectives of an event for one of two reasons. Either they see different aspects of an event or they see the same aspect but interpret it differently. Sometimes both factors are at play. For William Lyon Mackenzie and the rebels in Upper Canada, the rebellions of 1837 were an expression of revolt against an undemocratic government. This perspective stems from the vantage point of Upper Canada—the rebels "saw" primarily local concerns. For Louis-Joseph Papineau and the rebels in Lower Canada, the rebellions were not only a demand for responsible government but also an assertion of nationalism. This perspective stems from the vantage point of Lower Canada—the rebels "saw" primarily local concerns. For the government, though, the rebellions were the shenanigans of upstarts and criminal elements. The government authorities held power, the rebels were challenging it: they had different positions, which led to very different views of the event. By helping students seek out and compare different perspectives of historical events, we enable them to achieve a richer understanding of the past.

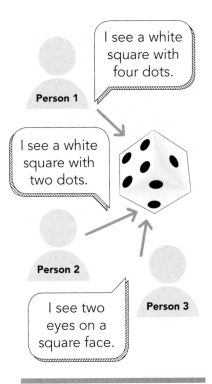

Figure 5.4 People have various perspectives for different reasons. Person 1 and Person 2 see different "sides," or parts, of an event. Person 2 and Person 3 interpret the same side differently.

Figure 5.5 The year 1870 saw the creation of Manitoba, the fifth province to enter Confederation. As with any event in history, there were diverse perspectives about the changes coming to the West. This 1870 painting by William Hind hints at two of them. Does the painting actually show these two perspectives? Which of the two is likely closer to the artist's perspective? A clue lies in Hind's title for the painting: *Civilization and Barbarism, Winnipeg, Manitoba.*

3 Note that the meaning of the French word *sauvage* at the time did not carry quite the negative connotation that it now does in English. The meaning was closer to "people of the forest."

Generating Powerful Understandings of Historical Perspectives

Use the lessons and activities in the second half of this chapter to enable your students to move from limited to powerful understandings of the ideas embodied in the guideposts.

> **Guidepost 1** An ocean of **difference** can lie between current **worldviews** (beliefs, values, and motivations) and those of earlier periods of history.

DEMONSTRATION OF LIMITED UNDERSTANDING	DEMONSTRATION OF POWERFUL UNDERSTANDING
Student assumes that the beliefs, values, and motivations of people in the past were the same as those of people today.	Student identifies examples of a vast **difference between worldviews** prevalent today and those prevalent in the past.

> **Guidepost 2** It is important to avoid **presentism**—the imposition of present ideas on actors in the past. Nonetheless, cautious reference to universal human experience can help us relate to the experiences of historical actors.

DEMONSTRATION OF LIMITED UNDERSTANDING	DEMONSTRATION OF POWERFUL UNDERSTANDING
Student assumes that people in the past had the same ideals, values, and worldviews that we have today, which makes it difficult to understand their actual motivations.	Student exercises caution when drawing on **universal human experiences** (e.g., love, death, hunger) to understand historical actors.

> **Guidepost 3** The perspectives of historical actors are best understood by considering their **historical context**.

DEMONSTRATION OF LIMITED UNDERSTANDING	DEMONSTRATION OF POWERFUL UNDERSTANDING
Student judges people in the past as dull-witted or weird, because the student ignores historical context.	Student explains or illustrates perspectives of people in their **historical context**.

> **Guidepost 4** Taking the perspective of historical actors means inferring how people felt and thought in the past. It does not mean identifying with those actors. Valid inferences are those based on evidence.

DEMONSTRATION OF LIMITED UNDERSTANDING	DEMONSTRATION OF POWERFUL UNDERSTANDING
Student equates perspective taking to flights of imagination, failing to consider evidence.	Student makes factually accurate, **evidence-based inferences** about the beliefs, values, and motivations of an historical actor, while recognizing the limitations of our understanding.

> **Guidepost 5** Different historical actors have **diverse perspectives** on the events in which they are involved. Exploring these is key to understanding historical events.

DEMONSTRATION OF LIMITED UNDERSTANDING	DEMONSTRATION OF POWERFUL UNDERSTANDING
Student fails to recognize differences among the perspectives of various peoples in the past.	Student distinguishes a **variety of perspectives** among historical actors participating in a given event.

Working with
HISTORICAL
PERSPECTIVES

Introducing Historical Perspectives

Critics claim that teaching approaches such as role-playing and writing historical fiction give students free rein to rely on imagination and feelings at the cost of historical accuracy. We assert that these approaches are key to understanding the people of the past, as long as suggested activities stress the importance of keeping inferences grounded in evidence, as do all the activities in this chapter.

ACTIVITY: What's in a Name?

Consider using the change in the popularity of names over time as a soft and subtle entry into the understanding of how the past is different from, but not necessarily inferior to, the present.

Begin by prompting students to discuss their own names: Do you know how you got your name? Do you have any nicknames? Do you like your name? At some point, direct students to shift their attention to the historical aspect of names by asking questions such as these:

- What names were used in the past that are no longer common today?
- What names are common today that weren't used much in the past?
- How have names changed? What might explain the changes?

Guide discussion toward a consideration of why certain names that are not common now were popular in the past. For example, ask "Were your grandparents less intelligent? Did they want to call their children 'funny' names?"

A Grade 4 teacher in a study by Levstik and Barton followed similar discussion questions with an assignment for her students to research the names of their parents and grandparents, and the reasons why they were given these names. Students in the study soon understood that some things change because of changing fashion and not because people of the past were "slow-witted." After the project, whenever the class encountered some puzzling belief or strange behaviour in history, some student would reliably say, "But it wouldn't seem that way to them, it just seems that way to us because we're not used to it."[4]

---

4 Levstik, L., & Barton, K. (1997). *Doing history: Investigating with children in elementary and middle schools* (p. 117). Mahwah, NJ: Lawrence Erlbaum Associates.

Teaching Guidepost 1

Prompt students to recognize differences between present and past worldviews by asking questions that highlight these broad differences and elicit wonder at them, for example

- If someone were transported from [era under discussion] to today, what would he or she make of our actions/this situation? (e.g., What might one of the anti-Asian politicians of this historical time period think if he or she walked the streets of Toronto today? How do you know?)
- How well do you think you really understand this person/event? (e.g., How well do you really understand the Great European Witch Hunt?) What more might you need to know to gain a better understanding?

Remind students that it is important to suspend judgment in order to interpret how people in the past understood the world, rather than deciding right away that some belief was foolish or sexist. Use the next activity to reinforce this frame of mind. If possible, introduce the following activity at the beginning of the year when you are discussing class rules. The activity provides a list of rules not for students, but for teachers.

ACTIVITY: Examining Rules for a Teacher, 1923

On the one hand, our individual experiences are limited, and, because of this, the beliefs and choices of people in the past may seem strange or inscrutable. On the other hand, we don't want students to assume that this difference shows people of the past to be backward or stupid. We want them to embrace the strangeness and inscrutability.

Ask students to consider what the rules in Figure 5.6 suggest about the perspective of members of one Ontario school board in 1923 about the role of women in education.

Students will readily infer the perspective of the school board that young women needed to be closely controlled and that teachers should model upright behaviour. Many students will label this perspective as sexist or weird. Invite them to suspend such judgments until they can more fully understand the perspectives of the school board officials.

Students will be better able to move beyond mere labelling if they understand some of the context. Explain that in Canada in the 1920s, most Canadians had a strict sense of appropriate behaviour. Canadians in general believed in not just a hierarchy of gender but also a hierarchy of class, religion, and race. At the same time, women were entering North American post-secondary institutions in dramatically high numbers from 1900 to 1930, largely because of the growing demand for schoolteachers. This meant that increasing numbers of young women were away from home at teachers' college or university and outside of parental control until marriage. (At this time, the median age of marriage for women in North America was 22.) Many authorities believed rules were needed to protect young schoolteachers. When a school was opened

MISS LOTTIE JONES AGREED THAT SHE WOULD...

1. not get married.

2. not ride in a carriage or automobile with any man except her brothers or father.

3. not leave town without permission.

4. not smoke cigarettes or drink beer, wine, or whiskey.

5. not dye her hair or dress in bright colours and wear at least two petticoats.

6. keep the school room clean and scrub it with soap and water at least once a week.

7. not use face powder or mascara, not wear dresses more than 2″ above the ankles, and finally, not loiter downtown in ice cream parlours.[5]

Figure 5.6 In 1923, when Lottie Jones agreed to teach at a school in Ontario for $75 a month, she agreed to follow certain rules, which are described here.

to train teachers in Vancouver, the *Victoria Times* warned that "children" would be "separated from home influence at a most critical time in their lives."[6]

The rule that most clearly expresses a vast difference in worldviews has to be the one against ice cream parlours. Young men and women socialized in these establishments, something that the school board may have wished to discourage. Beyond this, the rule also reflects widespread xenophobia of the time toward immigrants, as well as urban legends about "white slavery" and prostitution. Many ice cream parlours were owned by Italian immigrants who were imagined to be the ringleaders of slavery and prostitution. Bill Ellis argues that such rules were likely meant to protect female teachers from such "sexual predators."[7]

Most students should be able to identify at least some examples of vast differences between worldviews expressed in this 1923 set of rules and the worldviews of the present when you ask an open-ended question: "What differences between the past and present does this list of rules suggest to us?" You may need to prompt students to explore further by referring to examples, such as the worldviews about the position of teachers, "dangerous" colours and foods, ethnic groups, and so on. Caution students, however, that one set of rules cannot necessarily reveal the character of contracts elsewhere in Ontario and the country.

Advise students that many women schoolteachers in the 1920s were challenging the conventions expressed in these rules, and some became the feminist leaders of their generation. (Agnes Macphail, Nellie McClung, and Lucy Woodsworth all began as schoolteachers.) As one teacher reminisced,

---

5 Description of Miss Lottie Jones' contract, 1923. Marion Royce Papers. Centre for Women's Studies in Education, OISE. Cited in Light, B., & Roach Pierson, R. (Eds.) (1990). *No easy road: Women in Canada 1920s–1960s* (p. 270). Toronto: New Hogtown Press.

6 Cited in Calam, J. (1984). Teaching the teachers: Establishment and early years of the B.C. provincial normal schools. *B.C. Studies, 61*(Spring), 37.

7 Ellis, B. (2009). Whispers in an ice cream parlor: Culinary tourism, contemporary legends, and the urban interzone. *Journal of American Folklore, 122*(483), 53–74.

"It sounds like teachers had a hard life in those days but we thought of ourselves as adventurers—like Olympic Torch-bearers in our gumboots and mittens."[8]

Conclude the class discussion by asking, "What are some of the challenges that we should keep in mind when we look at beliefs of people in the past?" This exercise could also be used to consider some other powerful understandings, such as the risk of presentism and the importance of context with some explanation and questions. Ask questions such as the following:

- Many of you may have found these rules strange, especially the one against ice cream parlours, but do people today ever tell stories about establishments in the "wrong part of town"? Have you ever heard unfounded urban legends about ethnic groups?
- Are there any similar examples of measures to protect women today?
- Do our different attitudes give us the right to feel superior to people in the past?

Teaching Guideposts 2 and 3

> **DEMONSTRATION OF POWERFUL UNDERSTANDING 2**
>
> Student exercises caution when drawing on **universal human experiences** (e.g., love, death, hunger) to understand historical actors.

Students naturally tend to draw on universal experiences to tell them what people were thinking and feeling in the past. This tendency must be tempered because of the vast gulf that can exist between the worldviews of the present and those of the past. By drawing on our own experiences with death, for example, we can make inferences about what an historical actor might be thinking or feeling when a baby dies. In a period of history when many children died under the age of one year, however, perhaps people reacted to the death of babies quite differently from the way we do today. Historians have had protracted debates about this very question. Universal experience can sometimes be misleading, and so should be used with caution.

> **DEMONSTRATION OF POWERFUL UNDERSTANDING 3**
>
> Student explains or illustrates perspectives of people in their **historical context**.

Two specific dangers lie in wait for students who would draw on universal human experience to inform their understanding of the thoughts, feelings, and worldviews of people from the past. These are anachronism and presentism. To illustrate examples of anachronism for students, show examples of slip-ups in movies such as *Gladiator* and *Robin Hood*,[9] or anachronistic images on the Internet, such as photographs of Gandhi altered to show him wearing shades while listening to an MP3 player, or Che Guevara singing on *American Idol*.[10] Ask, How might these anachronisms, when taken seriously, create misunderstanding about the past?

Explain to students that presentism is the interpretation of the actions of people in the past through the filter of a contemporary belief system. It is like judging people of the past as boors because they rarely bathed, when it is likely that cleanliness was simply not a priority in times when life was

---

8 Letter from Edna May Embury to Paul Stortz, West Vancouver, March 11, 1988. Cited in Wilson, J.D. (1995). 'I am ready to be of assistance when I can': Lottie Bowron and rural women teachers in British Columbia 1928–1934. In Barman, J., Sutherland, N., & Wilson, J.D. (Eds.) *Children, teachers, and schools in the history of British Columbia* (p. 289). Calgary: Detselig.

9 Anachronisms! *The past—in the pictures.* Retrieved from http://www.thepastinthepictures.wildelearning.co.uk/Introductoryunit!.htm

10 Photo effects contests. *Worth 1000.* Retrieved from http://www.worth1000.com/contests/8779/contest#entries

harsh and survival was something to be won. Remind students of the introductory activity **What's in a Name?** on page 149, in which they reflected on presentism, although you may not have used the term at that point.

Consider providing further exploration of presentism by asking students to imagine what people in the future might think is strange about our society today. If Canadians 100 years from now are all vegetarians, would it be fair for them to condemn those of us who eat sushi or hamburgers today?

Using Historical Context to Avoid Presentism

How is a student to identify and avoid the dangers of anachronism and presentism? The answer lies in taking into account the historical context. Walk students through a few examples in which historical context provides the key to understanding a particular historical perspective. For example, you may wish to show students several examples of historical photographs in which the subjects are displaying stiff poses. Ask students what feelings the poses appear to reflect, for example, sadness or seriousness. Then ask them if the poses might merely reflect the limitations of the technology of the day. (The subjects needed to remain motionless for a long period in order to expose the film. It is difficult to maintain a smile for this length of time.) Show students a few recent passport photos. Discuss the expressions on the faces of the subjects, and ask what they might reflect (not seriousness or unhappiness, but an official requirement that the subject not smile). Help students recognize that it was the historical context of the official requirement that helped them interpret the expressions accurately. Speculate as to what conclusions people in the future might draw when looking at these passport photos.

Point out to students that knowing the historical context of language can help them understand perspectives more accurately. Written words in an historical document may not hold the same meaning today as they did in the past. One example is the word *gay*. Once connoting light-hearted or merry, the word eventually gained a new meaning: homosexual. Ask students to provide examples of other words from the past that are either no longer used today at all or have an entirely different meaning.

The list of inquiry questions on page 154 highlights the relevance of historical context in understanding historical perspectives accurately, and can be used to prompt or lead in to a particular lesson, unit, or activity. Although similar to those that you might have used to introduce Powerful Understanding 1, these inquiry questions are more directed to the particular features of time and place. They elicit wonderment at the *differences* between the perspectives of the present and those of the past, and at the same time lead students to a deeper and more critical understanding of the thinking that lay behind the decisions, actions, and beliefs of the people of the past. They help guide students to consider the perspectives of people *in their historical context*.

- If this action doesn't seem to make sense/isn't what you might expect/ is surprising, why do you think X took this course of action? (e.g., If throwing away expensive dishes, glasses, and cutlery doesn't make

---

CONNECTIONS BETWEEN CONCEPTS

The dangers of presentism apply to the ethical dimension concept as well. When examining ethical controversies, presentism may lead students to feel a kind of moral superiority and to think that people of the past have a kind of moral deficit because they did not believe in contemporary values such as multiculturalism or gender equality. Taking an historical perspective can help students understand—if not condone— the behaviours of the past.

sense, why did a wealthy Canadian family in the nineteenth century throw these things into their privy?)

- If this action appears to have been the best response, why do you think X did not take this course of action? (e.g., If vaccination was the best way to avoid catching smallpox, why did so many French Canadians refuse to get vaccinated during the smallpox epidemic of 1885?)
- What did this group/individual feel was most important in their life at this particular time? (e.g., What was most important to Nelson Mandela after release from prison?)
- Why might X have not really understood what Y was doing/believed in? (e.g., Why might Frobisher have misunderstood the Inuit?)
- What do you think made these people fight/refuse to fight/feel ashamed/feel proud? (e.g., Why did Canadians sign up so enthusiastically to fight in World War I? What led conscientious objectors to refuse to fight?)

Sentence prompts such as the following can be used to provide scaffolding for students attempting to use historical context to understand an historical perspective:

- This idea might have been popular because …
- This way of thinking might explain …
- This source suggests that people at the time were thinking that …

The following activity begins with the first inquiry question from our list, using it to explore intriguing clues about an event in the life of a family that occupied a picturesque home in nineteenth-century Upper Canada.

ACTIVITY: The Mystery in the Privy[11]

- Organize students into pairs and pose these inquiry questions:
  - It doesn't make sense to throw away expensive possessions, so why did a wealthy Canadian family in the nineteenth century throw the entire contents of their kitchen and dining room into their privy (outhouse)?
  - What does this tell us about the perspectives of the family?
- Ask students to write an initial hypothesis to explain the behaviour.
- Provide one copy of **BLM 5.1: The Mystery in the Privy** to each pair of students. Ask them to cut apart the clues.
- Students read each clue, one by one, and sort them into one of three or four categories, such as the family, the house, the privy contents, and disease. When clues have been sorted, students label each category and suggest hypotheses to answer the inquiry questions using the clues as evidence.
- Ask pairs to write down their answers, and then report and defend their answers to the class. Some may conclude, as most historians

PURPOSE

To practise using historical context to take an historical perspective

MATERIALS

- BLM 5.1: The Mystery in the Privy (1 per pair of students)
- scissors (1 per pair of students)

11 Thanks to John Myers of OISE/University of Toronto for the original version of this mystery game. For further information, see Doroszenko, D. (2006). Uncovering family history. *Heritage Matters, 4*(3), 14–15; or Grzybowski, S., & Allen, E.A. (1999). Tuberculosis: 2. History of the disease in Canada. *Canadian Medical Association Journal, 160*(7), 1025–1028.

have, that it is likely that the death of Edith Radenhurst's son Charles prompted her to dispose of all the objects in her kitchen and dining room to prevent further tragedy to her family from tuberculosis. The historical context reveals that the family was probably feeling a great deal of fear of further deaths from tuberculosis.

- Give students an opportunity to revise and improve their hypotheses.
- After sharing hypotheses as a class, discuss questions such as these:
  - What were the major differences in worldviews between Canada in the nineteenth century and now? What examples support your answer?
  - In what ways might these worldviews be similar? For example, how might the thoughts and feelings of the Radenhursts resemble those of a Canadian family today?
  - Look back at your original hypotheses. Were any of them close? How did learning about the context of the time change your thinking?
  - Did any of your first hypotheses suggest that this family was strange or lacking in common sense? (This would be an opportunity to explain presentism without, of course, denigrating students who did think the behaviour strange.)

Teaching Guidepost 4

"Sir John A. Macdonald was a loyal Canadian." As Macdonald was the architect of Confederation, most Canadians would accept this as true. But how do we really know? Back up the statement with evidence, and it increases in authority. For example, here is a comment made by Macdonald himself: "My sins of omission and commission I do not deny; but I trust that it may be said of me in the ultimate issue, 'Much is forgiven because he loved much,' for I have loved my country with a passionate love."[12] Surely, then, Macdonald believed in Canada as a country.

However, look further and another quote of his challenges our conclusions: "A British subject I was born, a British subject I will die."[13] We are brought up short, reminded of the limitations of discovering the truth about the beliefs and values of historical actors. Perhaps, however, the notion of "Canada as a country" was different in the nineteenth century, and it is our understanding of, and interpretation of, Macdonald's first statement that is at fault? Could a Canadian in the late nineteenth century combine a loyalty to Canada and loyalty to Britain? More research into historical context may be necessary.

Reinforce to students that they can make inferences about the beliefs, values, and motivations about people in the past, but that these cannot simply come from their imagination. Inferences need to be based on evidence. While beginning an exploration of a topic, chapter, or unit, use either of the following inquiry questions. Each question requires students to interpret evidence and draws their attention to the process:

> **DEMONSTRATION OF POWERFUL UNDERSTANDING 4**
>
> Student makes factually accurate, **evidence-based inferences** about the beliefs, values, and motivations of an historical actor, while recognizing the limitations of our understanding.

---

12 Retrieved from a quotation archive website: http://www.qotd.org/search/search.html?aid=8433&page=2
13 Retrieved from http://www.canadachannel.ca/macdonald/index.php/February_7,_1891

CONNECTIONS BETWEEN CONCEPTS

The evidence concept is so closely connected to historical perspectives that one is almost tempted to combine these two elements of historical thinking. Not only is evidence necessary for perspective taking, but perspective taking is necessary for interpreting evidence.

- Why is it difficult to determine the perspectives of people during this time? (e.g., Why is it hard to know what First Nations thought about the war?)
- How can we tell what X was thinking? (e.g., How can we tell what Mackenzie King was thinking?)

Many of the prompts used to teach the concept of evidence can guide students to use sources to interpret perspectives, for example:

- If you compare these two sources,...
- This source supports the evidence of ...
- Source X goes even further than Source Y in showing that ...
- Source X contradicts the evidence of Source Y in suggesting that ...
- These pictures show different perspectives on ...

Writing historical fiction is a good method for encouraging the use of evidence for perspective taking. For example, if students are writing a piece of historical fiction and doing it well, they will consider, and reflect on, the beliefs, values, and motivations of people in the time period they chose to write about. They will research details of the period in order to make factually accurate, *evidence-based* inferences about their characters, including what the characters might think; what they might do and why; and their response to the social, cultural, and political environment around them. Remind students that they do not have to agree with, or support, their characters' actions or beliefs, but merely gain an understanding of them. You may wish to require a list of supporting evidence used to inform the writing.

ACTIVITY: Reading Historical Fiction

Consider this fictionalized account of the Battle of Québec:

Figure 5.7 Simon Schama incorporates fact and fiction in this account of the Battle of Québec.

> We were tried, God knows, for as they came closer, the first musket shots came, cracking and hissing through the air and amidst the long grass and from behind the cover of trees to our right we could make out Indians coming closer, some of them creeping on their bellies. Some of our men fell to their shot without ever making a move like tin soldiers at a midsummer fair and this gall'd us so our hands trembled and shook at our muskets with mixt fear and rage, the more when we heard the Savages whooping and yelling. Then we made out the grey uniforms of the French coming at us at a trot and yelling and singing that they supposd us turning tail at the sight of them.[14]

PURPOSE

To appreciate the benefits of historical fiction and recognize its limitations

This fictionalized account by historian Simon Schama has a power and a richness of detail not offered by most social studies textbooks. A writer of historical fiction has the leeway to evoke a mood, with details and words such as *creeping* and *cracking*, for example. He or she also has "access" to the characters' internal thoughts and feelings, and can detail them for us. However, a writer

14 Schama, S. (1990). The many deaths of General Wolfe. *Granta, 32*(Summer), p. 55.

of historical fiction also has the responsibility to represent the era fairly—making up a character but not changing the course of historical events.

After students review the quotation, ask them to point out anything they believe an author would have to research before including. These might include whether First Nations were involved in the battle, the length of the grass at that time of year, and the colour of the French uniforms. Help students see that the author would also have to find evidence to determine the emotions that were felt by the soldiers. Help students realize the necessity of depending on evidence both for the supporting details of the story and for the beliefs, values, and motivations of the characters.

However, one must approach historical fiction with caution because, unlike history, it does not have to be completely faithful to the evidence. The first goal of a novelist, like that of a film director, is entertainment.[15] To help their young readers enter into the story, many authors of historical novels for youth portray their protagonists in ways that seem familiar and realistic to contemporary readers but may also be ahistorical. For example, the protagonist of an award-winning novel for middle school and junior high is an orphaned 15-year-old girl sent from London to York Factory in 1795 to work as a clerk for the Hudson's Bay Company (HBC). At that time, however, the HBC did not allow European women at any of its posts. Moreover, the novel reflects modern values of gender equality and multiculturalism, with the positive role models of a bright, open-minded English female protagonist who is helped by a romanticized, sympathetic First Nations girl.

The reading of *good* historical fiction, however, can help guide students to a deeper appreciation of historical perspectives. To conduct an historical fiction reading assignment related to a unit your class is studying, we recommend that you select, or at least vet, the literature. When students have read their choice of historical fiction, invite them to consider questions such as these:

- What makes a good historical story about this time period?
- How do the characters help us understand society at that time?
- What other options did the characters have, given the time and setting?
- What might be the point of view of the author of this story?
- How could this story have been told from another point of view?
- What does the novel/story suggest about society at the time the story was written (i.e., treating the fictional work as a primary source)?
- Is this story accurate? Plausible?
- How important is historical accuracy in a work of historical fiction?
- How does this story help us understand the past in ways that other types of sources do not?
- What do other sources offer that this fictional story does not?

For a thorough discussion of one example of good-quality historical fiction, see the essay about Lawrence Hill's *The Book of Negroes* in Chapter 6.

---

15 Clark, P. (2008). Teaching history through literature. In R. Case & P. Clark (Eds.), *The anthology of social studies: Vol. 2: Issues and strategies for secondary teachers* (p. 326). Vancouver: Pacific Educational Press.

PURPOSE

To demonstrate the use of evidence to write historical fiction that accurately conveys the beliefs, values, and motivations of historical actors

ACTIVITY: Writing Historical Fiction

If studying historical fiction can engage students and guide them to a deeper understanding of historical perspectives, then writing has the potential to help students put those understandings into practice. Writing journals and letters from the point of view of people from the past are the most common forms of historical writing in the classroom.[16] However, historical fiction can be written in an even wider variety of forms, such as scripts and poetry, and can also be combined with aural and visual media and role playing.[17]

Provide students with **BLM 5.2: On Writing Historical Fiction**, which can be used to guide students in any assignment involving the writing of historical fiction. You may wish to walk students through the following considerations:

- **Narrative mode**: Historical fiction is most easily written in the first person. However, if you wish students to include multiple historical perspectives in a story, suggest that they use third-person narration.
- **Research**: Emphasize that students must base their historical fiction on evidence. Provide access to contextual information and historical sources (including an array of primary sources) that students can use to develop historically plausible settings, conditions, and character motivation.
- **Plot**: Provide students with plot structure guidelines. Without limits, students may develop overly ambitious or confusing plots. For example, if they write a story, students should begin with a problem, such as something going wrong or some event that spurs a protagonist to action, and then focus on how the protagonist resolves the problem. The bio-poem in Figure 5.8 has an even more well-defined structure.
- **Characters**: Consider limiting the number of characters in students' narratives in order to help students keep their stories straightforward and focused. As well, remind students that they don't need to condone the behaviour, beliefs, or values of their characters. Rather, they simply must be able to provide evidence for why the behaviour would have occurred or for inferring these beliefs or values.
- **Language**: Teach writing techniques in order to accomplish two goals: (1) to help students see how they can engage their readers and develop historically plausible characters, and (2) to help them recognize how word choice and use of language shape our interpretation of the past.
- **Setting**: If students are writing a story, suggest that they consider all five senses when describing the setting. Point out that they may wish to consult the illustrations in their textbook as sources.

---

16 For example, the International School of Toulouse Humanities Website has a very well-developed journal assignment with supporting sources on a Nazi meeting held in March 1932. Retrieved from http://www.internation alschooltoulouse.net/igcsehistory/term2/rise_to_power/empathy/activity.htm

17 Lindquist, T. (n.d.). Why & how I teach with historical fiction. Retrieved from http://teacher.scholastic.com/ lessonrepro/lessonplans/instructor/social1.htm. This article by Terry Lindquist, a recipient of the Elementary Teacher of the Year award in the United States, gives thoughtful advice and creative examples of assignments, from a T-shirt template to a magazine interview.

BIO-POEM "BY" GALILEO GALILEI

I am loyal to my Church and loyal to science
I wonder about the heavens and how they move
I hear the lute my father used to play
I see with delight the four moons of Jupiter and stars of the
    Milky Way
as I touch and turn the lenses of my telescope
I want to share with the world these wonders
I am loyal to my Church and to science

I face the Inquisition and its dangerous folly
I accept its power: my ideas were wrong; the earth does not move
I worry that still it moves
I seek the help of Cardinal Bellarmine and Maria Celeste, my
    daughter
I am inspired by Copernicus and Kepler
I am loyal to my Church and to science

I understand that the moon is uneven, rough, and full of cavities just
    like the earth
But I say it is not so
I dream that someday we will see the truth together
I try to live a quiet life in my villa with my tools and telescope
I am loyal to my Church and to science

Figure 5.8 When writing this bio-poem, the author took the perspective of Galileo Galilei.

Writing a Bio-Poem: One Form of Historical Fiction

Encourage students to create their own bio-poem using **BLM 5.3: Write Your Own Bio-Poem**. Students write a "biography" in the voice of an historical actor, recognizing the barriers to change that have shaped his or her dreams and deeds. Show or read to students the sample bio-poem provided in Figure 5.8. Then give them the following instructions:

1. To create your own "biography" poem, first choose a person from the past and conduct research about him or her.
2. Find enough evidence to make accurate inferences about this person's thoughts, feelings, motivations, and beliefs.
3. Fill in each line as suggested. Try to write in this person's voice and from his or her perspective.

Teaching Guidepost 5

When we study history, we make evidence-based inferences about the beliefs, values, and motivations of historical actors. This can be challenging because each historical actor is unique. To begin, people are members of a society, so their perspective tends to differ from the perspective of a person living in a different society. In addition, people are influenced by their specific social, cultural, and political environments; for example, a union worker may have a different perspective from a manager who works in the same company. Further, each individual has a unique personality shaped by family, friends, and distinct events not shared by others. This means that historical actors may have a variety of perspectives on an event, despite their sharing a historical time and place.

An inquiry question such as the following can focus on the diversity of perspectives:

- Who supported and who opposed this action? Who celebrated and who mourned after this person was defeated? Who was excited, afraid, or content with this outcome?

ACTIVITY: Historical Perspectives in Role Plays

In Sam Wineburg's description of "models of wisdom in the teaching of history,"[18] he describes a wise American history teacher whom he refers to as the Invisible Teacher. In this teacher's classroom, students prepare for and then enact a role play that highlights the diverse perspectives of a variety of historical actors. With great passion and intelligence they debate whether, prior to the American Revolution, the British government had the authority to tax its American colonies. Some students play the role of rebels and others play Loyalists. A third group acts as judges.

The judges' verdict at the debate's conclusion stuns the class: the Loyalists win. One girl stares at the ceiling dazed, then begins to nod her head and says, "You know, … we could have been part of Canada." Wineburg explains that "the realization that, had the loyalists prevailed, Queen Elizabeth would appear on *our* stamps, as well as those of our northern neighbors, does not come easily to adolescents growing up in an era when America, not Britain, is the dominant world power."[19]

The verdict ended the debate but the lesson continued. The students went on to make sense of what they had learned in the role play with debriefing and follow-up assignments.

Although Wineburg dubs the teacher "invisible," this is true only in the sense that a choreographer who works tirelessly to prepare the performers to take centre stage is also invisible. "Backstage" support and guidance were crucial to the success of the performance.

---

18 Wineburg, S. (2001). *Historical thinking and other unnatural acts: Charting the future of teaching the past* (pp. 155–172). Philadelphia: Temple University Press.

19 Wineburg. (2001). *Historical thinking and other unnatural acts*, p. 163.

Conducting a Role Play

- To conduct a role play, divide the class into small groups and describe the assignment. Make sure students understand that they must ground their role plays in evidence, researching historical conditions and individual historical characters so as to give as accurate and plausible a portrayal as possible.
- Warn students against stereotypical interpretation. Even if students have developed a solid understanding of the perspective and context, when it is time to act out the play, they may resort to heavily accented speech and mannerisms that they think fit their character. Rule of thumb: no accents.
- Provide sufficient time and resources for students to prepare and practise. Offer guidance and encouragement as needed. Correct inaccuracies, but try to do so either when the role play is in script stage or after the role play has been presented.
- You may wish to provide students beforehand with a list of questions you will discuss after the role play is complete:
  - What values or ideas of the time was X reflecting?
  - How did X's understanding of the event vary from Y's understanding of the same event? Why was this?
  - How were X's and Y's beliefs different, and what would explain this?
  - Was this a plausible recreation of the past?
  - What other plausible choices might X have made?
  - Were there any opinions or actions that you found hard to understand?
  - Even though we research carefully, why will our abilities to reflect perspectives accurately always be limited?
  - What else do we need to learn about?
  - What does this whole process suggest to us about history?

In the Hot Seat

This type of role play follows a format that is similar to a television talk show. There is a host (you or a student), and an audience (students) who ask questions of the guests. The guests, who sit in the "hot seat," are either you or students in the role of historical characters. You may wish to play the role of guest as a means to explain the thinking and context of someone from the past in a manner more engaging than a formal lesson. If the students are the guests, debrief with questions such as those outlined above in Conducting a Role Play.

Debates and Trials

Students assume the roles of various historical actors, representing a variety of perspectives, to debate a controversial issue. The competitive nature of debate may have negative consequences, so at some point ask students to reverse their roles and take on the position of those whom they had previously opposed. Alternatively, recreate an historical trial or enact a "new" trial based on an accusation that you present. As with the other role plays, the keys to success are thorough research preceding the role play and thoughtful debriefing at the end. Evidence and historical context are the basis for presenting perspectives accurately.

Role Plays over Time

This type of role play combines the taking of historical perspectives with continuity and change. Successful execution lies in considerable organization and the collection of appropriate resources. Ontario educator Peter Kear, for example, has developed an array of role descriptions of various historical actors. Some of the roles are ordinary people, such as a Sikh sawmill worker. Others are prominent historical characters, such as Nellie McClung.

- Students adopt these roles at the beginning of the school year, as if the characters were the age of the students (for example, 15 or 16 years old).
- As the class travels chronologically through the course material, students "age" in their roles. They gain the opportunity to consider their characters' perspectives in dynamic situations within the larger historical context, such as the anti-Asiatic Vancouver riot of 1907 during the Laurier boom years or the field of battle during World War I or World War II.[20]
- Students reflect on whether their social position is changing as society changes, and if so, why and what effect this has on their perspective, if any. Are the beliefs, values, and motivations of their characters changing? If so, why?

Consolidating Understanding

One way for students to demonstrate their powerful understanding of historical perspectives is for them to create a tableau, which is a group of motionless figures representing a "still-life" scene from history. Although similar in some ways to a role play, a tableau can be less intimidating because, while all students take part, not all participants need to speak.

ACTIVITY: Setting the Tableau

Explain to students that they will work in small groups to prepare a tableau or a series of tableaux. In other words, they will use their bodies to illustrate a situation, event, or theme, and the perspectives of varied historical figures.

- Describe a tableau to students and explain its function.
- Divide the class into small groups of four or five. Provide each group with a topic (a situation, event, or theme)—either one that students have studied or one that they will need to research—as well as a perspective to represent. (If possible, suggest to students that they come up with the perspective themselves, perhaps using some previous

PURPOSE

To consolidate understanding of historical perspectives

---

20 Kear, P. (2011). *Come walk awhile in our shoes: A journey of ordinary—& some not-so-ordinary—Canadians, 1900–45 & 1945–99*. Available from the author at peterkear@vianet.on.ca

research they have done.) Consider giving each group a different topic—or giving each group the same topic but a different perspective. You may decide to keep these assigned topics and perspectives a secret and have the audience guess what is being depicted by each group.

- Explain that all students in the group must form part of each visual scene. If they do a series of tableaux, they may wish to include a narrator, possibly a different one for each scene, who can step out of the scene and provide a concise and dramatic explanation of the scene. This may assist the audience in appreciating the progression of events. Further, it may give participants a chance to further demonstrate understanding of historical perspectives.

- Ensure that students have studied or researched the time period and the historical actors in order to present plausible perspectives that are supported by evidence. Ask them to consider these questions:
  - What perspectives on the event do our characters, for example X, Y, and Z, have? How can we find out?
  - What is the key idea that we should concentrate on showing?
  - How can we show the perspectives of X, Y, and Z in visual scenes? (How will the audience understand what we are trying to convey?)
  - What beliefs, values, or opinions do our characters have that our audience might find difficult to accept or identify with? How can we make sure we support these with evidence in our visual scenes?
  - What actions can we portray to add drama and interest to our scene?
  - How can we bring historical context into our scene so the audience will better understand the perspectives of our characters?
  - How can we use a narrator to add context to the scene?

- Provide students with time to rehearse. Then, have the groups present their tableaux or tableaux series to the class. They must hold the pose for a defined amount of time, such as 10 or 20 seconds, or throughout the narrator's comments. This gives the audience time to examine the scene closely and arrive at an interpretation. Include "tapping-in," which permits you or other members of the audience to enter the tableau by touching one or more figures gently on the shoulder of a character and asking questions. Student participants then respond in role.

- Either after each tableau or series of tableaux, or at the end of the presentations, discuss with students questions such as these:
  - What values or ideas of the time was this group reflecting?
  - Was this a plausible recreation of the past?
  - What other plausible choices might the characters have made?
  - Were any opinions or actions hard to understand?
  - What else do we need to learn about in order to better understand the perspectives of these characters?
  - What does this exercise suggest to us about history?

- Conclude by letting students ask one another questions.

What makes an effective tableau?

- The most effective tableaux focus attention on one key idea and usually demonstrate some kind of action.
- Participants hold a pose, and generally do not speak.
- Props are optional.
- Participants pose at different physical levels to create visual interest.
- Participants exaggerate their poses to better convey a perspective.

Figure 5.9 A few characteristics of an effective tableau

BLM 5.1a **The Mystery in the Privy**

An outhouse was often called a privy in Canada during the last century.	The kitchen and dining room artifacts were thrown away by the Radenhursts.
Most of what we know of life at Inge-va in the 1800s comes from excavations made by archaeologists in 1988. More than 15 000 artifacts were found in the Inge-va privy.	The grounds of a stately mansion in Perth, Ontario, called Inge-va, contain the remains of a 160-year-old stone privy.
Seventy-six pharmaceutical bottles used by the Radenhursts were found in the privy.	After privies were no longer used as toilets, many were used as a kind of garbage dump.
In addition to the artifacts found in the privy, archaeologists were able to research the records of the town, and the oral histories and journals of townspeople.	Perth was founded as a military depot in 1816 and was settled by former soldiers. Later, as a government centre, it was a place for ambitious young lawyers to make their mark.
Those suffering from tuberculosis have flushed cheeks, fever, loss of appetite, weight loss, and, most of all, a cough that will not go away.	Expensive lotions and potions for hair care and to prevent hair loss were found in the privy.
A keg of oysters had been shipped from Toronto to Inge-va for Christmas in 1840. The shells were later used to seal the privy, since their lime composition helped to control odours.	The Radenhurst family moved into Inge-va in 1833. The father, Thomas Radenhurst, was a Reformer, a member of a movement trying to bring democracy to Canada, and a friend of Robert Baldwin, the Reform leader.
Edith and Thomas Radenhurst had ten children. After the death of Thomas in 1854, daughter Fanny died from typhoid fever in 1866. Son Charles died at the age of 27 in 1869 from tuberculosis, as did two sisters in 1873.	Tuberculosis (TB) or "consumption" killed more people in Canada in the nineteenth century than any other disease. It affected the poor more often than the wealthy. It was especially common among young adults.

It appeared that Edith Radenhurst buried the contents of her kitchen and dining room in the privy sometime in the early 1870s.	A baby mug with the name Charles inscribed on it was among the objects found in the privy.
Writers in popular magazines in the nineteenth century strongly recommended cleaning rooms where sick people stayed, removing unnecessary furniture and rugs, scrubbing walls, and burning and destroying anything likely contaminated by tuberculosis.	With the great rise in infectious diseases such as tuberculosis, typhoid, and cholera, social reformers began the Great Sanitary Awakening in Europe and North America in the nineteenth century. They identified filth as a cause of disease and began campaigns to enclose sewers, to collect garbage, and to take other sanitary measures.
After visiting her husband in Sri Lanka, where he was working, Ella Inderwick and her three sons moved into Inge-va in 1894. Ella named the house Inge-va, which means "come here" in the Tamil language of Sri Lanka.	The Reverend Michael Harris had Inge-va built in 1823–24. (At the time, the house did not yet have this name). He and his family were the first residents, and the house became a place for church and community gatherings.
Robert Lyon, a law student and nephew of Thomas Radenhurst, became involved in a feud with another law student over a local schoolteacher. In 1833, the two fought a duel. Robert Lyon was killed, the last Canadian to die in a duel. His body lay in the front room of Inge-va until the funeral.	Tuberculosis was seen as a "romantic" disease. It was thought to heighten sensitivity and it became popular among artists. Alexandre Dumas, author of *The Three Musketeers*, even pretended to have tuberculosis in order to be more popular.
The privy contained many wine glasses, tumblers for drinking liquor, and bottles that had once contained brandy, champagne, beer, hard liquor, and wine.	When someone with untreated tuberculosis coughs or sneezes, the air is filled with droplets containing the bacteria. Inhaling these infected droplets is the usual way a person gets tuberculosis.

BLM 5.2 On Writing Historical Fiction

Name: _____ Date: _____

Ground Rules for Writing Historical Fiction

- Unless otherwise instructed, you may include imaginary characters. However, the conditions within which these characters operate and the major events they witness must conform to the historical record. Do research so you can incorporate facts into your narrative and present accurate perspectives.
- Good historical fiction does more than describe events. Show how your characters saw those events at the time through their historical perspectives.
- Convince the reader that your characters are real. Give them depth. The reasons behind their actions or beliefs may be complex, or even contradictory.
- Remember that you do not need to agree with or support your characters' beliefs— you need merely to represent those beliefs accurately.

Questions to Think about When Writing Historical Fiction

- How can I use language and dialogue to create an authentic sense of the time period?

- How can I make my characters authentic, with perspectives that reflect the time and place in which they lived?

- What evidence do I have that this is what my characters would believe or do?

- What other options might my characters have, given this time and setting?

- What is my point of view?

- From what other point of view could I have told this story?

- How accurate or plausible is my story or poem?

- How does my story or poem help others understand the past in ways that other sources do not?

BLM 5.3 **Write Your Own Bio-Poem**

Name: _____ Date: _____

I am _____ (2 special characteristics you have)

I wonder _____ (something you are curious about)

I hear _____ (an imaginary or real sound)

I see _____ (an imaginary or real sight)

I touch _____ (an imaginary or real touch)

I want _____ (an actual desire)

I am _____ (repeat first line)

I face _____ (a barrier or challenge that you face)

I accept the power of _____ (a force or factor that is beyond your influence)

I worry _____ (a worry you have)

I seek the help of _____ (a person or people who help you)

I am inspired by _____ (a person or people who inspire you)

I am _____ (repeat first line)

I understand _____ (something you know to be true)

I say _____ (something you believe in)

I dream _____ (something you actually dream about)

I try _____ (something you really make an effort to do)

I am _____ (repeat first line)

Chapter 6

THE ETHICAL DIMENSION

How can history help us to live in the present?

Guideposts to the Ethical Dimension

> ### Guidepost 1
> Authors make **implicit or explicit** ethical judgments in writing historical narratives.

> ### Guidepost 2
> Reasoned ethical judgments of past actions are made by taking into account the **historical context** of the actors in question.

> ### Guidepost 3
> When making ethical judgments, it is important to **be cautious about imposing contemporary standards** of right and wrong on the past.

> ### Guidepost 4
> A fair assessment of the ethical implications of history can inform us of our **responsibilities to remember and respond** to the contributions, sacrifices, and injustices of the past.

> ### Guidepost 5
> Our understanding of history can help us make **informed judgments** about contemporary issues, but only when we **recognize the limitations** of any direct "lessons" from the past.

Figure 6.1 This photograph appears on the cover of Lawrence Hill's *The Book of Negroes* (2007), a work of historical fiction set in the time of the Atlantic slave trade. Sharon Kish, the book designer, chose a photograph that works not because it shows a captive during the eighteenth century but because it connects us at a visceral level to the Africans who experienced the barbarity of the trade. For fiction and photograph alike, we suspend disbelief to be caught in a woman's gaze demanding acknowledgment of the crime against humanity committed against millions of individuals whose memory she evokes. By helping us access the humanity of the captives, the author and designer alike help us recognize the ethical dimension of this period of history.

Thinking about
THE ETHICAL
DIMENSION

"Why are we learning about this?" The answer to this oft-repeated query emerges when we ask questions about the ethics of what has been done in the past and how we should respond. Thus, the ethical dimension of historical thinking helps to imbue the study of history with meaning. Remembrance of heroes' sacrifices, memorials to history's victims, reparations for mass crimes, and restitution for stolen goods and ruined lives are all attempts to come to terms with the past in the present. And because the past can never be fixed, all of these are also ways of helping us to move into the future, keeping in sight what we can learn from the legacies of horror and heroism bequeathed to us.

Like other historical thinking concepts, the ethical dimension of history poses a difficult conundrum. On the one hand, it is impossible to read about those who unleashed historical wrongs—using machetes, cat-o'-nine-tails, gas ovens, or box cutters—without making ethical judgments about both the horrific perpetrators and their heroic opponents, however complex and tangled those stories might be. Historical narratives about what we view today as inhumane and criminal events would be strange and colourless—perhaps even incomprehensible—without an implicit understanding between historian and reader that the perpetrators of those events were acting unethically. On the other hand, the historical perspectives concept suggests that we should avoid judging the past against the values and beliefs of today. Consequently, making ethical judgments about the past means walking a fine line indeed.

Before being introduced to the concepts of historical thinking, students tend to judge the actions of the past harshly: they divide the world into black and white, and miss the grey of real human experience. Instead of taking historical context into account, students tend to judge the ethics of past actions according to the standards and mores of the present day. By introducing students to historical thinking, we help them learn to judge the past fairly. Not only do students begin to distinguish what should be remembered, memorialized, or celebrated, they also learn how to judge what is an

CONNECTIONS BETWEEN CONCEPTS

The historical perspectives concept warns us to be aware that an ocean of difference may lie between the worldviews of the past and those of today. This warning is equally relevant to the ethical dimension of history, as we should be cautious about judging the past against the values and beliefs of today.

appropriate response in the present. Learning to think critically about the mistakes and the horrors—as well as the heroism—of the past contributes to the development of students' historical consciousness; they begin to see the links among the past, present, and future. In the process, they become more capable of negotiating the ethical dilemmas they will encounter in the course of their lives.

How One Author Approaches the Ethical Dimension

To find our way toward teaching the ethical dimension of history, we turn to Canadian Lawrence Hill, an award-winning author of historical fiction. In his novel *The Book of Negroes*,[1] Hill tells the story of fictional characters who take part in historically accurate events related to slavery in the eighteenth century. He borrowed the historian's hat, spending five years researching the slavery era to ensure he presented the events accurately. Of interest to our discussion is his success in bringing to life the ethical dimension of a period of history so far in the past that our connection to the raw human experience of slavery is many generations removed.

Hill's story of enslavement and resistance begins with the violent childhood kidnapping of his main character, Aminata Diallo, in West Africa in 1745. Both of her parents are killed in this episode, so the book begins by severing Diallo not only from her community and culture but also from those she loves. She endures a harsh journey to the coast and a horrific transatlantic passage, which many other captives do not survive. The crossing concludes with the humiliating and dehumanizing sale of Diallo to a plantation owner in Charles Town (now Charleston, South Carolina). She is forced to work on a southern indigo plantation, is raped at age 12 by the plantation owner, and has her first child torn away from her and sold.

Here the plot of Hill's book takes a turn toward Canada. Diallo makes her way north to New York in the midst of the American Revolution, escaping slavery in the process. She travels to Nova Scotia with other Black Loyalists who aided the British during the war. In Nova Scotia, the Black Loyalists live just outside the town of Shelburne, in the segregated shantytown of Birchtown. Their experience is difficult: they live hand to mouth in shacks made of scrounged materials. Even those are burned to the ground in anti-Black riots in the midst of a postwar recession. During these events, Diallo loses her second child ("I was in such agony I could barely speak") (p. 349).

Hill then embroils Diallo in an episode of history of which many Canadians are unaware: the British-sponsored exodus of Black Loyalists from Nova Scotia to Africa. Once in Freetown, Sierra Leone, Diallo realizes that both local slavery and the African side of the Atlantic slave trade are in full operation close to where the new migrants plan to settle. While trying to find her

KEY TERMS

debt of memory: an obligation to remember

ethical judgment: a decision about the ethics of an historical action

historical consciousness: awareness of the links among the past, present, and future that prepare one to negotiate the present

reparation: making amends for a wrong done

restitution: restoration or replacement of something taken away

---

1 Hill, L. (2007). *The book of negroes.* Toronto: HarperCollins Ltd.

childhood village, not far from Freetown, Diallo narrowly escapes being sold back into slavery. The book concludes with Diallo as an elderly woman, weary but wise. She testifies for the Commission on the Abolition of the Slave Trade in London, England.

Making Manifest the Injustices of History

Hill's work bears a number of parallels to the nonfiction book *Esther: The Remarkable True Story of Esther Wheelwright: Puritan Child, Native Daughter, Mother Superior*, which we explored in Chapter 5. Both tell the life stories of vulnerable yet unusually intelligent and capable protagonists whose lives were largely shaped by childhood kidnappings and multiple migrations from one society to another. These skeletal parallels only serve to make more striking the contrasts, the most important of which is that *The Book of Negroes* is historical fiction.

Hill's novel is written in the first person, from the perspective of Diallo. During the slavers' raid on her village, the girl's mother is clubbed over the head. "Other than in her sleep I had never seen Mama motionless," she tells us. "This had to be a dream" (p. 26). Through a feat of historical perspective taking on a grand scale, Lawrence Hill imagines himself into the conscious-ness of his fictional protagonist—and then shares this perspective with his readers through his narrative—in a way that Julie Wheelwright does not do with her nonfictional main character, Esther. Wheelwright adheres to the methods of the historian: she makes only those inferences clearly supported by documentary evidence. By clearly indicating the passages in which she is speculating, Wheelwright, like other historians, contributes to the public trust in the discipline of history.

TEACHING TIP

Students can become more engaged with the events of history by creating historical fiction of their own. As long as they ground their writing in evidence, they can help history come alive for those who read their stories. For more on reading and writing historical fiction, see the section Teaching Guidepost 4 beginning on page 155 of Chapter 5.

Hill has a different purpose; as he puts it, his novel is "about recognizing the drama and the sadness in our own history and bringing it to life."[2] He does bring it to life by using first-person narrative, making inferences about the thoughts and feelings of an *imaginary* young eighteenth-century woman thrown into slavery, and thereby creating an evocative story that hits us hard. We feel Diallo's pain and humiliation, and we understand that what was done to her—and to all the real captives of the slave trade—was utterly inhumane.

In the writing of his novel, Hill did not need to make an *explicit* ethical judgment. Yet *implicit* ethical judgment comes through in Hill's choices of what to tell about and how he tells it. Hill puts us right by Diallo's side. We feel the pain of her branding as if she were before us: "They aimed a finger's length above my right nipple, and pressed [the branding iron] into my flesh. I could smell it burning. The pain ran through me like hot waves of lava" (p. 52). Through Diallo, Hill provides us with a view not only of the condi-tions that this young woman endured, but also of her physical feelings and emotional states. After her sale to the plantation owner, she reflects, "All of

---

2 Lawrence Hill, quoted in Hickman, A. (2008). Merging history and fiction. *The Queen's Journal 135*(30). Retrieved from http://queensjournal.ca/story/2008-02-01/news/merging-history-and-fiction/

my sorrow was coiled in the very organs of my body, wanting to explode but with nowhere to go" (p. 120).

By way of contrast with Hill's approach, consider this densely quantitative paragraph about the slave trade in Virginia, the second most active British North American colony participating in the trade. The paragraph is quite typical of the entire work from which it is drawn: Herbert S. Klein's *The Middle Passage: Comparative Studies in the Atlantic Slave Trade*.

> Whereas in the 1710–1718 period the average annual importation from Africa was 236 slaves, compared with 300 from the British West Indies, the number of slaves of African origin rose to 1,228 per annum in the period from 25 March 1718 to 25 March 1727. By the third decade of the 18th century, African slavers were monopolizing the trade, and the basic patterns, which remained constant for the rest of the century, had been fully established.[3]

Klein's final observation, below, reiterates his purpose, and points ever so obliquely to Lawrence Hill's achievement:

> Though the individual African experience of surviving the forced migration and becoming a slave in America cannot be recaptured, the quantitative reconstruction of the mass migration of Africans to the shores of the New World helps to define the limits within which that experience took place.[4]

Klein's work is striking in its distance from the lives of people and the ethical issues around the human captives of the trade. This is not to say that Klein's work is less important than Hill's. Klein simply has a different purpose: to offer an interpretation of history that is grounded in evidence, so that future generations will know what happened, and so that the events do not get lost in the mists of time.

Nonetheless, it is Hill's approach that makes manifest the emotional impact of the experience of slavery. Through the fictionalized experience of an individual in chains and a neck yoke, the reader listens in on a captive's thoughts, feels the meaning of the loss of freedom, and understands viscerally the import of the large historical phenomenon of the trade in human captives. This gives us vivid material for an ethical response, and the novel becomes a sharp tool for the evocation of moral outrage.

---

3 Klein, H.S. (1978). *The middle passage: Comparative studies in the Atlantic slave trade* (p. 123). Princeton, NJ: Princeton University Press.

4 Klein. (1978). *The middle passage*, p. 251.

The Ethical Dimension in Historical Narratives

Hill successfully brings to light the ethical dimension of trading in human captives, yet historical fiction is not the only method for exploring the ethical dimension of history. Some historians, such as Klein, attempt to refrain from introducing judgment into their narratives, preferring to leave it to others to weigh the ethics of the past actions they document. Many historians, however, are more explicit than Klein—many of them incorporate ethical judgments, both implicit and explicit. A more typical example of historical writing can be seen in the following paragraph from Dr. Hakim Adi's 2011 article, "Africa and the Transatlantic Slave Trade."

> Historians still debate exactly how many Africans were forcibly transported across the Atlantic during the next four centuries [until the nineteenth century]. A comprehensive database compiled in the late 1990s puts the figure at just over 11 million people. Of those, fewer than 9.6 million survived the so-called middle passage across the Atlantic, due to the inhuman conditions in which they were transported, and the violent suppression of any on-board resistance. Many people who were enslaved in the African interior also died on the long journey to the coast.[5]

Not only does Adi cite figures to outline the parameters of the trade, he also uses phrases such as "forcibly transported," "inhuman conditions," and "violent suppression," to condemn the actions of the traders in human flesh. Note that the historian draws on evidence (he knows what conditions existed), but also adds a layer of ethical judgment (e.g., labelling those conditions "inhuman") based on his own perception of what constitutes "inhuman" treatment. Further, he refers to the victims of this crime as "Africans" and "people." Such nuances help the reader reject the dehumanizing capacity of words such as "slave" and recognize the humanity and dignity of the victims.

Historians' ethical judgments are by nature interpretations of the historical record. We will agree easily with some interpretations of the past, such as Hill's, as they are grounded in careful research. Other interpretations, when they pass into unsupported conjecture, invite doubt. To underscore this point, we need only turn to another contrasting narrative of the slave trade, J. Steven Wilkins's 1997 biography *Call of Duty: The Sterling Nobility of Robert E. Lee*. Wilkins offered his own ethical judgment of the Peculiar Institution, that is, slavery:

> Slavery, as it operated in the pervasively Christian society which was the old South, was not an

---

5 Adi, H. (2011). Africa and the transatlantic slave trade. *BBC History*. Retrieved from http://www.bbc.co.uk/history/british/abolition/africa_article_01.shtml

adversarial relationship founded upon racial animosity. In fact, it bred on the whole, not contempt, but, over time, mutual respect. This produced a mutual esteem of the sort that always results when men give themselves to a common cause. The credit for this startling reality must go to the Christian faith.... The unity and companionship that existed between the races in the South prior to the war was the fruit of a common faith.[6]

In 2011, a politician in the race for the Republican nomination for U.S. president recommended Wilkins's book as good reading. This fact casts into sharp relief the potential political implications of the ethical dimension of history. If Confederate General Robert E. Lee was a hero, fighting for the just

Figure 6.2 This illustration was created about 1830, before a British law ended slavery within the British Empire in 1833. It appeared in a British children's book. Like many historical narratives, it conveys an ethical judgment about the events of history. We can see the judgment in the portrayals: Who is doing harm in this image? What are they doing? Who are the victims? What ethical judgment has the artist made about the events in question?

6 Wilkins, J.S. (1997). Grant, Dr. G. (Ed.), *Call of duty: The sterling nobility of Robert E. Lee* (p. 303). Nashville, TN: Cumberland House Publishing Company. In a profile of Michelle Bachmann (who at one point was considered a plausible contender for the 2012 U.S. Republican presidential nomination), Ryan Lizza noted that Bachmann's recommended reading list on her website included *Call of Duty*. Lizza, R. (2011, August 15). Leap of faith: The making of a Republican front-runner. *The New Yorker*, 63.

cause of a Christian and benevolent slave-holding South—in other words, if slavery was actually good for everyone, including African Americans—then today's claims that racial injustice occurred must hold little water. One does not emerge from a reading of Lawrence Hill's novel ready to entertain such nonsense.

The Double-Edged Sword

Hill's condemnation of the perpetrators of the slave trade is effective and obvious. All of the characters—some historical, some fictional—play a role in relation to the trade. We can scan his book and easily identify the violent thugs, the "innocent" bystanders, and the hypocrites, as well as the damaged, the survivors, and the courageous. At the same time, as a skilled novelist, Hill builds complex three-dimensional characters.

Hill's strategy of writing in the first person helps us "feel" the indignities heaped upon the main character. Using this up-close-and-personal strategy, however, is a double-edged sword. It encourages the reader to draw on universal, "common sense" understandings of human relations that appeal to a reader's contemporary ethical sensibilities but that effectively trump any attempt the author or reader might make to take into account the foreignness of the people of the past. Hill would have had scant sources telling him what the eighteenth-century captives of the slave trade believed was ethically reprehensible. Was the African slaver or the European slaver more reviled? Was a yoke and chain or a whipping viewed as more undignified? Was purchasing a captive less compassionate than letting him or her die? How would people of the eighteenth century have answered these questions? Lacking evidence, Hill either answers questions like this by drawing on an understanding of universal human experience, which is prone to contemporary ethical sensibilities, or leaves it open to the reader to do so. Hill's strategy of writing in the first person thereby inadvertently undercuts the reader's ability to take into account the ocean of difference that can exist between the ethical standards of the present and those of the past. Consequently, *The Book of Negroes* illustrates that historical narrative in the form of historical fiction is effective in bringing the past to life but open to question regarding its veracity.

> ... universal, "common sense" understandings of human relations ... effectively trump any attempt the author or reader might make to take into account the foreignness of the people of the past.

In our secular society, we are aware of profound change in mores over time. It is generally accepted that social conventions and worldviews are different now than they were centuries ago. To what extent can we then legitimately assume that respect for human life and freedom constitutes a transhistorical and timeless ethical starting point? That is, are we justified in applying for all time standards that have—in the long view of human experience—only recently been articulated as a universal code of human rights?

Under Hill's guidance, the reader is led to assume that, yes, slavery was wrong in the past, just as we regard it as wrong today. What an historian can bring to the table, which Hill does not, is historical context for understanding *why* slavery and the slave trade were considered acceptable in the past, at least in some quarters. For example, European children learned in school and absorbed at the dinner table that Africans were inferior to Europeans, for any number of ill-founded reasons. The laws in many countries supported racism. When a child grows up in a culture that condones racism, he or she tends to become racist. It is true that African captives and abolitionists would have disagreed with the practice of slavery, but European Caucasian society generally did not.

Only by considering the context of the "normal" within which historical characters were operating can we make fair ethical judgments about their actions. In so doing, it becomes more difficult to blame individuals for their attitudes, and more logical to condemn the society that made slavery acceptable.

We can go further, though, to blame individuals by finding out if there were some people who acted against the norm of the time period. The existence of the eighteenth-century abolitionists, for example, is proof that it was *possible* to see things differently and choose an anti-slavery position, even when the dominant powers of the historical moment did not. This gives us more leeway to condemn those people who chose to take part in the slave trade in that time period.

Obligations to the Past

The ethical judgments we make about actions in the past can be thought of as part of a relationship we have with people and events in the past. What are our ethical obligations to the people of the past if they are dead? After all, we can neither thank deceased heroes nor punish dead villains. What, then, is the meaning of "history will be the judge" if those whom we might celebrate, memorialize, or condemn are no longer with us? Clio—Greek goddess and muse of history—seems an impotent judiciary!

But is she? Sometimes restitution and remembrance may be possible, if not with the participants themselves, then with their descendants. Some consequences of past actions ripple down into the present, having an intergenerational effect, which *can* be addressed. The legacies of slavery and its successor, the Jim Crow system that was dismantled in the American South within the past generation, continue to shape attitudes and social structures. More recently, Canada's system of residential schools, the last of which closed only in 1996, have a widely recognized impact on First Nations, Inuit, and Métis families today.

By making fair ethical judgments of events in the past, we can better cope with their repercussions in the present. Consider, for example, the implications of a judgment that the federal government policy of forced assimilation that created the residential school system was ethically reprehensible. That judgment informs how our society responds to the effects this schooling system has had on the generation who went to residential schools, as well as the succeeding generations. (These intergenerational effects include lost language, culture, and community, as well as parents ill-equipped to raise children because they didn't have their own parents'

CONNECTIONS BETWEEN CONCEPTS

What is worthy of remembering? To a great degree, this question is addressed by the historical significance concept—we should study events, people, and developments that either resulted in change or that reveal something significant. The ethical dimension adds a further layer, so that we can consider what events, people, and developments we should not only remember but also celebrate or condemn.

example to follow as role models.) Further, this ethical judgment and how we respond—for example, by offering an apology—helps us define contemporary Canadian values.

The fluid boundaries suggested by the term **contemporary history** can provide a rough dividing line telling us when we have an obligation to the past.

The fluid boundaries suggested by the term *contemporary history* can provide a rough dividing line telling us when we have an obligation to the past. On this side of the boundary are events that are connected to people alive today who identify with the heroes and victims of the recent past. That we have a responsibility to the recent past is clear. Across the boundary, on the far side of "contemporary," are events that are simply too distant to inspire the kind of ethical engagement we have been discussing. If no one remembers them well enough to feel wounded or triumphant, then our responsibility to respond to the crimes and victories of the distant past is diminished.

The complicating factor in this dividing line is the notion of cultural identity, which can tie a people today to events in distant history. Collective identities—whether inspired and transmitted along ethnic, racial, religious, or national lines—can generate a responsibility to respond even when the crime or victory occurred long before contemporary history. Examples pervade history, including the vilification of Turks by Armenians for actions in the early twentieth century, the veneration of the "Fathers of Confederation" in Canada in the nineteenth, the expulsion of the Acadians by the British in the eighteenth, or even the Serbs' loss of the Battle of Kosovo in the fourteenth.[7] The potency of these events allows them to be mobilized and retooled for contemporary political ends. To the extent that groups today tie their identities to people injured or victorious in long-ago events, we have motives for tangible forms of remembrance.

Coming to terms with the past often takes the form of reparations or restitutions. Before the modern era, these gestures were made between governments: the government of Germany paid "reparations" to the French government, for example, after World War I. A relatively new practice is for governments to compensate individuals and groups hurt by the actions of past governments. The first such responses were made by governments making restitution to Holocaust survivors and their relatives. These actions have subsequently been emulated in many other situations.

Truth and reconciliation processes, which are another form of response, were first initiated by South Africa as a means of addressing the legacies of the apartheid regime. These have been taken up by other governments attempting to address their own historical wrongs. The tradition of memorializing heroes has been ubiquitous in most societies, but now formal recognition of the victims of our history is becoming almost as common, as society gradually learns to recognize the wrongs of the past and how to redress them. Formal apologies and compensation programs all emerged from growing awareness of the

---

7 See Margalit, A. (2004). *The ethics of memory.* Cambridge, MA: Harvard University Press. Avishai Margalit makes a similar argument in his *The Ethics of Memory*, but restricts it to the obligations of memory *within* a community or identity group: if one desires to be remembered by one's descendants, then one must remember one's forebears. The ongoing identity of the group is crucial to this conception.

obligation of the present to recognize and respond to the ethical dimension of the past. The inclusion of particular events, such as the internment of Japanese Canadians during World War II, in Canadian school curricula, textbooks, and remembrance ceremonies stems from the same impulse.

Viewed through this lens, reading *The Book of Negroes* becomes a kind of remembrance through education: an attempt to learn about and remember the inhumanity of eighteenth-century slavery for readers in the twenty-first century. Learning about the survival, indeed the heroism, of Aminata Diallo does not provide reparation for past injustice, but it does help us recognize and remember its occurrence. Perhaps more important, it restores dignity to the memory of the many captives who had to endure so much.

What, then, can we glean about teaching students about the ethical dimension of history from this discussion of *The Book of Negroes* and other historical narratives? Primarily, this discussion demonstrates ways in which authors and historians include ethical judgments in the historical narratives that they write. After students recognize that judgment involves interpretation, they can begin to think critically about the ethical messages, implied or explicit, in the narratives of history. Awareness of the ethical dimension of history will help students develop an historical consciousness; they will become more capable of dealing with ethical issues in the present, including how to remember and respond to the crimes and sacrifices of the past.

Now that we have considered how one author brought the ethical dimension of history to life, let us examine five guideposts to the ethical dimension of history and how we can bring those big ideas into the classroom.

Ethical Positions: Implicit or Explicit

Ethical positions may be hard to identify in historical accounts, but they exist in many. The judgments may be explicit, as in Hakim Adi's article about the slave trade (2011, p. 174); implicit but fairly obvious, as in Hill's *The Book of Negroes*; or implicit but not so obvious, as in Herbert S. Klein's description of the numerical parameters of the Atlantic slave trade (1978, p. 173).

We can help students recognize and analyze the ethical positions implicit in historical narratives such as their own textbooks, historians' writings, historical novels, films, and museum exhibits. To do so, students need to understand the interpretive nature of historical accounts. These interpretations may be well grounded in historical evidence, defensible, and justifiable (as in Hill's work) or not (as in Wilkins's defence of slavery, 1997, p. 175). They may pack an emotional punch (as in Hill's work and many historical fiction films) or not (as in Klein's work). Give students ample opportunities to identify the ethical judgments made by creators of a wide variety of texts, including those in which the implicit ethical position of the author is difficult to identify. Remind students that the mere act of choosing, researching, and writing on a topic may open the door to an ethical stance.

> **The Ethical Dimension**
>
> **Guidepost 1**
> Authors make **implicit or explicit** ethical judgments in writing historical narratives.

Implicit but Not Obvious	Implicit and Obvious	Explicit
"In 2009–2010, 25 percent of junior players on two Ontario hockey teams have received concussions."	"Under the oversight of league officials, many teenaged hockey players have suffered concussions."	"Hockey league officials should be held accountable for not stopping on-ice fights, which so often result in concussions."

Figure 6.3 Three sentences on the same topic show varying degrees of explicitness of judgment.[8] In the first example above, the writer chose to reveal the high rates of concussions, a choice that implies judgment. The second example mentions the authorities in charge, implying criticism of their failure to prevent the concussions. Only in the third example is there a very clear charge laid against the authorities, who the writer believes were responsible for what occurred.

How Historical Context Leads to Fair Ethical Judgments

The Ethical Dimension

> **Guidepost 2**
Reasoned ethical judgments of past actions are made by taking into account the **historical context** of the actors in question.

After students learn how to recognize ethical judgments in historical narratives, they are better prepared for making their own reasoned ethical judgments about actions committed in the past. At first, students may have a tendency to think of historical actors as either evil villains or untarnished heroes, rather than as fallible people who made choices, for good or ill. To help students judge actions fairly, encourage them to always begin by considering the historical context within which an historical action took place. Otherwise, a fair judgment may not be possible.

Historical context can help us identify limitations on choices and possibilities that may have restricted people's actions in the past. How did fear of reprisal affect the actions of the ordinary citizen in Nazi-dominated Europe? The answer to this question affects the degree to which we condemn the "bystanders," as well as the degree to which we celebrate the "rescuers."

Taking the opposite tack, is there evidence that a variety of choices were possible? Does the presence of an abolitionist movement that decried the inhumanity of slavery even in 1800 indicate that people were relatively free to support or oppose the slave trade? Again, the answer affects the degree to which we condemn the plantation owners and celebrate those who recognized the evil of slavery and were willing to act on that recognition.

8 Data from Care, T. (2010, November 1). Junior hockey concussions at "alarming" rate: Study. *CBC.ca*. Retrieved from http://www.cbc.ca/sports/hockey/story/2010/11/01/sp-concussions-survey.html

Right and Wrong: Shifting through Time

Should it be acceptable to employ children in a dangerous occupation? Present-day Canadian society would deem this practice child abuse; the employer would be dragged into court. In earlier times, however, children worked in all kinds of dangerous jobs. Consider the thousands of boys as young as 12 who worked in the coal mines of Nova Scotia in the nineteenth century.[9] Canadian courtrooms in 1900 were not even reprimanding the employers of these boys. Just as it does not make sense to judge a person's actions today against the mores of the past, so too should we take care not to judge a person's actions in the past against the mores of the present.

The Ethical Dimension

> **Guidepost 3**
When making ethical judgments, it is important to **be cautious about imposing contemporary standards** of right and wrong on the past.

Figure 6.4 This photograph shows the last publicly viewable execution in Canada. On March 21, 1902, Stanislaus Lacroix was executed in Hull, Québec, for murdering his estranged wife. Studying this photograph helps us understand some of the problems posed by judging the past against contemporary standards of right and wrong. What is the matter with the following three judgments? (1) "How horrible—isn't executing people against the law?" (It was legal in 1902.) (2) "Hanging is cruel; death by injection is more humane." (This option was not available in 1902.) (3) "How shocking—why did they do this where people could watch?" Note the people on the rooftops, porches, and telegraph poles surrounding the gallows. (Punishment in the "public square" was the norm for thousands of years.)

---

9 McIntosh, R. (2000). *Boys in the pits: Child labour in coal mines* (Table 4.1, p. 71). Montreal: McGill-Queen's University Press, 2000.

Our judgment of historical actors should always be tempered by an understanding that their beliefs about what is right and wrong might vary markedly from our own beliefs. Sometimes acknowledging a worldview—such as the racist worldview of European and North American societies in the time of slavery—can help us understand (though not condone) the actions of slavers and plantation owners.

Remembering and Responding

Educators can help students grapple with the question of how to respond to the obligations that the past imposes on the present. In one sense, the writing, publication, and reading of Hill's novel are all the fulfillment of such an obligation. Educating oneself to more thoroughly understand the ethical dimensions of an historical period is one form of response. Reading an engaging novel is not the same as building a monument or paying reparations, but it exists on the same continuum. So does the teaching of the Atlantic slave trade.

In other words, there are a variety of ways to meet the obligations that the past imposes on the present. These include becoming more informed so that one can remember, informing others, memorializing, and taking action. Learning and teaching about the past help us gain an historical consciousness, which enables us all (citizenry and governments) to make informed decisions about what our obligations should be. Making these decisions in the absence of historical understanding is either irresponsible or impossible.

THE RESPONSE CONTINUUM

Remembering > Informing others > Memorializing > Taking action >

Figure 6.5 The many ways of meeting our obligations to the past all lie on a continuum.

History: A Continuum to Which We Belong

In the classroom, the ethical dimension opens students' eyes to a crucial way in which past experiences can shed light on present-day issues. Knowing about the history and human experience of the eighteenth-century slave trade, for example, supplies students with an otherwise inaccessible perspective on race relations in Canada today. Students should be discouraged from trying to see a direct "lesson" comparing racism in the era of the slave trade to racism in present-day Canada (which, of course, is not a slave-holding society). Yet after studying *The Book of Negroes*, students come away with a more nuanced and complex understanding of historical interracial tensions than can be supplied by the Historica-Dominion Institute's Heritage Minute vignette that presents

Figure 6.6 On November 14, 1998, 14-year-old Reena Virk was swarmed and murdered under a bridge in Saanich on Vancouver Island. Six months later, students from Frank Hurt Secondary School in Surrey, British Columbia, responded to Virk's death by performing "The Short Life and Lonely Death of Reena Virk." The students' drama instructor, Tim Trylinski, said, "We want to cast some light into the dark crevices of the human condition." In what ways could staging a play be a way of both remembering and responding to this case of extreme bullying?

Caucasian Canada as an unalloyed salvation for those who fled slavery via the Underground Railroad. It might also help students take more seriously the work being done in the present to overcome the legacies of racism and discrimination.

By developing awareness of the ethical dimension of history, students develop an historical consciousness that allows them to participate in social action with a more informed understanding of the connections among the past, present, and future—they will be aware of the past and more able to apply insights about how to live together in a peaceful, tolerant, humane society.

Generating Powerful Understandings of the Ethical Dimension

Use the lessons and activities in the second half of this chapter to enable your students to move from limited to powerful understandings of the ideas embodied in the guideposts.

 Guidepost 1 Authors make **implicit or explicit** ethical judgments in writing historical narratives.

DEMONSTRATION OF LIMITED UNDERSTANDING	DEMONSTRATION OF POWERFUL UNDERSTANDING
Student reads accounts for information and has difficulty "reading between the lines" to see the ethical position of an author or creator in a variety of media.	Student recognizes both **implicit and explicit ethical stances** in historical narratives in a variety of media (e.g., films, museum exhibits, books).

 Guidepost 2 Reasoned ethical judgments of past actions are made by taking into account the **historical context** of the actors in question.

DEMONSTRATION OF LIMITED UNDERSTANDING	DEMONSTRATION OF POWERFUL UNDERSTANDING
Student makes unsupported judgments about the actions of people in the past.	Student uses his or her knowledge of **historical context** to make reasoned ethical judgments about controversial actions of people in the past.

 Guidepost 3 When making ethical judgments, it is important to **be cautious about imposing contemporary standards** of right and wrong on the past.

DEMONSTRATION OF LIMITED UNDERSTANDING	DEMONSTRATION OF POWERFUL UNDERSTANDING
Student makes ethical judgments about the actions of people in the past based on present-day beliefs and mores.	Student **is cautious about imposing contemporary standards** of right and wrong when making an ethical judgment about the past.

 Guidepost 4 A fair assessment of the ethical implications of history can inform us of our **responsibilities to remember and respond** to contributions, sacrifices, and injustices of the past.

DEMONSTRATION OF LIMITED UNDERSTANDING	DEMONSTRATION OF POWERFUL UNDERSTANDING
When considering historical sacrifices and injustices, student's reaction takes one of two extremes: either seeing no relevance to the present or identifying totally with one side in the sacrifice or injustice.	Student makes fair assessments of the ethical implications of historical actions, and uses those to determine our **responsibilities to remember and respond** to the contributions, sacrifices, and injustices of the past.

 Guidepost 5 Our understanding of history can help us make **informed judgments** about contemporary issues, but only when we **recognize the limitations** of any direct "lessons" from the past.

DEMONSTRATION OF LIMITED UNDERSTANDING	DEMONSTRATION OF POWERFUL UNDERSTANDING
Student fails to consider links to current issues, or draws overly simple lessons from the past.	Student uses historical accounts to make **informed judgments** on contemporary issues, while **recognizing the limitations** of "lessons" from the past.

Working with
THE ETHICAL
DIMENSION

Introducing the Ethical Dimension

The textbook seems an unlikely starting place for introducing the idea of an ethical dimension in interpretations of history. Many students see it as the one true story; many teachers treasure it as an accessible source of necessary background information. When teachers are new to a course, it can be a lifeboat not to be tipped. Yet historical thinking requires us to see the textbook as just one possible source to understand the past and it, too, can be read critically. So let us rock the lifeboat of a Canadian history textbook a little bit.

ACTIVITY: When Is a Textbook Like a Movie?

Begin by considering ethics in the movies (or other medium with which students are familiar).

- Ask students to think of a movie they have recently watched, and pose questions such as these:
  - Did the movie have heroes and villains? Were they clearly good and bad, or did the hero have some flaws and the villain have a "good side"?
  - Did you care more about some characters than others right from the start? Why was that? Was there an imbalance of power among the characters? How did it affect your perception of the characters?
  - Was the movie trying to share a message, a lesson, or even a moral? If so, what was it?
- After students share examples, explain that when a film director portrays characters and actions as good or bad, powerful or weak, sympathetic or disagreeable, the film is communicating ideas about ethics—ideas about what is right and wrong. The director can communicate to us that a character is "good" through the character's appearance (e.g., pleasing, attractive). A slovenly character who scowls is "bad." Likewise, a character who steals a car seems bad if ominous music is playing in the background. But if a bumbling but attractive character steals a car while perky music plays in the background, he or she may be doing a "bad" thing but is probably "good." Often "bad" actions are not rewarded, but "good" actions are. Many movie plots revolve around ethical dilemmas that are resolved in a way that satisfies the audience, reinforcing our beliefs and values. The value judgments inherent in a movie may be obvious and clearly delineated or merely suggested and complicated, but they are usually there.

PURPOSE

To identify ethical positions in textbooks

MATERIALS

- passage from current history textbook that includes an ethical position to display
- **BLM 6.1: Spotting Ethical Positions** (1 per student)

- Ask students, "Does a textbook also have an ethical dimension or is it factual and neutral, just telling what happened?" Explain that they will investigate this question by examining several textbook accounts of the *filles du roi*. Provide a contemporary account of the *filles du roi* from a current textbook in your classroom, if one is available, so that students do not get the impression that ethical positions are only characteristic of older textbooks, or textbooks used in other places. Display the current account, or pass out the textbook, along with **BLM 6.1: Spotting Ethical Positions**. (Of course, you may instead wish to choose different topics and accounts that better fit your curriculum.)
- After students have finished considering the three historical accounts, discuss your original question again with the class: Does a textbook have an ethical dimension, or is it factual and neutral, just telling what happened? Ask, "If it does have an ethical dimension, is this position always clear? Why is it important to be aware of the ethical dimension in a textbook?"

ACTIVITY: Ethical Judgments on the Atomic Bomb

Distribute **BLM 6.2: What Is the Ethical Position?** to each student. Before students read, remind them to source each passage, that is, identify the country of origin and date of publication. Ask students, "How might this information have influenced the ethical position expressed in each text?" Then direct students to read the passages and underline phrases and sentences that might reveal each author's message or ethical position. This step will help students answer the questions on the blackline master.

Teaching Guidepost 1

Explain to students that ethical judgments, or positions, about historical actions are decisions about the rights or wrongs of those actions, based on principles such as honesty and loyalty. We can make many kinds of judgments about past actions; for example, we can make a political judgment that the *Chinese Exclusion Act* of 1923 was popular with many Canadians. However, the judgment becomes an ethical one when we apply a value such as fairness to decide whether the government was right or wrong to pass the act.

A key for students to understand the ethical dimension of history is to recognize that history *always* involves interpretation, no matter the medium. Films, historical novels, poems, paintings, songs, museum exhibits, and even obituaries are created by individuals who have interpreted the past and so hold ethical positions about historical actions. Through their respective medium, people convey these ethical stances, either explicitly—they are stated—or implicitly—they are implied. Ethical positions may not be explicit for various reasons. For example, the author may not realize that he or she has a position and is conveying it, or the author may believe his or her position is one shared by the audience, so it would be redundant or condescending to state it.

You can build inquiries for your curriculum on the questions in the activities **When Is a Textbook Like a Movie?** (page 185) and **Ethical Judgments on the Atomic Bomb** (page 186). The most direct inquiry question for recognizing the ethical stance in various media is to ask students, "What is the message of this film/exhibit/cartoon/painting/book?"

Supplementary questions can help students generate an answer:

- Who are presented as the heroes and who as the villains? Are there subtleties and complexities to the characters (e.g., are the heroes flawed, do the villains have a "good side")?
- To what extent do conditions at the time suggest that we should excuse or forgive the villains?
- What judgments does the book/film/exhibit convey about key actions? How does it convey those judgments?
- What are the consequences for those who commit crimes or injustices? Do they receive their "just deserts," or is their only punishment to be condemned by those who remember?

ACTIVITY: Message in the Museum

Museums hold a privileged position of trust in the public sphere. In exit surveys at Australian and Canadian museums, the majority of visitors saw museums as trusted and reliable. This was tied to a perception of them as apolitical and value neutral. As one visitor to the Canadian War Museum commented in a survey, "If history is facts why cloud it with viewpoints.... Museums have artefacts why cloud it with opinions."[10]

Yet most museum and history educators claim, as Barton and Levstik do, that "the exhibition of historical information is inseparable from interpretation, and museums and historic sites reflect a host of social, cultural, economic and ideological underpinnings."[11] Linda D'Acquisto, author of *Learning on Display: Student-Created Museums that Build Understanding*, argues that the presence of a "big idea" and a coherent story are the features that distinguish a museum project from a science fair or art show for both students and professional curators.[12]

To move students from a view that museums are value neutral toward an understanding that exhibits can involve an interpretation, a big idea, or an ethical judgment, plan a class trip to a museum or other exhibit location. There are multiple options:

- **An exhibit in a local museum**: This option is often the best resource for students to observe and identify the messages of an exhibit and the qualities of a good one.

PURPOSE

To recognize the ethical stance in an exhibit

MATERIALS

- **BLM 6.3: Message in the Museum** (1 per student)

---

10 Cameron, F. (2008). Safe places for unsafe ideas? History and science museums, hot topics and moral predicaments. Terwey, M. (Ed.), *Social history in museums*, *32*(6).

11 Barton, K. & Levstik, L. (2004). *Teaching history for the common good* (p. 121). Mahwah, NJ: Lawrence Erlbaum Associates.

12 D'Acquisto, L. (2006). *Learning on display: Student-created museums that build understanding* (p. 12). Alexandria, VA: Association for Supervision and Curriculum Development.

- **Historical displays in the public sphere**: If the previous option is not possible, students can study historical displays in shopping malls, libraries, or even the school hallway.
- **Online exhibits**: Alternatively, students can look at the Virtual Museum of Canada website,[13] which has more than 750 exhibits, or the Heritage Fairs website for ideas on Heritage Fairs projects.[14]

During the trip, whether actual or virtual, guide your class through the questions in **BLM 6.3: Message in the Museum** to help students recognize the ethical stance.

ACTIVITY: **An Enduring Controversy**

Invite students to consider another exhibit, *An Enduring Controversy*, which opened in 2005 in the Canadian War Museum. It focused on the Allied bombing of Germany in World War II. Explain to students that the institution was well aware of the controversy of the topic. Some 10 000 members of the Canadian airforce died in the campaign, as did hundreds of thousands of civilians. Many people questioned the rights and wrongs of the bombing.

PURPOSE

To analyze the controversial nature of a museum exhibit

MATERIALS

- **BLM 6.4: Ethical Controversy at the War Museum** (1 per student)

- Give a brief summary of the exhibit and introduce the inquiry questions (also included at the top of **BLM 6.4a: Ethical Controversy at the War Museum**): "What was the ethical position of the War Museum exhibit on the Allied bombing? Did it support, condemn, or excuse the bombing? Was it respectful to those Canadians who flew in the campaign?"
- Provide students with the blackline master. Ask them to read the original text, the explanation of the exhibit visuals, and the quotations, with the exception of the final section, The Fallout.
- Then ask students to analyze this exhibit by categorizing the phrases and images into three columns, using a chart modelled on the one shown at the top of **BLM 6.4c: Ethical Controversy at the War Museum**.
- After students have completed the chart, return attention to discuss the inquiry questions at the top of the blackline master.
- Next, ask them to speculate: How might this exhibit be judged by visitors to the museum? Might anyone take offence at this exhibit?
- After hearing their opinions, tell students that although the museum consulted both veterans and prominent historians while developing the exhibit, the exhibit did, in fact, provoke offence, even outrage among many other veterans. This led to a Senate inquiry. The "enduring controversy" was truly enduring.
- Ask for students' opinions about whether, in the face of this outrage and intense lobbying by veterans' organizations, the museum should have changed its exhibit or stuck to its interpretation.

---

13 Canadian Heritage Information Network. (2009). *Virtual Museum of Canada*. Retrieved from http://www.museevirtuel-virtualmuseum.ca/index-eng.jsp

14 The "Find Your Fair" link at *Canada's History for Kids* (2012) allows students to connect with regional heritage fairs across Canada, most of which feature photographs or videos of student projects. http://www.canadashistory.ca/Kids/Heritage.aspx

- To wrap up consideration of this exhibit, explain to students that after the controversy raged, the exhibitors relented and revised the text of the exhibit panel. Students can read this revised text in the section The Fallout on **BLM 6.4c: Ethical Controversy at the War Museum**. Ask students to compare the before and after versions and discuss which is more appropriate, and why.
- To extend this activity, ask students to investigate the controversy related to a Smithsonian exhibit about the Enola Gay.

Teaching Guideposts 2 and 3

To demonstrate the second powerful understanding, students must consider the values and beliefs of the past, as well as the political (or other) factors at play, before arriving at a reasoned ethical judgment about a controversial action in the past. The actions that invite an ethical stance are those that hold resonance today—actions that shaped the collective identities of groups today and those that have clear consequences in contemporary society.

Historical context of the time of the action can help us better understand how people acted in the past and thus make a reasoned judgment of their actions. The generic inquiry question for this is straightforward: "Did X (context) justify Y (action)?" For example,

- Did the legal history of rejected land claims justify the Mohawk actions at Oka?
- Did the fear of American expansion explain or excuse Macdonald's actions in the Northwest Resistance?

To answer these inquiries, students must demonstrate the third powerful understanding, that is, not imposing contemporary ethical standards on the past. This could also be addressed more directly with follow-up questions such as the following:

- This (e.g., child labour or judicial torture of the accused) was common at the time. So how should we judge this practice as we look at it today? Should we excuse it, condemn it, or do something else?

ACTIVITY: **Controversy over the Deportation of the Acadians**

Traditional debates can be fun, and many students like the competition. Other students, however, participate reluctantly because of the anxiety they feel in conflict situations. Introverts may have plenty to say, but express little of it in a debate. Still others develop a defensive adherence to their position when criticized and may show little intrinsic interest in the topic. In other words, traditional debates may lead to defeat rather than discovery.

DEMONSTRATION OF POWERFUL UNDERSTANDING 2

Student uses his or her knowledge of **historical context** to make reasoned ethical judgments about controversial actions of people in the past.

DEMONSTRATION OF POWERFUL UNDERSTANDING 3

Student **is cautious about imposing contemporary standards** of right and wrong when making an ethical judgment about the past.

PURPOSE

To consider historical context while avoiding imposing contemporary standards of right and wrong

---

A creative controversy offers an alternative approach through a small-group format that stresses criticism of ideas, not people, and encourages open-mindedness. Two pairs of students study two sides of an argument, present their positions, switch roles to argue the other side, and then drop their roles to prepare a common report.

The following creative controversy activity explains how you can use this procedure to guide students to consider context and historical perspectives in order to make a reasoned judgment about the ethics of deporting the Acadians in 1755, and avoid imposing contemporary ideas of right and wrong.

TEACHING TIP

Provide the following guidelines for students to generate good arguments:

• Criticize ideas, not people.
• Listen, even when you disagree.
• Try to understand all sides of the issue.
• Be willing to change your mind if the evidence convinces you to do so.
• Go for the best decision, not victory.

• Distribute **BLM 6.5: Developing a Fair Ethical Judgment**, and read aloud with students the first section, "What Happened," for a brief outline of the situation.
• After giving this introduction, write this inquiry question on the board: "Was the deportation of the Acadians a crime against humanity or a fair measure in time of war?" Provide a definition for *crime against humanity* or establish one together with the class. Before explaining the procedure for a creative controversy, ask why a question such as this might still be important today, so many years after the event (the continuing tension between francophones and anglophones in Canada, the position of francophones in Confederation, the continued strong identification of Acadians today with ancestors who were the target of the removal). This discussion establishes the contemporary significance of making a judgment about the ethics of events that occurred years before.
• Establish some guidelines for a good argument.
• Divide the class into teams of four, and then subdivide these teams into two pairs. Assign the first pairs Position 1 and the second pairs Position 2.
• Outline the following steps for the creative controversy activity:
  – Teams separate into pairs to read their handouts and prepare their positions.
  – Each pair meets with another pair who shares the same position as them in a new group of four (or six, if numbers warrant it) to rank their arguments in order of importance.
  – Pairs return to their original teams to present their positions. They advocate and refute arguments in an open discussion while you monitor, ensuring that students follow the guidelines for a good argument.
  – Pairs switch the positions they are defending (e.g., the Position 1 pair now defends Position 2), and repeat the whole process.
  – Teams drop their assigned points of view and try to reach a common decision. Teams report to the class and explain their reasoning. (Note that one of the two sides in this controversy has more points than the other. Some students will assume that this makes it the better argument. Monitor the discussion to see if this is the case and explain how this strategy is unreliable for ethical judgment.)

- Teams reflect on the group process with questions such as the following:
  - To what extent did we follow the guidelines of a good argument?
  - What could we do better (if anything) in the next group discussion of a controversy?
- In a concluding discussion, ask students to consider the role of context and shifting ethical standards in deciding on this issue, and discuss once more the relevance of the issue today:
  - How did the historical context influence your decision about the actions of the British?
  - Did your knowledge that standards of right and wrong have shifted over time influence your decision? If they did, in what way(s)?
  - Why do we care, if we do, about right and wrong (i.e., the ethical dimension) in this case? Why aren't we simply trying to understand what went on?

This creative controversy activity can be followed with an inquiry to develop the Demonstration of Powerful Understanding 4 about how we should respond to the past. For example, "How should we remember the deportation of Acadians?" or "What would be an appropriate commemoration (e.g., song, poster, monument) to recognize this event?" As an assignment, students could choose the most appropriate commemoration from the selection of monuments and works of art on the University of Moncton website *1755: L'histoire et les histoires*.[15] (Note that in 2003, the federal government adopted a Royal Proclamation making July 28 the annual day to commemorate the Great Upheaval.)

Teaching Guidepost 4

These broad inquiry questions can guide students toward the fourth powerful understanding:

- What heroic actions/contributions/sacrifices/tragedies deserve to be remembered? How should we remember them?
- How should we judge each other's past actions? What obligations does my group owe to others or do other groups owe to mine? How should we fulfill those obligations?

Although the words *ethics* and *morals* do not appear in many curriculum documents, both teachers and students expect to celebrate the good and condemn the bad that we discover in the past. We celebrate Nellie McClung's fight for the vote for women; we condemn the Nazis; we commemorate the war dead at Remembrance Day. In answering the inquiry questions above, students become more aware of the decisions behind these celebrations, condemnations, and commemorations—they begin to come to terms with the past. Answering these questions can also be extremely engaging; for example, students are fascinated by topics that involve the unfair treatment of people in the past.

> **DEMONSTRATION OF POWERFUL UNDERSTANDING 4**
>
> Student makes fair assessments of the ethical implications of historical actions, and uses those to determine our **responsibilities to remember and respond** to the contributions, sacrifices, and injustices of the past.

---

15 Centre d'études acadiennes, Université de Moncton. (2007). *L'histoire et les histoires, 1755: Stories.* http://www2.umoncton.ca/cfdocs/etudacad/1755/index.cfm?axe=2&lang=en&style=G

Step 1: Making a Fair Assessment

The first step for students is to decide if we owe something to the people of the past, such as those who contributed or sacrificed themselves in some way. As well, when considering our obligations to other groups, we must consider if we have a *responsibility* for the injustices of the past. For example, does Canada have obligations today to the First Nations for the injustices of the past?

Students may be enraged by the clear unfairness of past trickery, such as the forced removal of Inuit to the High Arctic where there was no game to hunt, or by abuse that took place in many residential schools. However, they may also think that all this happened a long time ago and that those treated unfairly should just "get over it." The challenge is to expand students' concept of fairness so they learn to recognize that past injustices can endure into contemporary society. For example, relocating a people from their ancestral territory had long-term economic, social, and psychological effects, and the residential schools led to intergenerational trauma.

Step 2: Remembering and Responding

After making a fair assessment of past events and deciding they have a responsibility to remember and respond to a contribution or to an injustice, students can then decide how to respond. It can be meaningful and engaging for students not only to decide where a debt of memory is owed but also to decide on appropriate and creative responses.

As stated in the introduction, there is a wide range of appropriate responses, from education programs to truth and reconciliation commissions, and from reparations to memorial ceremonies. In the past, society built traditional monuments to honour heroic deeds and exemplary figures. Statues or imposing monuments or buildings proclaimed a clear message that both the characters of our great men and women, and their contributions to society, should be remembered and celebrated. These individuals were a model for future generations to follow. More recent monuments, such as Swing Low, shown on page 194, reflect changing ideas about historical significance.

Memorials, in contrast, were the traditional responses to tragedies and injustices. These were not only structures but also songs, plaques, street signs, moments of silence, parades, proclamations, and building dedications. Just as more recent monuments have changed in both substance and purpose, so have memorials. In trying to convey the horror of a terrorist attack or genocide, they tend to be more abstract and artistic—and often controversial. Both monuments and memorials, in whatever form, are attempts to preserve memory and respond to a deep need for a moral response to the past.

Students can explore why and how we can remember and respond through the activity below, which focuses on the internment of Ukrainian Canadians during World War I.

ACTIVITY: Responses to the Ukrainian Canadian Internment

- Ask students a series of questions that moves them from considering personal obligations to considering societal obligations to the past:
  - Have you ever done anything harmful to someone?
  - Can you think of a time when someone really went out of his or her way, or made a sacrifice of some kind, to help you?
  - Do you feel, or can you imagine ever feeling, that you owe a debt of some kind to anyone? (At this point, you may wish to introduce the concept of debt of memory—an obligation to remember what happened.)
  - How long might a feeling of debt last? Could it ever pass down from one generation to another and so on, from your ancestors to you? For example, if your grandparents passed along property to you that they had stolen from someone years earlier, would you feel indebted to the people whose land had been stolen? If a religious group gave your grandparents assistance when they immigrated to Canada, would you owe a debt of gratitude?
  - Could a government owe a debt to someone or some group for actions the government took in the past?
- Describe the internment of 4000 Ukrainian immigrants and Canadians of Ukrainian origin during World War I from 1914 to 1920. Another 80 000 Ukrainian immigrants and their children were registered as "enemy aliens" and required to report regularly to the police. Here is a summary of the context:

  During World War I, Canadians were beginning to fear "enemy aliens"— people from countries, regions, or empires that were Canada's enemies during the war. One of those enemies was the Austro-Hungarian Empire, and the Ukraine was part of that empire. Yet most Ukrainians had actually fled their homeland. They had no loyalty to Austria-Hungary. Many Ukrainian immigrants and Canadians of Ukrainian origin had joined the Canadian army. They were interned, not because of anything they had done, but because of where they or their parents had come from. In addition, they were put in isolated camps in often harsh conditions, and many were used for forced labour. Beginning in 1985, some Ukrainian Canadian community groups sought official acknowledgment of this internment and redress for an historical wrong.

- Introduce the inquiry question for this activity: "How should the federal government, acting on our behalf, respond to demands for redress for the internment of Ukrainian Canadians in World War I?"[16]
- Before deciding on the ethical implications of what occurred, students should conduct some research to find out what happened and the historical context, including the values that were current at the time.

PURPOSE

To make a fair assessment of the ethical implications of an historical action, and to choose an appropriate response

---

16 This narrative can also be personalized by basing it on the story of a Ukrainian Canadian survivor, such as Mary Manko Haskett. She was born in Montréal but interned with her family when she was six years old at Spirit Lake in Abitibi, Québec. See Transcript of CBC Radio. (2007, November 26). *The Current*. Retrieved from http://www.ucc.ca/2007/11/26/transcript-of-cbc-radio-the-current-26-november-2007-the-ukrainian-canadian-redress-campaign-50-minutes-with-anna-maria-tremonti/

Figure 6.7 Recent monuments that celebrate heroic deeds reflect a changing sense of historical significance. Examples are the Women Are Persons! monument in Winnipeg, Manitoba (shown on page 111) and Allison Saar's Swing Low statue in Harlem, New York, shown here. It is the centrepiece of a memorial to Harriet Tubman (who is featured in the activity **Who or What Makes Historical Change?** on page 123). A class discussion of this photograph could emphasize attention to the details (Tubman's stance and expression, the emerging faces on her skirt, the base with a quilt-like pattern, the three-metre height). What do they communicate? What message is the artist sending? How does this memorial connect today's society with the past?

- Before deciding on the ethical implications of what occurred, students should also consider the possibility that we might be imposing our present-day values on the past. When we look back at the internment, we might see it as a violation of our values. But was it a violation of the accepted values of wartime Canada in 1914?
- Tell the class that even if they do not feel strongly about the past injustice, you want them to consider what would be an appropriate response, if any, for those who do.
- Explain to students that answering several questions will help them decide *whether or not* to respond to a past injustice:
  - Do we have a responsibility to the victims and their descendants that has endured over time?
  - Should we accept that we cannot change the past, and move on?
  - Should we, through our government, respond at all?
- The next step is to decide *how* to respond. Point out the lobbying by Ukrainian Canadian community groups for redress. Begin by considering the following questions:
  - If we do have a responsibility, what would be an appropriate response?
  - Should we simply offer an apology?
  - Should we compensate the descendants of the victims, but in so doing require a generation that didn't do anything wrong to pay for the injustice?
- Next, establish with students criteria for determining a response similar to the following. For example, the response should
  - be fair to historic victims and their offspring
  - not impose a burden on present-day citizens who may be innocent of wrongdoing
  - serve a useful social purpose
- Introduce these four possible responses that the federal government could make to the criticism of the World War I internment:
  1. offer financial compensation to any surviving victims and their descendants
  2. establish a memorial to the victims, or a memorial day
  3. provide education programs in the name of the victims to fight discrimination and promote human rights today
  4. recognize the injustice but offer no concrete response
- You may wish students to use Corners—a cooperative learning structure—to decide which of these responses would be best. In Corners, you explain the question and the four possible options and place a sign representing each option in a different corner of the room. Students choose, and record, the option they favour and then move to the corresponding corner. In the corner, students team with a partner to discuss their reasons. In a follow-up class discussion, ask pairs of students to paraphrase what was said between them.
- Ask students if they have any other possible government responses that meet the criteria for determining a response.
- Reveal to students that, in 2005, the federal Parliament recognized the Ukrainian Canadian internment as a "dark chapter" in Canadian

history. It passed an act in which it "express(ed) its deep sorrow for those events" and made plans for the development of commemorative plaques and educational resources. It did not express an apology. (The Ukrainian Canadian community had not asked for one.) In 2008, the federal government established a $10 million fund for memorials and educational exhibits about the Ukrainian Canadian internment. Ask students to share their responses to the government's actions.

Teaching Guidepost 5

There are so many, many similarities [between the present and the past], but we're always imprisoned if we try to make it a one-to-one comparison.[17]

—Documentary filmmaker Ken Burns comparing the United States in the Prohibition era to the United States today

> **DEMONSTRATION OF POWERFUL UNDERSTANDING 5**
>
> Student uses historical accounts to make **informed judgments** on contemporary issues, while **recognizing the limitations** of "lessons" from the past.

Why study history? Many people, both children and adults, say that we should study history to learn lessons from the past. The philosopher George Santayana famously said, "Those who cannot remember the past are condemned to repeat it." This leads us to ask what kinds of guidance, if any, the past provides for the present. Physicians collect histories of their patients' diseases to make better diagnoses. Generals study old wars to prepare for the next war. Stockbrokers and weather reporters are also keen to learn lessons from the past to help them make decisions for the future. But historians, less so.

According to many historians, the innumerable dynamics and combination of causes from each time and place make it impossible to synthesize the past into clear "lessons." History is too messy. They point to examples of self-serving or lazy analogies between the past and present. One famous example of this was the use of the "Munich analogy" to justify military action against Iraq. According to the American government, appeasing Saddam Hussein in 2003 would have had the same consequence as appeasing Hitler in 1938. Was the comparison fair? The analysts in the American government made little effort to see whether the policies and positions of the two dictators and the balance of power were comparable.

Although it is true that many so-called lessons stem from self-serving or lazy thinking, there are some regularities in history that can be helpful to guide our actions. Just as we find it beneficial to use past personal experience to make personal decisions, it can be helpful to use historical events and experience to guide larger questions of policy and action. For example, in 1939, almost everything that the Canadian government did was borrowed from experience in World War I: a board to control inflation, crown corporations to prevent profiteering, and skillful finessing of conscription by Mackenzie King. History does matter.

---

17 Cited in Doyle, J. (2011, August 2). The battle of Prohibition was fuelled by the fear of a new America. *The Globe and Mail*, p. R2.

However, we want students to have a nuanced view of history's lessons. There is a middle ground between a denial that history provides any lessons at all and a certainty that history always offers obvious and direct lessons. There are no hard and fast rules to learning lessons from history, but there are the virtues of history emphasized throughout this book:

- a commitment to a thorough examination of as much of the relevant evidence as possible
- a critical approach to all sources
- an honest assessment of the limits to our certainty in our conclusions[18]

We share Margaret MacMillan's thinking: "to use it, enjoy it, but handle history with care."[19]

The overarching inquiry question for learning cautious lessons from the past is, "What kinds of guidance, if any, does the past provide for the present?" The question could be rephrased to more directly address comparisons: "In what ways are the events and actions of X comparable to events and actions of Y today? What can X teach us to help make sense of Y?" It could also be made more engaging by rewording Santayana's principle: "Are we condemned to repeat the past? Or could we learn something?"

Using the past to understand the present begins with a comparison, and comparisons are familiar territory for our students. They begin comparing very early in their schooling, when teachers ask them, for example, to compare the lives of the pioneers with the lives of the First Nations of the time or with their own lives. By secondary school, history exams feature questions that begin with "Compare and contrast...." But just because territory is familiar to students does not necessarily mean they will travel skillfully over it. Comparing the past with the present demands considerable knowledge of both the past and present, as well as systematic reflection on what is worth comparing and what is comparable.

ACTIVITY: Comparing Natural Resources Industries

- Introduce this activity with a comparison from students' lives; for example, ask, "How might your experience last year at school help you understand how to deal with similar situations this year? What happened last year that was similar to this year that you could learn from?"
- Pause to see if students can suggest points of similarity. If not, give them prompts such as, "Did you learn anything about how to deal with your teacher? with friends? cliques? school work? sports teams? clubs?" Ask students to share their thoughts, but be sure to probe with care as some students may have had recent painful or negative experiences.

PURPOSE

To use an historical account to make an informed judgment about a current ethical issue

---

18 Adapted from Sheehan, J. J. (2005). How do we learn from history? *Perspectives Online, 43*(1). Retrieved from http://www.historians.org/perspectives/issues/2005/0501/0501pre1.cfm

19 MacMillan, M. (2008). *The uses and abuses of history* (p. 187). Toronto: Viking.

- Next, ask students to make some general statements about learning from the past that you might refer to later: "How can we best learn from experience? What are some advantages in looking to the past for answers or guidance? What problems might there be? Can we learn lessons from the past?"
- The next step is to use some of these personal examples and insights as reference points for an academic topic. Explain to students that, in the upcoming activity, they will be doing something similar—thinking about how best to use the past to inform the present, but they will be comparing two controversial issues instead of their own past experience. Because most Canadian curriculum documents and textbooks have learning outcomes about sustainability and depletion of natural resources both historical and current, we will use the depletion of the Atlantic cod stocks to inform a powerful current controversy: the Alberta oil sands.
- It is desirable for students to have studied the Atlantic cod fishery beforehand. Here is a brief summary:
  - For over 400 years, the cod fishery was a sustainable industry that gave a livelihood to thousands of people on the east coast of Canada.
  - Foreign fishing fleets overfished the offshore cod, especially factory ships in the 1960s and 1970s.
  - In 1977, Canada declared authority over fishing up to 200 nautical miles (370 km) offshore.
  - The federal government modernized the fleet and subsidized big companies to increase fishing.
  - There was strong political pressure from some groups to build the fishery industry—Newfoundland was poor and needed employment.
  - The scientists of the Department of Fisheries and Oceans (DFO) set limits on fishing but, in retrospect, the limits were too high.
  - The DFO ignored warnings from the local inshore fishers about the declining catch of cod.
  - In 1992, the federal government declared a moratorium on cod fishing because cod stocks were seriously depleted.
  - The cod stocks have yet to recover, and most experts think they will never come back.
- Brainstorm with students what might be some possible ethical lessons we can draw from the history of the Atlantic cod fishery to apply to ethical issues related to the Alberta oil sands industry. For example,
  - New technology can lead to over-exploitation of a resource.
  - Governments should listen to the locals.
  - Governments should be careful about subsidies.
  - Even scientists make mistakes.
  - Environmental damage can be forever.
  - Greed gobbles guppies (and other fish).
- Pose your inquiry: "What can the history of the Atlantic cod fishery teach us about issues related to Alberta oil sands development?" In other words, which of the lessons you brainstormed might apply to the oil sands, or are the two cases just not comparable?

- Be sure to have ample resources available about both the Atlantic cod fishery collapse and the mining of the Alberta oil sands, since both topics are complicated (and politically charged).
- If students are quick to make judgments, review ideas such as the importance of a wide range of evidence, the critical look at sources, and the limits to certainty.
- Focus on the features of the collapse of the cod fishing industry that have the potential to cast light on the development of the oil sands. You may wish to create a chart similar to the one below in Figure 6.8, to help guide students to make comparisons as a whole class or in small groups.
- As students research sources of information, pause at various points to consider the reliability of these sources and to reflect periodically on the inquiry question: "What can the history of the Atlantic cod fishery teach us about issues related to Alberta oil sands development?"
- At some point, pose the more general question, "What insights does comparing the ongoing oil sands development with the collapse of the Atlantic cod fishery in the past give you about the challenges of trying to learn from the past?" Relate students' answers to the earlier discussion about learning from experience in their personal lives.

As a culminating task for this comparison, students can write a letter to the prime minister expressing their opinions on the oil sands, including comparisons with the cod fishery collapse. Alternatively, you may wish to stage a "hot seat" activity as described on page 161. Students could take on the roles of the premier of Alberta, an oil company executive, an oil rig worker, a Chipewyan fisher, an environmentalist, and a government economist.

Feature	Similarities between the cod fishery and oil sands development	Differences between the cod fishery and oil sands development	Possible lessons
Role of government			
Economy			
Science and technology			
Environment			

Figure 6.8 The history of the Atlantic cod fishery has both similarities and differences with the current Alberta oil sands development.

Consolidating Understanding

This consolidating activity invites students to grapple with the ethical issues about the past's presence in our lives today and to develop a personal stance—that is, an historical consciousness.

ACTIVITY: Memorials and Monuments

The activity has two parts. The first part, Assess a Memorial, consolidates the first powerful understanding—recognizing an ethical stance—and reflects on how the memorial's creators have remembered and perhaps drawn lessons from the past (our fourth and fifth powerful understandings.) The second part of this activity, Create a Memorial, builds on the first part. Students make a reasoned ethical judgment to choose a subject worthy of remembrance, and determine what the most appropriate type of memorial should be.

As stated earlier, there are many forms for memorializing an event or person from the past. The wording for the following assumes that students will be considering a physical monument, but it could be changed to consider some other form. For example, a particularly engaging activity of memorializing is to have students help plan the school's Remembrance Day ceremony.

There may well be a monument of some sort near the school that could be used for the first part of the activity, Assess a Memorial. Alternatively, in recent years, spontaneous memorials have been created at roadsides where people have been killed in car accidents. If students are familiar with one of these locations, this may make a good starting point to open the discussion. As well, a wide variety of monuments are also displayed online.[20] Alternatively, you may simply assess the memorial *Swing Low*, shown in Figure 6.7 on page 194.

Assess a Memorial

Introduce the inquiry questions: "What makes a powerful memorial? How do the best of them create the power to move us, make us think, or fulfill a duty of memory?"

Distribute **BLM 6.6: Assess a Memorial** and show or visit an appropriate memorial. "Think aloud" with the class about how to answer the questions on the blackline master, making links back to the powerful understandings.

You can use this activity to explore what should be the criteria for a powerful memorial, and have the establishment of criteria as your wrap-up to the lesson. Alternatively, you may wish to establish criteria at the outset. Examples of appropriate criteria include clarity of purpose, artistry of construction, and wisdom or inspiration of message or lesson.

On completion of the chart on the blackline master, return to consider the inquiry questions. Decide if this example is a powerful memorial and why.

20 The *Facing History and Ourselves* website has thoughtful ideas for studying memorials and examples of student-created ones. (2004). Memory, history & memorials. Retrieved from http://www2.facinghistory.org/campus/memorials.nsf/Home?OpenFrameSet

Show students other examples of memorials to assess in small groups and independently. The more memorials that students explore prior to creating their own, the greater the possibility that they will create a meaningful memorial.

Create a Memorial

Tell students they are going to expand on their reflections about history's relevance to the present by creating a memorial. School assembly, collection of historical fiction, or hallway display—the form will depend on your teaching context. Distribute **BLM 6.7: Create a Memorial**. The questions in this step-by-step guide will help students organize and complete their projects efficiently, but you may also wish to refer to the project directions in the **Creating a Classroom Museum** activity on page 65.

After they complete their design of a memorial in step 2 of the blackline master, individuals should submit their proposals to you. Give feedback to ensure that they have a fair and thoughtful plan.

Be sure to establish an authentic audience for the memorials, such as another class or parents and the principal (always a strategic choice). Building some ceremony into the "unveiling" of the projects based on student answers to step 4 can be an important part of the act of remembering and responding.

During the unveiling or at another appropriate moment, discuss the questions in step 5 about the changing and often controversial nature of memorials, and the overarching question of how learning history and paying a debt of memory can help us to live in the present.

Ask students to consider the likely responses of different audiences to their monument. In so doing, they are challenged to think about how different people today find meaning in the past, that is, an historical consciousness.

As with most projects, there are several possible pitfalls here,[21] many of which are extensions of the limited understandings described in this and other chapters. First, students need to overcome presentism and not impose contemporary values on the past. Toward this end, they need to recognize the distance between themselves and people of the past, and not assume that they understand what "really happened" or how people "really felt."

A problem common to many learning projects is that students think the memorial should convey as much information as they can fit on it. They need to be reminded that memorials are historical accounts and accounts are, by their nature, selective. This project is not just researching and reproducing information, nor is it trying to create a period piece. It is an interpretation and needs an image or metaphor that responds to the focus question on the meaning of the past for our lives today, such as the faces about to break free in Harriet Tubman's skirt in Swing Low (Figure 6.7).

---

21 For a more extensive discussion of the benefits and problems with memorial projects, see Duraisingh, L.D. & Mansilla, V.B. (2007, December). Interdisciplinary forays within the history classroom: How the visual arts can enhance (or hinder) historical understanding. *Teaching History, 129*, 22–30.

BLM 6.1a Spotting Ethical Positions

Name: _____ Date: _____

Read these passages from different textbooks about the *filles du roi*, women who came to New France in the seventeenth century. Underline words that describe the *filles du roi*.

Passage A

Section Title: "Wives for Homesteaders"

Through Normandy, Brittany, and other parts of France, they [the government] searched till they found a number of young girls who were willing to go to New France. Often they were daughters of men with very large families who could hope to do little for them at home. Sometimes they were orphans brought up in homes or convents. Strong, healthy girls were chosen. They must have had brave hearts as well as strong bodies to dare, all alone, the ocean, the wilderness, the savages, and a land of strangers.

The young women chosen gathered at Rochelle, where they were put in [the] charge of two nuns, with whom they sailed to Canada. Very lonely they must have been as the ship put out to sea, and the pleasant shores of France faded from their sight forever. It was indeed forever, for well they knew they were never likely to return. No doubt they wept long and sadly, comforting one another as best they could, while the nuns reminded them that the good God was as near to Canada as to France.[22]

(The story continues for two more pages.)

Passage B

Section Title: "Jean Talon, 'The Great Intendant'"

Talon next recruited settlers from France.… He also had shiploads of young women—orphaned girls and the daughters of poor families—sent out over the years (perhaps a thousand women in all) in order to provide wives for the men of the colony. As a further encouragement of marriage, wedding presents of money or goods were made by the Council, relief from taxes for a certain number of years was granted young married men and family-allowance payments were made to large families. As a result of all these measures, the census for 1673 showed 6705 inhabitants, more than double the 1666 population.[23]

(The *filles du roi* are not mentioned further.)

---

22 Dickie, D.J., & Palk, H. (first published 1928; revised 1951). *Pages from Canada's story* (pp. 100–101). Toronto: J.M. Dent.
23 Lower, J.A. (1970). *A nation developing: A brief history of Canada* (p. 26). Toronto: McGraw-Hill Ryerson.

BLM 6.1b Spotting Ethical Positions

Name: _____ Date: _____

After reading the textbook passages on the *filles du roi*, respond to these questions.

1. How are these passages similar? How are they different?

2. What specific words or phrases create the differences?

3. Who is taking action in these passages? Who is being acted upon?

4. In each passage, what are the ethical messages conveyed about the following?

   a) the *filles du roi*

   b) the recruitment of the *filles du roi*

   c) Jean Talon

5. Explain whether or not you think textbooks have ethical positions, and why.

BLM 6.2a What Is the Ethical Position?

Name: _____ Date: _____

After you read each of the following three passages,[24] answer the questions to help identify the textbook authors' ethical position.

> *American scientists with the aid of British and European colleagues had developed a new bomb of unprecedented destructiveness. Two of these atomic bombs were dropped on the Japanese, ending their fanatical resistance and beginning a new nuclear age where the human species had, for the first time, the technological means of obliterating itself.*
>
> —*Roberts, M. (2001). Britain 1846–1964: The challenge of change.*
> *London: Oxford University Press.*

- Who are the possible heroes, villains, or victims? How do you know?

- What message is the author sending? How do you know?

> *The Potsdam Declaration, made in the names of the U.S., Britain, and China, called for Japan to surrender and submit to democratization. However, the Japanese government ignored the declaration and urged the Japanese people towards a fight to the finish.*
>
> *As a result, the U.S., which had succeeded in experiments to create the world's first atomic bomb and motivated also by the desire to come out of the war more powerful than the Soviet Union, dropped an atomic bomb on Hiroshima on August 6, and another one on Nagasaki on August 9. Both cities were annihilated in a flash. By 1950, it was estimated that more than 200 000 people in Hiroshima and 140 000 in Nagasaki had died as a result of the atomic bombings, making this the worst tragedy in the history of mankind.*
>
> —*Japan in modern history, junior high school textbooks. (1994).*
> *Tokyo: International Society for Educational Information, 515.*

VOCABULARY

unprecedented—never seen before

fanatical—frenzied; zealous

obliterating—destroying completely

annihilated—destroyed completely

- Who are the possible heroes, villains, or victims? How do you know?

- What message is the author sending? How do you know?

---

24 Lindaman, D. & Ward, K. (2004). *History lessons: How textbooks from around the world portray U.S. history* (pp. 238–243). New York: New Press.

On August 6, 1945, the world was changed forever. On this day, the Japanese city of Hiroshima was obliterated by the world's first atomic bomb. Three days later a second Japanese city, Nagasaki, faced the same fate. About 110 000 people were killed and an additional 10 000 injured by the two bombs, known as "Little Boy" and "Fat Man." The bombing had the desired result—Japan was forced to surrender, and the war was over. The nuclear age had begun....

Canada provided a safe haven, far from the battlefields, for British scientists working on the Manhattan Project (that developed the atomic bomb). Also, Canadian scientists played a crucial role from its beginning. They discovered uranium 235 (the basic element of the atomic bomb), helped to create the first chain reaction using uranium 235, and discovered how to purify uranium 235 ...

Some Canadians were unwilling participants in the development of the atomic bomb. Men of the Sahtugot'ine people, a nomadic group of Aboriginal people who lived near Great Bear Lake, were hired as transporters for the uranium. Despite warnings from the ... scientists about the dangers of radioactive substances, the Sahtugot'ine were allowed to carry tonnes of uranium without being provided any protective clothing and were not warned about the dangers they faced. The men, covered in uranium dust brought the radioactive material into their tents, thereby unknowingly contaminating their families.

The long-term effects of their work in transporting uranium have been devastating for the Sahtugot'ine community. Gina Bayha, from Deline, N.W.T., noted: "Men from my grandmother's generation regularly lived into their nineties or one hundreds. But we hardly have any men past the age of sixty-five. They all died of cancer."

> **VOCABULARY**
>
> radioactive—irradiated; deadly

—Newman, G., et al. (2000). Canada: A nation unfolding.
Toronto: McGraw-Hill, 244.

- Who are the possible heroes, villains, or victims? How do you know?

- What message is the author sending? How do you know?

- What might explain the differences and similarities in the interpretations of the authors of these three passages?

BLM 6.3 Message in the Museum

Name: _____ Date: _____

Museum: _____ Exhibit Title: _____

1 **Features:** What are the key objects and images? How are they organized? What other features are used (e.g., text explanations, lighting, sound)?

2 **Story:** What story does the exhibit tell? Who are the main figures (individuals and groups) in this story? How are they portrayed? Who is in the margins, that is, left out or given little importance?

3 **Messages:** Does the exhibit portray messages about injustices, tragedies, or crimes? Alternatively, does it portray messages about triumphs, accomplishments, or heroism? What are the main messages (if any)? What are the complexities or counter-examples (e.g., flaws in a hero)?

4 **Techniques:** How does the written text convey these messages? How do other features, such as the choice and arrangement of objects and visuals, convey them?

5 **Implicit vs. explicit:** Which parts of the messages are up front and clearly stated, that is, explicit? Which parts are suggested by the storyline or techniques, that is, implicit? Explain your reasoning.

BLM 6.4a Ethical Controversy at the War Museum

In 2005, the Canadian War Museum opened an exhibit on the Allied bombing campaign in World War II, in which some 10 000 members of the Canadian airforce died. The curators called it "An Enduring Controversy." After reading about the exhibit, consider these inquiry questions:

- What was the ethical position of the War Museum exhibit on the Allied bombing?

- Did it support, condemn, or excuse the bombing?

- Was it respectful to those Canadians who flew in the campaign?

The Exhibit Text

This appeared on the text panel:

> *The value and morality of the strategic bomber offensive against Germany remain bitterly contested. Bomber Command's aim was to crush civilian morale and force Germany to surrender by destroying its cities and industrial installations. Although Bomber Command and American attacks left 600 000 Germans dead, and more than five million homeless, the raids resulted in only small reductions in German war production until late in the war.*[25]

The Perspectives

To the right of the text panel were quotations.

VOCABULARY
civilian morale—public mood
industrial installations—factories

- One from Sir Arthur Harris, head of Bomber Command, insisted that the campaign had been a vital contribution to ending the war.

- Another, from John Kenneth Galbraith, a famous Canadian-American economist, stated that while the bombing campaign did not win the war, it helped the ground troops who did.

- A third quotation came from Canadian airman Flight Lieutenant W.E. Vaughan who said, "More than once I wondered 'How many people will those bombs kill?' However, you couldn't dwell on it. That's the way war is."[26]

---

25 Dean, D. (2009). Museums as conflict zones: The Canadian War Museum and Bomber Command. *Museum and Society* 7(1), 4. Retrieved from http://www2.le.ac.uk/departments/museumstudies/museumsociety/volumes/volume7

26 Dean, D. (2009). Museums as conflict zones, 4.

The Big Six Historical Thinking Concepts

The Visuals

Accompanying the text and quotations were a number of aerial photographs showing the effects of Allied bombing of several German cities, as well as photographs of corpses of German men, women, and children, dead from the blasts. Other photographs in the exhibit revealed the destruction of industries and residences.

Figure 6.9 This photograph, which appeared in the exhibit, shows the state of Münster, Germany, which was bombed by the Allies on October 10, 1943.

The Analysis

Phrases and images that support the bombing	Phrases and images that condemn the bombing	Phrases and images that excuse the bombing

The Fallout

After the controversy raged, the exhibitors relented and revised the text of the exhibit panel, as follows:

The strategic bombing campaign against Germany, an important part of the Allied effort that achieved victory, remains a source of controversy today. Strategic bombing enjoyed wide public and political support as a symbol of Allied resolve and a response to German aggression. In its first years, the air offensive achieved few of its objectives and suffered heavy losses. Advances in technology and tactics, combined with Allied successes on other fronts, led to improved results. By war's end, Allied bombers had razed portions of every major city in Germany and damaged many other targets, including oil facilities and transportation networks. The attacks blunted Germany's economic and military potential, and drew scarce resources into air defence, damage repair, and the protection of critical industries. Allied aircrew conducted this gruelling offensive with great courage against heavy odds. It required vast material and industrial efforts and claimed over 80 000 Allied lives, including more than 10 000 Canadians. While the campaign contributed greatly to enemy war weariness, German society did not collapse despite 600 000 dead and more than five million left homeless. Industrial output fell substantially, but not until late in the war. The effectiveness and the morality of bombing heavily-populated areas in war continue to be debated.[27]

> **VOCABULARY**
>
> **objectives**—goals
>
> **razed**—completely destroyed
>
> **industrial output**—goods produced

---

27 Dean, D. (2009). Museums as conflict zones, 11.

The Deportation of Acadians: What Happened[28]

They came from France to trade furs around the Bay of Fundy in the early 1600s, but within a few years *les Acadiens*, the Acadians, started to build dikes and carve out farmland on the rich, marshy soil surrounding the bay. By 1755, the population of *l'Acadie*, or Acadia, was about 13 000 people. Long isolated from France by that date and highly influenced by the Mi'kmaq Nation, they had developed their own sense of community.

Since the Treaty of Utrecht in 1713, the Acadians had lived under British rule. They had tried to remain neutral in the continuing conflicts between Britain and France. However, their farms lay in a strategic area between British settlements at Annapolis Royal and Halifax, the important naval base, and New France, which at this time included New Brunswick, Prince Edward Island (Isle St. Jean), and Cape Breton Island (Isle Royale).

Although it was not yet official, another war between Britain and France, and thus their colonies, had begun. The British Lieutenant Governor at Halifax, Charles Lawrence, saw the French-speaking Acadians as a security risk. This fear increased when, in June 1755, an Anglo-American force captured the French fort of Beauséjour and found some 200 Acadians inside.

Britain had asked Acadians before to swear loyalty to the British Crown. In 1727, they had agreed, but their oath had been made with the understanding that they would not be required to take up arms against the French or the Mi'kmaq. After the fall of Beauséjour, Lawrence ordered an unqualified oath of allegiance under the threat of deportation south to other British colonies. The Acadians refused to take this oath, promising only to remain neutral.

Lawrence refused to accept the promise of neutrality in lieu of the oath. The British seized the Acadians' crops and cattle and burned their homes, barns, and churches. They separated families and shipped the Acadians away to different colonies to the south. Conditions on the boats were dreadful and many Acadians died en route. Authorities in the colonies did not expect the Acadian refugees and offered little help. Some refused even to accept the "boat people." Many Acadians began a life of wandering throughout North America and even to the West Indies and France, trying to return to their homeland.

---

28 Material adapted from Morton, T. (1992). The Acadians. In Johnson, D. & Johnson, R. *Creative controversy: Intellectual challenge in the classroom* (pp. 6:45–6:48). Edina, MN: Interaction Book Co.

BLM 6.5b Developing a Fair Ethical Judgment

Position 1: The deportation was a crime against humanity.

Your assigned position is that the action of the British was a crime against humanity. Whether or not you agree with this position, argue for it as strongly as you can. Consider the arguments below and prepare a statement of your position. Listen carefully to your opponents' viewpoints and learn their thinking as well. Insist that they support their position with facts and reasons. Determine where you both need more information.

Arguments:

1. For more than a century, France and Britain repeatedly attacked and counterattacked each other. Control of Acadia shifted back and forth. For the Acadians to commit to one side one day might mean punishment from the other side the next day. Given this context, it made sense for them to insist on being neutral.

2. The Acadians had taken an oath of loyalty in 1729 and had kept their word. They were entitled to stay on their land.

3. The French and their Mi'kmaq allies had threatened the Acadians with attacks and burned an Acadian village to force them to take refuge in Fort Beauséjour. Given this context, it is hard to say whether the 200 Acadians found at the fort were truly in support of the French.

4. Why should 13 000 people lose their homeland for the supposed crime of 200? It was unjust to punish all Acadians for the risk posed by a few.

5. A previous British governor, Peregrine Hopson, firmly believed the Acadian claims to neutrality and was convinced that if the Acadians were treated fairly, they would be loyal British subjects.

6. Governor Lawrence did not just want to defend Nova Scotia. He scattered the Acadians to many different places and burned their homes. These actions were meant to destroy them as a people, so he could give their valuable, developed farms to British newcomers.

7. Even though we live in a different time and place, there are some basic principles of justice that endure over time. The right to one's homeland, and not to be forced into life as a refugee, is a universal human right.

Position 2: The deportation was fair in the context of the time.

Your assigned position is that deportation was fair in the context of war and the Acadians' refusal to meet reasonable British requirements. Whether or not you agree with this, argue for it as strongly as you can. Consider the arguments below and prepare a statement of your position. Listen carefully to your opponents' viewpoints and learn their thinking as well. Insist that they support their position with facts and reasons. Determine where you both need more information.

Arguments:

1. Consider the context: war with France was coming. Acadia was on the front lines. The survival of the British colonies was at stake. Any reasonable military commander of a country today or in the past would want full loyalty of all those in its territory, as Lawrence did.

2. The capture of 200 Acadians inside the French fort of Beauséjour showed that the Acadians were not neutral. This fact supports Governor Lawrence's decision to protect the lives of his people.

3. Britain was tolerant toward the Acadians for years. Although the Acadians were a conquered people, the British let them keep their land, practise their Catholic religion, and generally live as they pleased. Until this threat to Nova Scotia and other British colonies, they were even allowed to refuse to defend the colony. The Acadians should have repaid British kindness.

4. The Acadians were given a clear choice—swear full allegiance or be deported. They chose their fate.

5. Ideas such as human rights, equal rights, or the right to a homeland did not develop until the 1760s and the American and French revolutions. We should not expect that people of this time period would be familiar with the modern belief in the right to a homeland, let alone uphold it.

BLM 6.6 Assess a Memorial

Name: _____ Date: _____

Name or description of memorial: _____		
1	What, or who, does this memorial commemorate?	
2	Who built this memorial? When was it built, and why?	
3	Describe the appearance of the memorial (e.g., materials, size, composition). What does its appearance suggest to you?	
4	What symbols and/or imagery are used in the memorial, if any?	
5	What words are on the memorial, if any?	
6	Is the location of the memorial important? appropriate? In what ways?	
7	What is the purpose of the memorial? What message does it convey? What did the creators of the memorial want us to think about or learn from the past?	
8	How effective is this memorial? How well does it achieve its purpose? How does it represent the people it commemorates?	
9	How do you feel about this memorial? What is your reaction to it?	
10	How does the memorial reflect the historical context of the time when it was made or when the events occurred? Are the ethical standards of today different from those at the time it was made?	
11	If you were to recreate this memorial, what features would you change, if any?	

BLM 6.7 **Create a Memorial**

Step 1: Choose the subject and decide the purpose of the memorial
- Why is this person or event worth remembering?
- Which of the following purposes will your memorial serve?
  - (1) change the way people usually think about the subject
  - (2) suggest a lesson to be learned
  - (3) fulfill a duty of memory
  - (4) inspire action on a contemporary issue
  - (5) any other purpose you can think of
- What would you like people to feel or think about when they see your memorial?
- Who will your audience be?
- What story do you want to tell?
- In what ways might your memorial upset some people or cause controversy?

Step 2: Design the memorial
- Where should your memorial be displayed?
- What materials should be used?
- What will the memorial look like?
- What words or quotations might be inscribed on it?
- What should it be called?
- How will the memorial convey your chosen message or lesson, if any?
- How will the design achieve your purpose?

Step 3: Create the memorial

Step 4: Plan the unveiling
- When will you display the memorial, and for how long?
- Who will be invited to your unveiling?
- What publicity will you seek, and why?
- What will people do at the unveiling?
- What ceremony will be appropriate?

Step 5: Reflection
- What has this project taught you about the role of history?
- Why are some memorials controversial?

Glossary

account: a narrative or story

agency: the power to act

anachronism: a practice or technology represented outside of the time period in which it existed

cause: an action or condition that contributes to a result

change: an alteration; possibly evolutionary erosion or sudden collapse, gradual building, or revolutionary upheaval

chronicle: a list of events; a timeline

condition: a broad societal, political, economic, or cultural circumstance

consequence: an outcome that results from actions or conditions

construction of historical significance: making connections among evidence and themes to create meaning within an historical narrative

context: the circumstances at the time of the creation of a source; the society and belief system in which the source was created as well as the historical events taking place at the time

continuity: staying the same; an uninterrupted succession or flow

corroboration: crosschecking; comparing and contrasting one or more sources with an interpretation, with the intention of confirming or refuting the interpretation

debt of memory: an obligation to remember

decline: the erosion of conditions

diverse perspectives: the different ways that various people can view an historic event

durability: how long a change lasts

ethical judgment: a decision about the ethics of an historical action

evidence: what a source becomes when it is analyzed, thereby becoming pertinent in an historical inquiry

historical actor: a person who existed in the past

historical consciousness: awareness of the links among the past, present, and future that prepare one to negotiate the present

historical perspective: the viewpoint of an historical actor

inference: conclusion based on "reading between the lines" of a source

interpretation: an account of the past reached by making inferences from sources; a single event can have multiple interpretations

making inferences: developing evidence-based estimations of the thoughts and feelings of historical actors

periodization: the process of using themes to divide history into chunks of time with beginning and end dates

perspective: a mental outlook influenced by worldview—how one sees and interprets reality

presentism: imposing the thoughts, beliefs, and values of today onto historical actors

profundity: the level of depth or intensity of a change

progress: the betterment of conditions

quantity: the number of people affected by a change

reparation: making amends for a wrong done

restitution: restoration or replacement of something taken away

source: a trace, relic, record, written account, oral testimony, archaeological artifact, or even DNA, that is being analyzed in the course of an historical inquiry

sourcing: asking questions related to the creator of the source and the intended audience

structure: another word for *condition*; specifically, the societal, political, economic, and cultural conditions within which actions play out

taking an historical perspective: using evidence and historical context to infer the thoughts and feelings of an historical actor

trace: a scrap left over from the past, anything from a menu to a telegram or an email

unintended consequence: a result that is unexpected, and never planned for

Index of Activities

Chapter 1: Historical Significance

Chapter 2: Evidence

Chapter 3: Continuity and Change

Chapter 4: Cause and Consequence

Chapter 5: Historical Perspectives

Chapter 6: The Ethical Dimension

Credits

This page constitutes an extension of the copyright page. We have made every effort to trace the ownership of all copyrighted material and to secure permission from copyright holders. In the event of any question arising as to the use of any material, we will be pleased to make the necessary corrections in future printings. Thanks are due to the following authors, publishers, and agents for permission to use the material indicated.

Photos

Chapter 1. 13: © Fine Art/Corbis **18:** Winnipeg Free Press/The Canadian Press (Mike Aporius) **20:** Tony Bock/GetStock.com **23:** © Stephane Guidoin/Caroline Pilon **27:** Courtesy of Adele Chamberland **Chapter 2. 41:** The Canadian Press (Chuck Stoody) **44:** The Protected Art Archive/GetStock.com **48:** Library and Archives Canada, C-103527 **54:** *Deffaite des Yroquois au Lac de Champlain, planche tirée de l'ouvrage Les voyages du sieur de Champlain Xaintongeois...*, Paris, Jean Berjon, 1613. CA BNC Réserve FC330 C3 161. Accessed at: http://www.champlain2004.org/html/11/01_e.html **57:** George Bird/Montreal Star/Library and Archives Canada/PA-129838 **67:** © Marcel Laforce/Library and Archives Canada, PA-185843 **71:** Library and Archives Canada, PA-001332 **Chapter 3. 75:** © Hulton-Deutsch Collection/Historical/CORBIS **83:** Luis Argerich/Stocktrek Images/Glow Images **84:** (top) The Course of Empire: The Consummation of the Empire, c.1835–36 (oil on canvas), Cole, Thomas (1801–48)/ © Collection of the New York Historical Society, USA/The Bridgeman Art Library **84:** (bottom) The Course of Empire: Destruction, 1836 (oil on canvas), Cole, Thomas (1801–48)/© Collection of the New York Historical Society, USA/The Bridgeman Art Library **90:** Courtesy of Adele Chamberland, Makaela DeClude, Madelaine Hodges, and Jada Kinnaird **Chapter 4. 103:** © McCord Museum, MP-1979.111.212 **105:** © jiangkehong/Xinhua Press/Corbis Wire/Corbis **107:** © Mike Grandmaison/Terra/Corbis **111:** The Canadian Press (Winnipeg Free Press/Ken Gigliott) **113:** © Historical/CORBIS **Chapter 5. 137:** © Penny Wheelwright/ Wheelwright Ink Ltd. **142:** Ford Madox Brown/The Bridgeman Art Library/Getty Images **145:** © Bettmann/CORBIS **147:** Courtesy of the Toronto Public Library, JRR 2294 **Chapter 6. 169:** David Lees/Taxi/Getty Images **175:** © Bettmann/CORBIS **181:** Library and Archives Canada, C-014078 **183:** Maclean's/The Canadian Press(Bayne Stanley) **194:** © Frances Roberts/Alamy **208:** Library and Archives Canada, e002344098.

Text

Chapter 1. 28: Canadian Museum of Civilization, Social Progress Gallery: http://www.civilization.ca/cmc/exhibitions/hist/progrese .shtml. Reproduced with permission. **37:** Excerpts from *BURY THE CHAINS* by Adam Hochschild. Copyright © 2005 by Adam Hochschild. Used by permission of Houghton Mifflin Harcourt Publishing Company. All Rights Reserved. **Chapter 2. 50:** Reprinted with permission. Copyright © 2009 Designed Instruction, LLC. All rights reserved. You may visit Designed Instruction online at: http://www.designedinstruction.com/learningleads/teacher-support-traces.html **64:** © Canadian Broadcasting Company **67–68:** © Canadian Broadcasting Corporation **68:** Reproduced with permission of Matthew Coon Come **69:** Courtesy of the Canadian War Museum **Chapter 3. 91:** From the Schools History Project, Leeds Trinity University College. Reproduced with permission. http://www.schoolshistoryproject.org.uk/index.php **92:** Reprinted with permission from How Students Learn: History, Mathematics, and Science in the Classroom, 2005 by the National Academy of Sciences, Courtesy of the National Academies Press, Washington, D.C. **94:** From the Schools History Project, Leeds Trinity University College. Reproduced with permission. http://www.schoolshistoryproject.org.uk/index.php **Chapter 5. 139–147:** pp. 55, 92, 112, 134–135, 136, 137, 149–150, 271, 251–252, 177, 77 from *Esther: The Remarkable True Story of Esther Wheelwright: Puritan Child, Native Daughter, Mother Superior* by Julie Wheelwright. Copyright © 2011 by Julie Wheelwright. Reprinted with permission of HarperCollins Publishers. **151:** Marion Royce Papers, Centre for Women's Studies in Education, OISE, cited in Light, B. and Roach Pierson, R. *No Easy Road: Women in Canada 1920s to 1960s.* Toronto: New Hogtown Press, 1990. Reprinted with permission. **156:** Simon Schama, "The Many Deaths of General Wolfe," *Granta* 32, Spring, 1990, 55. **159:** "Bio-Poem 'by' Galileo Galilei" courtesy of Tom Morton **164–165:** Reproduced with permission of John J.C. Myers **Chapter 6. 205:** From Newman, Garfield et. al. *Canada: A Nation Unfolding.* Toronto: McGraw-Hill, 2000. Reproduced with Permission of the McGraw-Hill Companies. **207:** (middle quotation, bottom quotation) Courtesy of the Canadian War Museum **209:** Courtesy of the Canadian War Museum **210:** Johnson, David, and Roger Johnson. The Acadians. *Creative Controversy: Intellectual Challenge in the Classroom.* Interaction: Minnesota, 1992. Reproduced with permission of Interaction Book Company: 5028 Halifax Ave. So. Edina, MN 55424. (952) 831-9500.

DVD-ROM Table of Contents

---

* Formative assessment tools. Easily modifiable for summative assessment by adjusting the criteria to suit specific assignments

---